Becoming BROWNING

The Artist Depicting Himself Sketching a Landscape in Southern France

Becoming BROWNING
The Poems and Plays of Robert Browning, 1833–1846

CLYDE DE L. RYALS

Ohio State University Press
Columbus

Portions of chapters 1 and 2, under the titles "Browning's *Pauline*: The Question of Genre" and "Browning's *Paracelsus*: 'A Poem, Not a Drama,' " were published in the fall 1976 and summer 1979 issues of *Genre*. Reprinted by permission.

An earlier version of chapter 3, under the title "Irony in Browning's *Strafford*," appeared in *The Humanities and Human Conduct: Essays Presented to Morse Peckham by Some Friends and Colleagues*. It is reprinted with the permission of Camden House.

The Afterword originally appeared, in somewhat different form, under the title "Browning's Irony," in *The Victorian Experience: The Poets*, ed. Richard A. Levine. Reprinted by permission of Ohio University Press.

Excerpts from Friedrich Schlegel, *Dialogue on Poetry and Literary Aphorisms*, trans. Ernst Behler and Roman Struc, are reprinted by permission of the Pennsylvania State University Press.

The poem "Browning Resolves to Be a Poet" is from *The Gold of Tigers,* by Jorge Luis Borges, trans. by Alastair Reid. English trans. copyright © 1976, 1977, by Alastair Reid. Reprinted by permission of the publisher, E.P.Dutton, Inc.

Copyright © 1983 by the Ohio State University Press
All Rights Reserved.

Library of Congress Cataloging in Publication Data

Ryals, Clyde de L., 1928-
   Becoming Browning: the poems and plays of Robert Browning, 1833-1846
   Bibliography: p.
   Includes index.
   1. Browning, Robert, 1812-1889–Criticism and interpretation. I. Title.
PR4238.R86   1983   821'.8   83-4140
ISBN 0-8142-0352-3

FOR ANNA CATHERINE THUN SCHEFFEY

Ernst ist das Leben. J. C. F. von Schiller, Prologue to *Wallenstein*

Ach, . . . es ist garzu aufregend und festlich! Und mit festlichem Spass soll es ausgeführt sein aufs Allerheiterste. Denn die Heiterkeit . . . und der verschlagene Scherz sind das Beste, was Gott uns gab, und sind die innigste Auskunft vor dem verwickelten, fragwürdigen Leben. Gott gab sie unserem Geist, dass wir selbst dieses, das strenge Leben, mögen damit zum Lächeln bringen. Thomas Mann, *Joseph, der Ernährer,* Chapter 6

CONTENTS

Preface	ix
Introduction	3
I. *Pauline*	9
II. *Paracelsus*	25
III. *Strafford*	53
IV. *Sordello*	66
V. *Pippa Passes* and *King Victor and King Charles*	119
VI. *Dramatic Lyrics*	146
VII. *The Return of the Druses, A Blot in the 'Scutcheon,* and *Colombe's Birthday*	170
VIII. *Dramatic Romances and Lyrics*	201
IX. *Luria* and *A Soul's Tragedy*	230
Afterword	247
Notes	257
Selected Bibliography	281
Index	287

PREFACE

ALTHOUGH BROWNING IS UNIVERSALLY ACCLAIMED as a major poet, his fame rests on the work of his middle years. In an earlier book—*Browning's Later Poetry, 1871–1889* (Cornell University Press, 1975)—I attempted to chart the *terra incognita* of his later work. In this book I propose to explore land slightly better known but still, in my opinion, inadequately mapped—the poems and plays of his earlier years. Beginning with his first published poem and ending with the last of the *Bells and Pomegranates*—the work of his years before marriage—I attempt to trace Browning's poetical development by studying his growth as an ironist. In the process I hope to show that some of the works of the young Browning are worthy of a higher critical esteem than they have enjoyed.

I should like to record my thanks to Herbert F. Tucker, Jr., who gave this book a rigorous reading in typescript and who kindly permitted me to see parts of his recent book—*Browning's Beginnings: The Art of Disclosure* (University of Minnesota Press, 1980)—before its publication. I am also appreciative of the careful typing of Dorothy Roberts, who on this occasion as on past ones improved the quality of my typescript by correcting mechanical errors that I otherwise should have let slip past.

Portions of this book have been previously published. Parts of Chapters 1 and 2 appeared in *Genre* (Fall 1976 and Summer 1979 respectively); of Chapter 3 in *The Humanities and Human Conduct: Essays Presented to Morse Peckham by Some Friends and Colleagues,* ed. H. W. Matalene III (Camden House, 1983); of the Afterword in *The Victorian Experience: The Poets,* ed. Richard A. Levine (Ohio University Press, 1982). I thank the editors of the journal and the university presses for their kind permission to reprint this material.

All quotations from Browning, except as otherwise noted,

All quotations from Browning, except as otherwise noted, are taken from the first London edition. Line numbers have been added to correspond with the Camberwell Edition, *Complete Works of Robert Browning*, ed. Charlotte Porter and Helen A. Clarke, 12 vols. (New York: Thomas Y. Crowell, 1898).

Browning's stylistic use of ellipses in his early work poses a problem in distinguishing authorial omissions in the quotations. Browning's ellipsis points, ranging in number from two to six, are here typeset closed up, without space between (...); authorial omissions are indicated by the customary spaced points (. . .).

Becoming BROWNING

BROWNING RESOLVES TO BE A POET

In these red London labyrinths
I find that I have chosen
the most curious of human professions,
though given that all are curious, in their way.
Like alchemists
who looked for the philosopher's stone
in elusive quicksilver,
I shall make ordinary words—
the marked cards of the sharper, the people's coinage—
yield up the magic which was theirs
when Thor was inspiration and eruption,
thunder and worship.
In the wording of the day,
I in my turn will say eternal things;
I will try to be not unworthy
of the great echo of Byron.
This dust that is me will be invulnerable.
If a woman partakes of my love,
my poem will graze the tenth sphere of the concentric heavens;
if a woman shrugs off my love,
I will make music out of my misery,
a vast river reverberating on through time.
I will live by forgetting myself.
I will be the face I half-see and forget,
I will be Judas who accepts
the blessed destiny of being a traitor,
I will be Caliban in the swamp,
I will be a mercenary dying
without fear or faith,
I will be Polycrates, horrified to see
the ring returned by destiny,
I will be the friend who hates me.
Persia will grant me the nightingale, Rome the sword.
Agonies, masks and resurrections
will weave and unweave my fate
and at some point I will be Robert Browning.

☐ Jorge Luis Borges

INTRODUCTION

BROWNING'S WORLD IS EVER IN MOVEMENT. IN his verse energy, motion, and change are the salient traits of nature, character, and the consciousness of the poet himself. Only the physically or spiritually dead are fixed. The "principle of restlessness" iterated in his first published poem (*Pauline*, 277) finds expression throughout his work, even to his last poem, wherein men are urged to "strive and thrive" in this world and the next ("Epilogue" to *Asolando*). For Browning an entity becomes something so as to become something else, is created so as to be de-created, is formed so as to be transformed. Chaos → cosmos → chaos and so on *ad infinitum*—the principle of becoming is at the very heart of his thought and practice as a poet.

Browning's belief in dynamicism and change was part of his Romantic inheritance. But where his immediate poetic predecessors envisioned change as part of a revolutionary process leading to a new heaven and a new earth, Browning views change as a process without *telos*. The idea of an open, evolving universe is, to a certain degree, antithetical to the Romantics' notion of union of self and nature and of the work of art as a revelation of the meeting of the self and the Absolute. Coleridge, for example, speaks in chapter fourteen of the *Biographia Literaria* of the imagination as the means of synthesizing or reconciling opposites. And Shelley alludes everywhere in his work, both in his prose and poetry, to the encounter of the self with the Absolute in moments of harmonious union. To both men the poetic act was the enclosure of the chaotic world within a perfect sphere. Neither had fully emerged from the closed world represented by Platonic philosophy and medieval Christianity. Browning, on the other hand, maintains that it is the function of the imagination not to reconcile opposites but to transcend them by accepting them as antinomies, thereby substituting for the Romantics' circle of enclosure an upward-tending spiral. It is, I believe, this idea of nonteleological becoming that from the beginning sets Browning off from Shelley and other Romantics from whom he is traditionally said to be descended, first as an eager son and then as a rebellious heir.[1]

As far as his basic thought is concerned, Browning owes far more to German than to English philosophers and poets. Whether or not he got his ideas directly from the German is a matter for speculaton, about which I shall have more to say later. I am, in any case, less interested in tracing the sources of his thought than in explaining its essential nature. His belief in the principle of becoming marks him as one embracing philosophical irony, which is grounded on the denial of any absolute order in natural or human events as they occur in the fertile abundance of the phenomenal world.[2] According to Friedrich Schlegel, the foremost theoretician of philosophical irony, the essence of reality is not *being*, a substance in itself, but *becoming*. In his view infinity is an ever-growing center of finite expressions and finitude a momentarily limited infinity. An exhaustless fund of life is constantly developing itself in nature, which itself is characterized by an ever-flowing vital energy, each one fueling the other. Reality is thus an interplay between the finite and the infinite, and in the creative process everything is simultaneously itself and something other. Ontologically the finite can never encompass the infinite, for to do so would cause life to cease. Epistemologically man can never attain full consciousness, an infinite self, so that any theoretical formulation or system of reality that he makes can only be an approximation, which ultimately must be transcended. When translated into psychological terms, this conception of the universe entails a tension in the individual, who simultaneously desires order and coherence—being—and chaos and freedom—becoming. The drive toward stability is usually experienced as love, the drive toward change as power. As we shall see, the conflict between love and power is dramatized in all of Browning's early poetry.

Life, then, persists in, and is developed by, a continual reversal of order and disorder; the world is always being shaped so as to be destroyed and shaped anew. Correctly perceived, this constant flux permits man opportunity for increasing self-realization by self-transcendence, demanding that he hold the double vision of himself as limited and also as able to transcend these limits through self-conscious acknowledgment of them. Schlegel's philosophical irony thus offers triumph to the self that hovers between system and chaos.

Schlegel termed this philosophy of infinite becoming ironic because on the one hand it urges the individual forward toward the infinite while on the other hand it pulls him back by making him aware of his finite limitations. In the case of the poet, the irony of such a philosophy is most evident, for it energizes him to seek a perfect system—a poem—that accurately depicts the beauties of the world while at the same time making him realize that any such perfection, which must belong to the inifinite alone, is impossible.[3] A poet can never fully comprehend the fertile yet chaotic abundance of the phenomenal world not only because of his limited perceptions but also because language, which itself is a structured system, never can fully or adequately deal with the unstructured world of becoming.

Philosophical irony involves then a dialectic of order and change, love and power, the conditioned and the free, the finite and the infinite. Schlegel's dialectic allows for no synthesis; his contradictions remain always unresolved. It is the function of philosophical irony as he expounds it to permit an individual to hold the two contrary states of being and becoming in mind at the same time and to recognize that they cannot be harmonized. Browning too espouses this view, but he introduces the element of progress, which is not clearly a part of Schlegel's philosophy. Insofar as he adopts the notion of progressive evolution, Browning is more nearly akin to Hegel. But he does not share with Hegel the notion that every thesis generates its antithesis, which is then resolved into a higher synthesis. Browning does not envision a synthesis; for him the dialectic remains unharmonized. He sees, however, a growth of consciousness resulting from the dialectic interplay that allows the individual and the race to evolve into ever higher spiritual, moral, and artistic states or conditions; for him becoming involves the notion of creative evolution.

As we shall see, Browning's conception of philosophical irony has profound implications for his art, ultimately determining not only the content of his verse but its form as well. Perhaps the least oblique statement of his poetic theory and the philosophy upon which it is based may be found in his *Essay on Shelley*, which was composed in 1851, fairly soon after the period of his career in which I am here interested, and thus may be taken as a summary of what he as a poet had been about during his early years.

Using the nineteenth-century commonplace critical terms "objective" and "subjective,"[4] he contrasts two different kinds of poets. The objective poet is mimetic, his concern being for men and their actions. A "fashioner" who shapes his art out of the multitudinous world around him, he is impersonal and his poetry is distinct from himself. His mode is narrative and dramatic. The subjective poet, on the other hand, is an illuminator who looks beyond things external to perceive their essence, his concern being with God and "what God sees," not with humanity in action. A "seer," he is personal, and his poetry is projected from, but not separate from, himself. His mode is essentially lyric. Having defined the two types of poets, Browning then proceeds to show that literary history has proceeded dialectically, in alternating cycles when one or the other type was dominant. But, Browning suggests, there is no reason why these two modes of poetic faculty might not be combined in the "the whole poet" who fully displays the objective and subjective modes.

Underlying the concept of the whole poet, of his perception and expression, is the idea of evolutionary advance or becoming. The whole poet beholds the universe, nature, and man "in their actual state of perfection in imperfection"; looks to "the forthcoming stage of man's being"; and presents "this ideal of a future man." Rejecting "ultimates" and aspiring always toward a "higher state of development," he strives "to elevate and extend" both himself and mankind. All this is embodied in a language "closely answering to and indicative of the process of the informing spirit." In brief, the whole poet is the poet of becoming, the kind of poet that Browning himself evidently wished to be.[5]

"Certainly," says Browning, "in the fact of any conspicuous achievement of genius, philosophy no less than sympathetic instinct warrants our belief in a great moral purpose having mainly inspired even where it does not visibly look out of the same." What urges a poet on is ever greater insight into the nature of reality that he then reveals to "the masses." "An absolute vision," Browning hastens to state, "is not for this world, but we are permitted a continual approximation to it. . . ." But what kind of approximation? A *mythus*, a provisional system or conception, something never fully to be believed in but to be embraced as a structure of belief.[6] As Schlegel said, "It is equally deadly for a mind to have a system or to have none. Therefore it will have to combine both" (*Athenaeum* Fragment no. 53).

The *Essay on Shelley* shows that historically Browning dwells on an isthmus between the old religious view of life and the new positivist view. This was not for him, however, a cause for lamentation, as it was, for example, for Tennyson and Arnold.[7] He wrote to Elizabeth Barrett: "The cant is, that 'an age of transition' is the melancholy thing to contemplate and delineate—whereas the worst things of all to look back on are times of comparative standing still, rounded in their impotent completeness" (Kintner, 2:710). The very indeterminancy and openness of the present is a cause for joy, offering opportunity for greater self-understanding and self-realization not only on the part of the individual but for mankind as a whole. Browning proclaims his liberty from the limitations of time by calling on its revolutionary potential: in a minute man can change his mind and revise all that he had thought or stated before; meaning is always in the making, man is always making and unmaking himself. In short, man is always in a state of becoming.

In the pages that follow, I propose to study this drama of becoming in Browning's poetry to 1846, the year generally accepted as marking the close of his early career.[8] By this time, with roughly one-third of his total work behind him, he was well on his way to becoming "Browning." I shall draw special attention to his constantly evolving forms, to his preoccupation with language, and to the consciousness of his characters that they are themselves *dramatis personae* in the process of constructing and deconstructing scripts. In brief, I shall trace his growth as an ironist. Others have dealt frequently with Browning's irony but with specific or particular ironies—that is, corrective ironies and the ironies of paradoxes, dilemmas, and other impossible situations. I am not, however, mainly interested in his local ironies. I want to show his irony to be of a more general nature and of a greater magnitude. For Browning's essential irony is not polemical; it is, rather, a disposition or a state of mind. It originates, as I have suggested, in his double vision of man as caught between the rival principles of objectivity and subjectivity, between the dualities of power and love, finitude and infinity. From one point of view, man as an individual is seen as a finite creature in a multitudinous world whose complexities he can never penetrate, whose contradictions he can never reconcile, and whose myriad possibilities he can never realize. From another point of view, man, endowed with the power of the imagination, is himself creative and free of dependence upon finite objects, which he can deal with as he will; he alone creates value and meaning. Which then is the true view? Neither one nor the other but both, says Browning, as in his art he gives us a composite image of man as infinite and free in imagination and thought but finite and bounded in understanding and action. "The spiritual comprehension," he writes in the *Essay on Shelley,* "may be infinitely subtilised, but the raw material it operates upon must remain." A "whole" poet represents the real and the ideal—the objective and the subjective—and comes to terms with both. He shows, in other words, both the irony of the world against man and the irony of man against the world—man as victim and as savior. And in presenting them ironically in his art, he transcends both. Browning shared Goethe's belief that "art is the individual's attempt to preserve himself against the destructive power of the whole."[9] It was because he embraced the philosophy of becoming that Browning became an ironist, and it is as an ironist that he is becoming in every respect.

CHAPTER I
PAULINE

TRADITIONALLY *PAULINE* HAS BEEN CATEGORIZED as lyrical and subjective, "thoroughly autobiographical" to the extent that "Browning is the speaker, hardly disguised at all" (DeVane, *Handbook,* p. 42).[1] Recent criticism has tended to veer in the opposite direction and hold that the poem is dramatic and impersonal, representing "the interior life of a character, not that of the poet himself."[2] In my opinion both views, though contradictory, are valid. To explain the paradox, let me begin with some thoughts on the genesis and composition of the poem.

In all likelihood Browning had been thinking of a confessional poem for some time, probably a lyrical narrative in the manner of Shelley's *Alastor*.[3] It was to be the means by which the young man could trace his own development imaginatively and so view his past, which he seems to have regarded guiltily, with some degree of objectivity. As a genre the lyric confession was fraught with danger: first, he might reveal too much of himself, and second, and probably more importantly, he might not gain sufficient distance from his putative speaker or narrator. Then one evening in the autumn of 1832 Browning went to the theater to see Edmund Kean as Richard III. Kean had, as everyone knew, fallen on hard times—alcoholic and tuberculous, he was a shadow of his former self—but he somehow managed to get a grip on himself and hide his infirmities long enough to give a captivating performance as Shakespeare's hero. As Browning walked home after the play, he marveled that such weakness could display such power—by playing a role. The answer dawned on him how he could accomplish the poem that had been lurking unformed in his mind: "I will tell / My state as though 'twere none of mine" (585–86).[4] He would play the role of an unnamed speaker of a dramatic confession addressed to a woman called Pauline.[5] Between 22 October 1832, the night on which the work was conceived and dated at the end, and January 1833, the date affixed to the epigraph, he wrote the poem—as he said, "on one leg" (Orr, *Life,* p. 55). It was published anonymously, at his aunt's expense, in March 1833 as *Pauline; A Fragment of a Confession.*

From its inception the poem involved a concept of irony, though probably at the beginning Browning did not clearly understand the extent to which he was to engage in an ironic exercise. The consciousness of the distinction between an empirical self and a separated self necessitates the mediation of language, a *dédoublement,* as Baudelaire called it in his essay "De l'essence du rire," accomplished only by the linguistic process of signs. That is why *Pauline,* which Browning in a note to the 1888 edition labeled the "first of my performances," is cast as an auricular confession, why his separated, aesthetic self speaks his "sad confession first" before he can find "pardon" (25–26): it is an attempt to gain self-knowledge and self-definition, showing in his aesthetic self some of what he is and much of what he perhaps wishes not to be. His words may be poisonous, as the epigraph from Agrippa indicates, but until he speaks them "it were vain / To hope to sing" (16–17). Urged into song by Pauline, who is to a certain extent identifiable with the empirical self, the aesthetic self will tell not of "truth and love" (87) but of "struggling aims" (811) and "all the wandering and all the weakness" (125–26). The "shame" of his thoughts, it turns out, is that they have not hitherto been allowed issue. But if he (or his author) had not repressed them, then of course there could be no song. Now, however, he must "cast away restraint" (41) because "nursed up energies . . . will prey" (481–82). In giving voice to his guilty thoughts, the "I" believes he has control over them and can "look up and be what I had been" (73–74). As we shall see, this end is delusory, totally at variance with the motto from Marot, which (in translation) tells, "I am no longer that which I was nor will ever know how to be again." The poem is a record of the growing disjunction between the aesthetic self and the empirical self, which will "be the first to deny all, and despise / This verse, and these intents which seem so fair" (991–92).

The sense of playing a role in a world constituted out of language from a script not of his own devising involves the speaker in a kind of irony, for he knows that he has only the freedom allotted to an actor on the stage. He recognizes that his "words are wild and weak" (904) and that only provisionally is he "won by a word" (237). Yet he is not cast into utter oblivion because the playwright who is the empirical self may redeem a dark mood by "some little word" that will "light it up again" (1011) and call him once more into play. The sense of dependence of the aesthetic self on the empirical self serves throughout to underscore the ironic view of the poem.

The drama in which Browning engages his *dramatis persona* takes place in the arena where souls are formed. "Je crois que dans ce qui suit," says Pauline, in a note, which is the only time she speaks *in propria persona,* "il fait allusion à un certain examen qu'il fit autrefois de l'ame ou plutot de son ame, pour découvrir la suite des objets auxquels il lui serait possible d'atteindre."[6] Browning shows that we come into the world as "selves" and that we become "souls" as we establish relations with the world external to self. The pheonomenal world is thus what Keats called a "vale of soul-making."[7] The more we partake of exterior reality, the greater soul we become.

Soul-making, however, involves us in a moral problem. For the self is restless and aggressive in its attempts to increase the soul's wealth. As it encounters the not-self, it may be overcome and thus live only as a reflection of the object encountered; or it may attempt to absorb the not-self into its own orbit of value, thereby robbing the not-self of its freedom and distinctiveness. In the case of human encounter, the will of the one violates the will of the other. Considered morally, action of this sort must be condemned. Yet if the self does not engage in such activity, the soul can never grow; which is to say, the self can never be a soul—a moral entity—unless it engage in immoral conduct. It is a paradoxical situation, the self being damned if it does, damned if it doesn't. The dialectic of self and other is the basic theme of *Pauline*, and the ironies that it entails are heavily informative of the early verse.

In his first published poem, Browning vicariously seeks self-definition by examining the soul in its relation to poetry, love, and religion. The emphasis is mainly on the artistic aspect of his development, but, at least by implication, he is also concerned to show that his aspirations to be a new and distinctive kind of poet can come to fruition only if he has what in the *Essay on Shelley* is called "an adequate instrumentality"—that is, a developed moral and religious soul. He has his dramatic persona begin with childhood, when he shared the religious and cultural beliefs of his elders. Then restraints and imitation are cast aside; "a change was coming on, / . . . the past was breaking / Before the coming, and like fever worked" (394–96). This was a time when "schemes and systems went and came" (399). He seeks out "some one / To be my own," and his choice fell not so much on a scheme or system as a man—the Sun-treader, Shelley. In Browning's own life this was a period of emotional turmoil when, says his earliest authoritative biographer, he "set the judgments of those about him at defiance and gratuitously proclaimed himself everything that he was, and some things that he was not" (Orr, *Life,* pp. 45–46).[8]

What attracted the speaker to the Sun-treader and Browning to Shelley was the older poet's exquisite lyricism. Before he encountered the Sun-treader, the speaker had been much given to the lyric mode, his verse a kind of effusion indifferent to verbal meaning: "I sang, as I in dream have seen, / Music wait on a lyrist for some thought, / Yet singing to herself until it came" (377–79). He is first caught by "passion's melodies" in the Sun-treader's verse and attempts "to gather every breathing of his songs." But then he notices that "woven with them there were words, which seemed / A key to a new world" (410–14), a beautiful idealism, both political and philosophical. For the first time it occurs to him forcefully that the lyric strain can be set to serve a prophetic purpose.

The Romantic poets, and Shelley especially, believed that the physical world is in essence like the spiritual world, phenomena being veiled shows of the noumena behind. It is possible, however, to discern appearances as signs or symbols of the spiritual realm. He who can read this language intermediate between the actual and the ideal is a seer. He who not only sees but reveals what he sees is a bard. Thus Shelley offers his work as the record, in the complex language of analogies and symbols, of the authentic meeting of his mind with the universal mind, what he calls the unseen Power.[9]

To the "I" of *Pauline,* the discovery of Shelley–Sun-treader was thrilling. It meant coming upon a new heaven and a new earth. First struck by his music and then by his words, the speaker "went on, and . . . soon the whole / Of his conceptions dawned" (416–19). He adopts the Sun-treader's libertarian ideals: "Men were to be as gods, and earth as heaven" (425). As for himself personally, he would be a bard, among that small but mighty band who are the unacknowledged legislators of mankind. He would be like the Shelley of whom Browning wrote later in the *Essay on Shelley*: able to perceive Power and Love in the absolute and Beauty and Good in the concrete and to throw, "from his poet's station between them both," swift, subtle, and "numerous films for the connection of each with each." Like Shelley's his verse would be a "sublime fragmentary essay towards a presentment of the correspondency of the universe to Deity, of the natural to the spiritual, and of the actual to the ideal." "And I—ah! what a life was mine to be, / My whole soul rose to meet it" (427–28).

Believing himself a true visionary, a bard "who had the key to life" (425), he turned his gaze from the ideal "to look on real life, / Which was new to [him]" (440–41), to see how his goal for the perfection of mankind might be attained. What he discovered was a fallen world that seemed utterly devoid of those seeds that would burst forth in blossoms of perfection. What he had envisioned as a reality was "but a dream; and so adieu to it" (449). First went his hopes of perfecting mankind and with them his trust in men and his belief that liberty or virtue are soon to be attained. Then he lost faith even in his "motive's end, / And powers and loves; and human love went last" (460–61). Having put his whole faith in the realization of a beatific vision, he is bereft when that proves false; his idealism supplanted by cynicism, he yields up moral questions in despair.

The crisis described in *Pauline* is remarkably similar to those recounted in *The Prelude* and *Sartor Resartus,* although neither work was available to Browning at the time *Pauline* was written.[10] What is noteworthy is that the crisis and the recovery from it came early in Browning's career and at an age much younger than for other young men who experienced similar crises—Wordsworth, Carlyle, or Mill, for instance. It was doubtless the most important event in the poet's life[11] (*pace* those who claim his marriage to Elizabeth Barrett was), not because of its intensity but because of its effect on his fundamental outlook: the rejection of the all-or-nothing attitude epitomized by Shelley and, as we shall see, the embracing of the idea of change as the basic law of life.

It was not only Shelley's philosophy that Browning recoiled from: it was also his whole mode of poetry. For Shelley the lyric was the chief means of expression, and what he sang of was himself, sometimes under other names but always recognizably Shelley. What he aimed to do was to elevate himself into a mythic role as poet and redeemer of the world, and what he presented in his verse was an ideal of himself, which he considered to be representative of mankind, as, for example, when in the preface to *Alastor* he says that his poem "may be considered as allegorical of one of the most interesting situations of the human mind." With himself as his hero and his own inner experience as his subject matter, his poems are works of mythopoeic creation.

Such songs are beautiful, but are they true? That is, are the visions that they unfold anything more than lovely dreams of wish fulfillment? When the speaker in *Pauline* attempts to act on them, he finds that he is like a wanderer who sees dimly in the distance strange towers and walled gardens thick with trees "where singing goes on, and delicious mirth, / And laughing fairy creatures peeping over"; but when on the morrow he comes there to live forever, he discovers that they are not there (450–56). No, the Sun-treader's "sweet imaginings are as an air, / A melody, some wond'rous singer sings" (221–22). They can be prized as the sweetest songs ever sung, expressions of man's highest and noblest aspirations, but as mythic allegories their truth is personal and private.

This is why Browning hereafter is deeply suspicious of the allegorical mode and contemptuous of bards. He cast aside forever all notions of the self as representative of mankind and of poetry as allegorical. Endowed with an acute consciousness of self, Browning regarded himself as unique. "This is myself," the speaker of *Pauline* says three times—not myself as representative of anything, only myself as me. To be sure, he does not disavow the imagination, but his, unlike Shelley's, comes "not / In fitful visions, but [is] beside me ever" (285-86) to control and shape experience. He makes no pretense to rise to Shelley's lyrical mythicism. As the epigraph reads (in translation), "I AM NOT SAYING THAT THESE THINGS ARE GOOD FOR YOU, I AM ONLY TELLING THEM."

Browning also recognized that the equation of personal expression and lyric intensity yields lyric emotion at the expense of phantasms, melodramatic poses, and extreme irrational, emotional states. The expression of self as hero can produce not only visions but also hallucinations. In a word, turning inward can lead to madness. "I'll look within no more," says the speaker of *Pauline*. "I have too trusted to my own wild wants— / Too trusted to myself—to intuition" (937-39). Turning away from Shelley and other Romantic visionaries, Browning disavowed idealized autobiography and the subjectivity of lyric expression for the objectification of self offered by the dramatic mode: "I will tell / My state as though 'twere none of mine" (585-86). Here and hereafter, though there might be occasional resemblances between Browning and his characters, he and his hero were never to be one.

Browning did not, however, openly repudiate Shelley. On the contrary, *Pauline* closes with the speaker's apostrophe to the Sun-treader and his admission that he will lean on the older poet. What happens is not repudiation but a swerve away from Shelley, what Harold Bloom calls a *clinamen*.[12] The process is subtle and complex, and Browning releases himself from the pervasive influence of Shelley by freezing the poetic visionary into the distant perfection of a star. First, however, the speaker in *Pauline* distances himself not by elevating the bard but by stressing the depth of his fall from the Sun-treader's ideals: "For I have nought in common with him—shapes / Which followed him avoid me, and . . . I feel how low I am to him" (212-15). The descent means that as a poet he can no longer aim "even to catch a tone / Of all the harmonies which he called up" (216-17). But is this so bad?

Losing the Sun-treader has he lost everything? As he looks back, the speaker sees that even earlier, when he lost his faith in mankind, he had been aware of a compensatory gain: "new powers / Rose as old feelings left"(462–63). Furthermore, even at the height of the hold of the Sun-treader's ideals, he doubted their validity for him: "I had oft been sad, / Mistrusting my resolves" (464–65).

There then occurs a great sense of liberation; he was at last his own man; "My powers were greater" (469). In the temple of his soul, nought was changed except that the idol was gone and a new, although darker, spirit had taken his place. As the newly freed poet wanders through the temple, shadowy troops rise to greet him as their king: "We serve thee now, and thou shalt serve no more!" (475). As for himself: "I felt once more myself—my powers were mine" (491).

This process of disentanglement and self-assertiveness engenders, however, a certain amount of guilt: glad to be free, he is also sad that an idol once adored is no longer worshiped. It is the "curse" of guilt "to see our idols perish" (545–46). Moreover, it is a question not only of guilt but also of *amour-propre*: one cannot admit that one was so foolish as to have revered a false idol. What is necessary for one's psychic well-being is, then, to adopt a strategy that will retain the idol, but as the sun, whose light to seek at close range would be blinding: Shelley must be hyperbolized as the Sun-treader.[13]

First in the strategy comes the process of self-abasement. We, being lowly, made of clay—we may wither; but our fate should not extend to our idols. To witness paintings fade not only in color but in significance, to hear music that no longer moves us as it once did, to discover, in other words, that art wears out like everything else—this is a "curse" indeed! It is the curse of betrayal. "And I, perchance, half feel a strange regret, / That I am not what I have been to thee" (191–92), the speaker says to the Sun-treader. "For never more shall I walk calm with thee" (220). But most unsettling is the thought that one's own work of the present is perhaps as meaningful as that of once-idolized predecessors of the past "whom trustingly / We sent before into Time's yawning gulf"—"I'd be sad to equal them." To preserve them, "keep them for ever / In beauty," the speaker denies emulation of his idols by choosing a deferential position, "contented lowness": "I'd feed their fame e'en from heart's best blood, / Withering unseen, that they might flourish still" (545–59).

The second step of the strategy is elevation of the idol, now deposed from the altar in the temple of the soul, to a distant sphere in the heavens, transcendence erasing immanence. A series of metaphors accomplishes this. Once worshiped as "a sacred spring," the divine water turns out to be "the fountain-head, / Long lost, of some great river," which engulfs everything in its path (172–85). Rocks may try to turn or stay its course, but in vain. "So / Wert thou to me," says the speaker, employing the past tense; and had he not removed himself from the vicinity of this river, he would have been drowned, sucked into the stream and made permanently a part of it, having no distinction of his own (190–91). Not to be admired as a close and mighty river, the Sun-treader is made a "Spirit" which, "its long task completed, . . . hath risen / And left us, never to return" (158–59). Yet though elevated, the Sun-treader still "seems bright with thy bright presence" (161):

But thou art still for me, as thou hast been. (162)

But thou art still for me, who have adored. . . . (168)

The repetition suggests both continuity and stasis, the fixity of the "star" (171) that the Sun-treader has become, something immovable and therefore not of this world:

And if thou livest—if thou lovest, spirit!
Remember me, who set this final seal
To wandering thought—that one so pure as thou
Could never die.
                                    (206–9)

The Sun-treader is sealed into eternity, unchangingness, and perfection, as the speaker—"a watcher, whose eyes have grown dim / With looking for some star"—perceives a heavenly light "which breaks on him, / Altered, and worn, and weak, and full of tears" (227–29). Shelley is steadfast, Browning is vacillating; but Shelley is fixed forever and thus dead, whereas Browning is protean and alive.

The swerve away from Shelley allowed Browning to become a new and distinctive kind of poet. It did not, as I have said, entail repudiation of the older poet, whom Browning continued to regard with admiration and affection, as the *Essay on Shelley* makes abundantly clear. By the end of *Pauline*, Shelley is gathered into the artifice of eternity where dwell God and truth and love (1020–21). He can now be invoked as a figure permanently enshrined, on whom the speaker will hereafter "lean" (1023). Shelley can be "leaned" upon not for method or mode but for the vision of perfection that the poet must have ever before his eyes but that he knows he can never reach.

The irony of willed dependency that we notice in the case of the poet with regard to the Sun-treader is also discernible in his relation to Pauline. When Romantic ideals proved to be chimerical, he was left with nothing to cling to. It is almost a commonplace of Romantic literature that love for a woman is a means of validating human existence. As Shelley states in the preface to *Alastor*, it is through love of a woman that his hero "unites all of wonderful, or wise, or beautiful, which the poet, the philosopher, or the lover could depicture." Having failed him in poetry and philosophy, Shelley might still be right about love. So the speaker turns in his despair to Pauline: "Thou lovedst me, and I wondered, and look in / My heart to find some feeling like such love" (578–79). But he finds no love there. The reason is that he cannot chain his soul to "its clay prison; this most narrow sphere" (591). Why love only one object when he can love many? His "love would pass . . . reason," but since "love must receive its objects from the earth, / While reason would be chainless," he cannot find an object that will embody all that he can imagine love and beauty to be. Thus his imagination has "sufficed to quell / All love below" (637–41). Poor inadequate Pauline, who fails her would-be lover not, like the Sun-treader, from soaring too loftily but from inability to get off the ground.

Where is, then, that love which "would quell / Reason, tho' it soared with the seraphim?" (642–43). It can only be self-love, the self finding value only in its unchained subjectivity: "And yet I seem more warped in this than aught, / For here myself stands out more hideously" (646–47). But "thus it is that I supply the chasm / 'Twixt what I am and all that I would be" (676–77). He is not at ease in the situation and begins to feel self-love turn to self-hate (650–52). Why has he sought refuge in himself? Because of "the woes I saw and could not stay— / And love!—do I not love thee, my Pauline?" (688–89).[14] Obviously in loving Pauline he loves himself. "I cherish prejudice, lest I be left / Utterly loveless" (690–91).

Pauline is not, however, his only "prejudice" or pretended love. He still loves liberty, poets ("tho' sad change has come there too"), and his native England (692–97), where apparently he will take Pauline to reside. But England, like Pauline, cannot encompass his fancies of where a home should be. So instead of England it must be "a home . . . , out of the world; in thought" (730); whereupon he takes her on a magical mystery tour of England's green and pleasant land, finally settling among Wordsworthian hedgerows and smoking cots (732–807). But the England of Romantic nature poetry does not offer the imaginative freedom that his soul requires. For among the hedgerows "the bushes close, and clasp above, and keep / Thought in" and his "soul saddens when it looks beyond" (807–9). Once again the reality does not measure up to his preconception of it.

Throughout the poem there are images of expansion and contraction that reflect the speaker's urges and inabilities to transcend self. His position is a paradoxical one. When his soul is most contracted "into the dim orb / Of self" (91–92), it is also least bound; for it is all potential. When most expanded, it is least free; for it has had to restrict its possibilities. Of his first encounter with the Sun-treader's philosophy, he says: "My whole soul rose to meet it" (427). Yet instead of expansion of his powers, he experiences only the limitations of servitude. When he rebels against the Sun-treader, he says: "I felt once more myself" (491); "my powers were greater" (469). Likewise when he meets Pauline, he feels his soul rise up, only soon thereafter to feel suffocated. "And thus I know this earth is not my sphere, / For I cannot so narrow me, but that / I still exceed it" (634–36). It is this alteration—"this wavering will" (653), "these struggling aims" (811)—that is the chief matter of the "confession"; and nowhere is it more notable than in the passage devoted to the English home "in thought," where open spaces are "walled in with a sloped mound of matted shrubs" (750) and "tall trees over-arch to keep us in" (754) only to expand to vast spaces until the bushes of the copses and hedgerows close in again. Wordsworthian nature, domesticity, Pauline—all are signs of the "home," enclosure and fixity, that the speaker fears.

Yet he recognizes that Pauline is "a last / Resource—an extreme want" (907–8). If in fact he had remained constant to her earlier, he would have been spared the "shame" he now feels (28). Yet still he can give her "not love, but faith" (43). Nevertheless, she must remain with him and shut him in from fear (1–5, 925–27). Earlier he had said that he could love nothing: "but sense supplies a love / Encircling me and mingling with my life" (311–12), and it is this very erotic "sense" that he now clings to as the redeeming aspect of his relationship with Pauline:

> thy soft breast
> Shall pant to mine—bend o'er me—thy sweet eyes,
> And loosened hair, and breathing lips, and arms
> Drawing me to thee.
> (1–4)

> How the blood lies upon her cheek, all spread
> As thinned by kisses; only in her lips
> It wells and pulses like a living thing,
> And her neck looks, like marble misted o'er
> With love-breath, a dear thing to kiss and love,
> Standing beneath me—looking out to me,
> As I might kill her and be loved for it.
> (896–902)

> Leave me not,
> Still sit by me—with beating breast, and hair
> Loosened— . . .

Look up.   kissing me when I

(925–29)

It will be noted that in the second of these quotations the speaker stands in a position superior to Pauline. This is, however, but momentary. He can refer to her as a frail winter flower, "offering / Its frail cup of three leaves to the cold sun" (712–13). He can say that he sustains his inamorata, who "lives in loving me, / Lives strangely on my thoughts, and looks, and words" (239–40). He can promise: "I have / Much yet to gladden you—to dawn on you" (934–35). But he can no more be a sun to Pauline than he can be equal to or rise above the Sun-treader. He knows full well that his must be a position of dependency, that his soul must "rest beneath / Some better essence than itself—in weakness" (818–19). It is his nature to adore (833). He will do anything, "only believing he is not unloved" (859). So, "No more of this—we will go hand in hand, / I will go with thee, even as a child, / Looking no further than thy sweet commands" (948–49). She will choose what and where their life will be, and he will lean on her as on the Sun-treader. The psychology of dependency in love adumbrated here will become more obvious and more pathological in much of Browning's subsequent early work.

The leaning is, however, here as in the other case, provisional. Although at the moment he can "make an end in perfect joy" (994, 1007), he may also "be first to deny all" (991) because he remains "one half afraid / To make his riches definite" (998–99). Any end that is fixed can never claim his full allegiance. Deferment, openness, change—these are for him the aspects that make life vital. This is why Pauline must remain content to be the provisional redemptress of one who does "doubt not [that] many another bliss awaits" (1009).

The speaker's relation to both Pauline and the Sun-treader involves a concept of love and power: he can love only that to which he attributes power. This puts him in an anomalous position because he feels a strong sense of power within himself. In his self-analysis he states that he possesses an intense consciousness of self. This self is felt to be supreme, existing as a center to all things and aiming to create, rule, and call upon all things to minister to it. Allied to this is a sense of restlessness "which would be all, have, see, know, taste, feel, all" (269–78). The self in other words would subjugate and violate all things so as to penetrate, possess, and know them fully. At the same time the self needs to feel that it is not the omnipotent entity that it wishes to be, needs something to give direction and purpose to the exercise of power: "never acting from myself" but "trusting in a hand that leads" (306–7). The soul first says, "I should rule" (343), but then, on second thought,

> The soul would never rule—
> It would be first in all things—it would have
> Its utmost pleasure filled,—but that complete
> Commanding for commanding sickens it.
> (814–17)

As we have seen, Pauline and the Sun-treader are both granted command, but the power they have over him proceeds only from himself, not from them. What he requires is a power over which he can have no control: "And what is that I hunger for but God?" (821).

The God-hunger has long been with him. As a boy he "saw God every where" (302), but during adolescence he came to doubt God's "being" (305). Now he feels "a need, a trust, a yearning after God," although accompanying and "reconciled" with this feeling was "a neglect of all . . . deemed his laws" (295–98); and "this feeling still has fought / Against . . . reason and resolves" (308–9). The speaker does not pretend to any direct experience of the divine; his is simply the expression of a need, and because of the need he can work himself up to an emotional state that allows him to say, "I need thee, and I feel thee, and I love thee," this in spite of the fact that he disclaims any rapture at God's work or any belief in immortality: "but there is that in me / Which turns to thee, which loves, or which should love" (821–30). As in the instances of the Sun-treader and Pauline, the speaker returns to God not so much out of love for Deity as out of the necessity for a superior power who can love him and be a support on which to lean. If there is not this power, then it is impossible to escape solipsism. The imagination can be "an angel" (285), but it can also be a demon that causes "a mind like this [to] dissipate itself" (291) while "draining the wine alone in the still night" (940). "Take from me powers, and pleasures," he pleads to God, "so I . . . see thee" (845–46). God's "being" may be doubted but his "presence" (305–6) is a necessity of "soul."

Until he locates this "presence" that is power, the speaker cannot hope to love. For the divine presence alone can sanction the immediate and the imperfect, which he would but cannot love. He has attempted to foist this role on Pauline and the Sun-treader but discovers that they can be no more than mediate figures to be idolized until he reaches God. "Do I not feel a love which only ONE.....?" he asks, in an unfinished question (837). The answer must be yes, an affirmation not of feeling but of will. And having so willed, he can turn to Pauline and say: "And now, my Pauline, I am thine for ever!" (860).

The God affirmed is, however, no more than a convenient (if necessary) fiction. He is "the last point" that turns the soul that "would be first in all things" into a dependent that would "rest beneath / Some better essence than itself—in weakness" (815–19); the God of Pauline's lover is "the last point" where "tend—these struggling aims" (811). As the "end in perfect joy" (994, 1007), God is distanced into stillness and eternity, and thus out of this world into a realm of abstractions where dwell beauty, truth, and love (1006, 1020–21). But this is Deity conceived by "one half afraid / To make his riches definite" (998–99): it is Deity that, in a special sense, is both Alpha and Omega and thus allows for expansion as well as enclosure. "I shall again go o'er the tracts of thought," says the speaker, "As one who has a right" (1013–14), and in doing so may reconceive Deity, "the last point" that is but a provisional "end in perfect joy."

By confessing the means and ends of his soul's development in respect to art, love, and religion, the speaker in *Pauline* arrives at the point of self-definition. "This is myself" (279); "these make myself" (313); finally, "this is 'myself'—not what

I think should be" (820). The self is ultimately defined in terms of the will. In his relation to the Sun-treader, Pauline, and God, the speaker resigns his will so as to place himself in a position of secondariness, but always with the knowledge that the possibility remains for the will to reassert its priority: "the sole proof / Of a commanding will is in that power / Repressed" (621-23), the power in hiding being a "bright slave" of which he "cannot be but proud" (633). What the will represses can of course be rediscovered later on, summoned up by "a commanding will." Much of what the speaker confesses is, by his own declaration, foul and shameful, and hence to be willed away. Yet this which "lies in [him] a chained thing" is "still ready / To serve if [he] loose its slightest bond" (631-33).

What the "I" learns from his "confession" that the will is at the center of the self is that the most contrary statements that can be made about his soul are alike true. For the soul wishes both continuity and change, primacy and secondariness, openness and enclosure, expansion and contraction. It finds itself always in the present, which is the gap between desire and realization, repression and reclamation, oblivion and recovery, the moment of something ever about to be: "And thus it is that I supply the chasm / 'Twixt what I am and all that I would be" (676-77). For such a soul nothing is fixed, all conclusions being but new points of beginning.

The belief in change embraced here is not developed into a philosophy, as it will be in Browning's next poem. We see, nevertheless, that allied to it is a belief in progress, which is figured as the ascent of a mountain. Pauline in her note speaks of the plateaus that her lover achieves and that then become points of departure to attain yet other heights that in turn must be surmounted. Because it is conceived linearly, the advance must have an end; but as we have noticed, the terminal point recedes with each advance toward it so that there is never any possibility of its being attained. Nowhere is this clearer than at the close of the confession. Having given his "vision" of himself, the speaker thereupon asserts, almost in passing, that he will be the first to deny all and despise this verse that incorporates "these intents which seem so fair" (991-92). His visions are quickly subject to revisions.

At the end we witness the increased disjunction between the empirical self of the poet and the separated self of the poem. For it is in the nature of a joke that the poet has his fictional speaker say twice that he can "make an end in perfect joy" (994, 1007). In the first place, this is not an end in any conventional sense of the word. As the speaker tells us, this is but the "first stage" of his life (885). In the second place, for one embracing the doctrine of becoming there can be no "last point." In the third place, the achievement of perfection is vitiated, as the speaker himself asserts, by the fact that in a dynamic universe perfection is a sign of death and decay. In the fourth place, the joy is more than offset by "a lurking fear" (995) of one "half afraid" (998) who feels "this weak soul sink, and darkness come" (1010). Whatever joy there is in this "end" is purely delusory, self-induced. "I shall be priest and lover, as of old" (1019), or, in the revised text, "I shall be priest and prophet as of old"—we have just witnessed his farewell to any claim to the bardic throne when he shed the mantle of the Sun-treader. "I believe in God, and truth, / And love" (1020–21)—we have noted how he believes in them only as necessary fictions.

Not realizing the ironic nature of the poem, commentators have more often than not attributed the speaker's confession to Browning himself. But it is increasingly clear as the narrative progresses that the empirical self of the poet withdraws from this linguistic entity that is the "confession." Believing it possible to be redeemed by language into the state where he can once again be "trusting in truth and love" (87),[15] the dramatized self does indeed claim that, through verbal reenactment and repetition of the past, he has reached the point of self-control where he is "won by a word again / Into my old life" (237–38) of believing in God and truth and love. We have just noted how such an affirmation is based on a willed repression of thoughts and feelings revealed in the confession. He can be the "perfect bard" (893)—the "priest and lover, as of old" (1019)—only by committing himself to the imagined life that is the world of language. As Browning discovered, the self that exists only in the form of language may aid the empirical self in achieving differentiation and definition; but it is no more than a linguistic construct whose authenticity must be denied. Language can be psychologically therapeutic, a step forward in self-articulation. The separated self suggests this when he says that in future dark moments of the soul "some little word shall light it up again, / And I shall see all clearer and love better" (1011–12), just as this "little word" that is his confession has done in this instance. But that language has reality or meaning of its own is called into question by the assertion of the aesthetic self that this is an "end" in which he speaks as a bard, whose words are of doubtful authenticity.

It is indeed Browning's strategy to distance his empirical self from his separated, linguistically realized self. He does this not only in the "affirmation" at the close but also in other parts of the poem. The note in French signed by Pauline, the Latin headnote from Agrippa, the motto from Marot in French, the affixed dates at the beginning and end—all these are signals that the confession is not the poet's; they may even be signals of Browning's intention as to genre—that is, signals that the work should be regarded as a fictional edition.[16]

In her role as editor, Pauline has presumably performed several services. First, she has prepared the text for publication. She may even have arranged and rearranged certain sections of the confession—she speaks of considering "à mieux coordonner certaines parties." Second, she has provided a critical note in which she emphasizes the importance of genre in evaluating the poem and also points out its artistic defects.[17] Third, she has attempted to illuminate the confession by prefixing two quotations. The motto from Marot on the title page suggests that change is the basic theme of the poem. The quotation from Cornelius Agrippa on the reverse title page cautions the (learned) reader that the poem is the work of a youth and that its emotional extravagances should perhaps not be taken too seriously. Fourth, Pauline has supplied the place and date of the poem's composition and of her final editorial work.[18]

Editing is of course a way of distancing experience, setting the fictional self at a still further remove; it is a technical means of separating story from narration and thereby asserting the essential negativity of the fiction; in brief, it is an obvious artifice that obviates any confusion about the coincidence of life and art. In her note Pauline tells us that the confession is not fully intelligible and perhaps not fully trustworthy, and she tries briefly to give us her understanding of the poem. But is Pauline's judgment to be accepted? She herself says that it would be best to burn the "fragment"—"mais que faire?" The fact remains that she does not burn it but undertakes to have it published. Only through her does her lover have his say. From one point of view, Pauline as editor represents the empirical self as it comes to an articulation of itself when the confession is completed. Yet from another point of view, she is as much a fiction as the "I" of the confession, the one no more and no less real than the other. In her role as editor, she provides another perspective and so keeps the poem within Browning's ironic view of the world. For she maintains the double vision that the speaker of the confession seeks in the final phases of his song to surpass. Pauline's role is to keep open and dynamic (even though by her editorial work she ironically encloses the "fragment,") the dialectic of self that is ever being threatened by closure and stasis.

Pauline shows us clearly the double vision that characterized Browning from beginning to end. In his last works he was still posing the same question implied in *Pauline*: "Advantage would it prove or detriment / If I saw double?" he asks in the parleying "With Gerard De Lairesse" (118–19). Browning like the lover of Pauline had a soul that he could not chain:

> it will not rest
> In its clay prison; this most narrow sphere—
> It has strange powers, and feelings, and desires,
> Which I cannot account for, nor explain,
> But which I stifle not, being bound to trust
> All feelings equally—to hear all sides:
> Yet I cannot indulge them, and they live,
> Referring to some state or life unknown. . . .
> (593–600)

Fortunately he learned early that no life can indulge the desire to view an object or an event from all sides not sequentially but simultaneously. Only God can assume this supreme stance. Yet, as Mrs. Orr suggests, Browning could never entirely forgo what Hillis Miller calls "a central adventure of romanticism—the attempt to identify oneself with God."[19] He did not forgo it, but neither did he yield to it. He turned from an outmoded Romantic vision, represented in this first work mainly by Shelley, to an ironic double vision that accepts certain opposites as antinomies and therefore irreconcilable. As we see in *Pauline* and as we shall see hereafter, the self, calling on the revolutionary potential of time, is always in process, always glorifying its own self-activity and therefore is its own lord and master.

I do not claim that in *Pauline* the poet has accomplished all he purposed to do. After all, this is Browning at twenty. The style is not yet distinctive, although sufficiently characteristic for Rossetti to come upon the anonymous work in the British Museum almost fifteen years later and recognize it as Browning's.

> Night, and one single ridge of narrow path
> Between the sullen river and the woods
> Waving and muttering—for the moonless night
> Has shaped them into images of life,
> Like the upraising of the giant-ghosts,
> Looking on earth to know how their sons fare.
> Thou art so close by me, the roughest swell
> Of wind in the tree-tops hides not the panting
> Of thy soft breasts.
>
> (732–40)

That is not Browning; it is a kind of general Romantic style. Moreover, the fusion of the dramatic and the lyrical elements in the poem is not entirely successful because the speaker's utterance is not conditioned by the presence of the auditor, who is to a large extent spoken of as though she were not present. The speaker is, on the other hand, more dramatically portrayed than are those of Romantic confessions or monodramas:[20] he cannot be ignored as a character, but at the same time he does not sufficiently engage our sympathy in this monologue of 1,031 lines. It was to require further experimentation in the dramatic mode before Browning learned how to individualize character to the extent that he could elicit our sympathetic interest in foolish or despicable speakers. In addition, the attempt to achieve a perspective other than the speaker's is so inadequately handled that readers have not even recognized what the poet aimed to do. This rudimentary attempt at a fictional edition lacks technical expertise.

But in spite of its deficiencies, *Pauline* is more than the "abortion," "crab," and "eyesore" that Browning later called it.[21] In my opinion it is much better than modern critics have been wont to allow. Many passages of its blank verse are powerfully dramatic and lyrical, as for example:

> But I begin to know what thing hate is—
> To sicken, and to quiver, and grow white,
> And I myself have furnished its first prey.
> All my sad weaknesses, this wavering,
> This selfishness, this still decaying frame...
> But I must never grieve while I can pass
> Far from such thoughts—as now—Andromeda!
> And she is with me—years roll, I shall change,
> But change can touch her not—so beautiful
> With her dark eyes, earnest and still, and hair
> Lifted and spread by the salt-sweeping breeze;
> And one red-beam, all the storm leaves in heaven,
> Resting upon her eyes and face and hair,
> As she awaits the snake on the wet beach,
> By the dark rock; and the white wave just breaking
> At her feet, quite naked and alone,—a thing
> You doubt not, nor fear for, secure that God
> Will come in thunder from the stars to save her.
> Let it pass—I will call another change.
>
> (650–68)

That is poetry which is meant to be read aloud; it is speech which suggests the nervous, vacillating, almost schizophrenic character of the speaker. And formally the whole has sophistication and breadth of conception. The idea of an open-ended "fragment" enclosed within an editorial apparatus, a form reflecting the imagery of expansion and contraction adumbrated in the confession—this shows an intellectual maturity and an artistic daring that belie the author's mere twenty years. We should not accept Browning's epithets of opprobrium for his first work any more readily than we accept Keats's dismissal of *Endymion* (in the preface) as "a feverish attempt, rather than a deed accomplished."

CHAPTER II
PARACELSUS

IN THE NOTE APPENDED TO *PAULINE*, THE EDITOR says that the only merit to which "une production si singulière" can pretend is "celui de donner une idée assez précise" of the genre that has been merely sketched. In his next work Browning wrote in the foreword: "I am anxious that the reader should not, at the very outset—mistaking my performance for one of a class with which it has nothing in common—judge it by principles on which it was never moulded, and subject it to a standard to which it was never meant to conform." The fact is, he says, no matter how the text might otherwise appear, "I have endeavoured to write a poem, not a drama." Nor, he goes on to say, has he written a dramatic poem, which, as he understands the genre, means accepting the limitations of acted drama without any compensatory benefits. To help us understand this work that looks like a play but that its author disclaimed as a drama and insisted was a poem, perhaps it would be salutary to begin with a brief consideration of the drama and dramatic literature earlier in the century.

With its emphasis on causality in the moral as well as in the physical world, the philosophical empirical tradition laid great stress on investigation of the motives of action. Extended to drama, it was to lead actors and critics alike to suspect that human action has no meaning unless referred to the mental state that prompted it. The acting styles of Garrick, Mrs. Siddons, Kemble, and especially Kean sought to reveal a character's nature by exposing his motives to the audience; in the plays in which they acted, character consequently tended to predominate over action.[1] Action or plot, which Aristotle had found the "soul" of tragedy, yielded primacy to thought and feeling. Addressing himself to modern drama, A. W. Schlegel spoke of "a new definition in the conception of action, namely, the reference to the idea of moral liberty, by which alone man is considered as the first author of his determination."[2] Coleridge, contrasting modern literature with that of the Greeks, observed that the modern achieves an opposite effect from the ancient "by turning the mind inward on its essence instead of letting it act only on its outward circumstances and communities."[3] By 1829 John Henry Newman could say, with the air of one uttering what had never been doubted, "The action then will be more justly viewed as the vehicle for introducing the personages of the drama, than as the principal object of the poet's art; it is not in the plot, but in the characters, sentiments, and diction, that the actual merit and poetry of the composition are found."[4]

Stressing character over action, the actor reserved his talents and energies for the big scenes when motives are disclosed, so that a play like *Richard III, Hamlet,* and *Macbeth* became, in the hands of Sarah Siddons or Edmund Kean, a series of "moments." Writing of their acting styles, Joseph Donahue says: "Plunged into the immediate situation, [the actor] has no time to meditate on his reactions; they burst forth at the instant they are formed in the mind, impelling him into the future. Subsequent moments, drawing forth repeated demonstrations of his responsive nature, reveal the struggle of the mind with the varying forms of passion. Only these moments, as they occur, are real."[5] Henry Siddons's *Practical Illustrations of Rhetorical Gesture and Action, Adapted [from the German] to the English Stage* (1807) presupposes that dramatic reality consists entirely of a sequence of "moments," each revealing the character's nature by eliciting a reaction to a situation. Coleridge said of Kean: "To see him act, is like reading Shakespeare by flashes of lightning."[6]

An acting style emphasizing the moments of passion served to reinforce, and be reinforced by, a general demand throughout the first part of the nineteenth century for a literature of lyrical intensity. Wordsworth's emphasis on poetry as the "spontaneous overflow of powerful feeling," Coleridge's insistence on the intuitive nature of the creative act, Shelley's belief in the evanescence of artistic inspiration, Keats's claim that "the excellence of every Art is its intensity"[7]—all such statements attest to the prevalence during the first two decades of the century of the idea that all literature, but especially poetry, properly aims at brief lyrical effects. By 1835 these sentiments had hardened into dogma. Newman, in the essay (1829) referred to earlier, was intent upon establishing a critical theory based on the "essence" of poetry rather than its "externals" and maintaining that a poem is the result of the poet's "rush of emotions" and "feelings" instead of his logical constructive powers.[8] In two essays of 1833—"What is Poetry?" and "The Two Kinds of Poetry"—John Stuart Mill denigrated narrative and praised lyric as "more eminently and peculiarly poetry than any other," it being "the poetry most natural to a really poetic temperament."[9] Alexander Smith, writing on "The Philosophy of Poetry" in 1835, spoke on the subject with the assurance of one summing up orthodox doctrine: "The essential character . . . of a poetical narrative or description . . . is this—that its direct object is not to convey information, but to intimate a subject of feeling, and transmit that feeling from one mind to another." Hence "the interest derived from story, incident, and character, can be equally well conveyed in prose composition, nay, infinitely better, from a variety of causes, and chiefly from the inadmissibility, in poetry, of the mention of any fact not calculated to be spoken of *with emotion.*"[10]

In the drama of the early 1800s, such attitudes resulted in the lyrical dramas of the great Romantics that center almost exclusively on the moral development of the protagonists, in the works of playwrights like Joanna Baillie and Henry Hart Milman that reduce action to a minimum and concentrate on dialogue as a means of exposition of motive, and in the dramatic scenes and fragments of Landor and Barry Cornwall. Looking over the state of the English theater in 1823, George Darley observed in one of his "Letters to the Dramatists of the Day": "Action is the essence of drama; nay, its definition. . . . But that essence . . . you, Gentlemen, seem with one consent sedulously to avoid meddling with. . . . You seem to think that the whole virtue of tragedy lies in its poeticity."[11] At the end of the next decade, a French observer of the English stage made almost the same comment.[12]

The theory and practice of a literature of dramatic

"moments" was to have a strong effect upon Browning's early career. *Pauline* had "shadowed out" the "first stage" (884–85) of a man's life. In *Paracelsus* Browning's aim was more ambitious: to recount all stages in the life of his protagonist. A work in the narrative mode must surely have first suggested itself; but Browning found narrative technique tedious, and, in addition, he seems to have shared Mill's view that, considered as poetry, narratives are "of the lowest and most elementary kind," appealing mainly to those "in a rude state" of society or to the "idle and frivolous" in more advanced societies. Eschewing conventional narrative technique, he decided to cast the poem that was to "shadow out" all stages of his hero's life in dialogue form. To do this, he would choose the most important events in the career of his protagonist so as to make them moments of lyrical intensity.[13]

The advantages of such a form were numerous. First, it would relieve him of the tedious part of narrative writing, what Tennyson wearily referred to as "the perpetual 'said' and its varieties."[14] Second, it would reduce the "prose" parts of his narrative by focusing only on critical moments, thus becoming a discontinuous narrative. Third, it would permit the development of a "soul" to be witnessed without the distracting incidents and descriptions in conventional narrative or dramatic writing. The result—a series of dramatic fragments or moments organized around the life of one person and presented discontinuously—would be a new genre permitting the poet to achieve what other poets and critics had been proclaiming as an ideal during the first third of the nineteenth century: a narrative that was both lyric and dramatic.

In the work, as indeed in Browning's future works, character is dominant over action, which is reduced to a minimum. Somewhat like Wordsworth, in whose *Lyrical Ballads,* according to its preface, "the feeling therein developed gives importance to the action and the situation, and not the action and situation to the feeling," Browning attempts in his poem

> to reverse the method usually adopted by writers whose aim it is to set forth any phenomenon of the mind or the passions, by the operation of persons and events; and that, instead of having recourse to an external machinery of incidents to create and evolve the crisis I

desire to produce, I have ventured to display somewhat minutely the mood itself in its rise and progress, and have suffered the agency by which it is influenced and determined, to be generally discernible in its effects alone and subordinate throughout, if not altogether excluded. . . .

This means that each scene catches Paracelsus at a critical moment in which he examines and reveals his inner life, or "mood," and is brought by the utterance to new insights allowing him to act. In effect, the five scenes are like five monologues. To be sure, there are other characters who are not mere auditors as in *Pauline*; but the focus being exclusively on Paracelsus, the other figures do not enlist the reader's interest. The reviewer of *Paracelsus* for the *Spectator* (15 August 1835) perceived this when he observed that "the fundamental plan renders the whole a virtual soliloquy, each person of the drama *speaking up* to Paracelsus, in order to elicit his feelings, thoughts, or opinions." To use Henry James's term, Festus, Michal, even Aprile are mere *ficelles*.

Like *Pauline*, *Paracelsus* focuses on soul-making and the ironies involved. "I go to prove my soul," says the protagonist (1. 559), and in doing so he comes to a conclusion whose "drift and scope," said the poet, "are awfully radical."[15] For in the process he discovers that the "principle of restlessness" disclosed in *Pauline* (277) is not only characteristic of the soul but is also the creative principle of the universe: nothing is; all—nature, mankind, God—are ever becoming. Having apparently interrupted composition of a longer poem, *Sordello,* to work out a statement of the philosophical irony upon which his subsequent work was to be based, Browning wrote *Paracelsus* hurriedly, in late 1834 and early 1835, and published it, at the expense of his father, several months later, in August 1835.

For his protagonist the poet chose the Renaissance scientist and mage Paracelsus—"the father of modern chymistry" and also a "theosophist" as he is called in the note to the poem. One of the first empirical scientists, Paracelsus was among the early expounders of the modern scientific view of life, one that called into question the medieval Christian view of the universe as perfectly structured and enclosed. But he was also the practitioner of magic who relied on an older view of the world for spiritual insight. As Browning uses him, he is a restless seeker after knowledge who aims to delve into all aspects of the physical and spiritual universe until he comes to "the secret of the world" (1. 277), "to comprehend the works of God, / And God himself, and all God's intercourse / With our own mind" (1. 533–35). In other words, Browning's Paracelsus begins with the belief that the world is mind, that the individual consciousness can encounter universal consciousness—Wordsworth's Nature, Shelley's unseen Power—and that the encounter can be recorded in language.

Paracelsus unleashes what the speaker of *Pauline* had "repressed"—"a craving after knowledge," which had been "chained" but which remained "still ready / To serve, if [he] loose its slightest bond" (*Pauline,* 620–33). Once unleashed, it becomes for Paracelsus a monomania, "one tyrant all- / Absorbing aim" (2. 152–53) that has "made life consist of one idea" (2. 140). Having no purpose other than itself, "in itself alone / Shall its reward be—not an alien / Blending therewith" (2. 285–87). And supercharged with this idea, Paracelsus has rejected all help: the emotions of love or fear and the work of sages of the past. As though he were a new Adam, he asserts his own priority. It is not until he, like Pauline's lover, recognizes his dependency and secondariness that he penetrates to the perception that his quest was misconceived.

In Paracelsus as in Pauline's lover, the principle of restlessness is linked to an intense consciousness of self that keeps him constantly aware of his empirical self acting in the natural world: he is forever looking at himself going about certain activities. This ironic consciousness of role-playing provides the basic metaphor of the poem and, as we shall see, dictates its mode. In order to play his role correctly, Paracelsus must first come to terms with the text of the play, which he discovers to be written partly by himself and in the language of poetry instead of prose.

The protagonist believes himself called by God "to be his organ" (1. 295), "singled out" (1. 369) to play the role of "God's commissary" (1. 609). As the would-be "star to men" (1. 527), he will have no supporting cast, his script being a one-man play "loaded with fate" (1. 552). What he is called to do is to release the "mind" and "truth" imprisoned within himself so that it can meet the One Mind that is Truth (1. 726–37). In this way alone can he comprehend "God himself" and consequently "the works of God" (1. 533–34) that are nature. But, asks his friend Festus, if Paracelsus has undertaken to read the physical universe as the text where God has revealed himself, why does he not begin with the books in which other men have recorded their experiences of truth? Paracelsus replies that he has been permitted vision in which he has "gazed / Presumptuous on Wisdom's countenance, / No veil between," and now he cannot be guided by others, "whom radiance ne'er distracts" and whose eyes are "unfed by splendour" (1. 515–22). He will follow no prints but will see his way "as birds their trackless way," God directing them both (1. 560, 565). The mediation of print is not required for those who wish to read beyond the thing to the Thing-in-itself.

In scene one Paracelsus views the phenomenal world as the robe or veil of the noumenal world, and believes it possible to transcend the thing (the world as it is perceived by the human mind) to reach the Thing-in-itself (the world as it actually is). Like Carlyle's hero in *Sartor Resartus,* which appeared in serial form in 1833–34 and may well have influenced the composition of the poem, Paracelsus aims to know the world out of clothes, the form without the vesture. "Perfect and true perception" is prevented only by "a baffling and perverting carnal mesh" (1. 731–32). "By searching out the laws by which the flesh / Accloys the spirit," one may "win some day the august form / Of truth" (1. 775–78). Insofar as he is concerned at this time with the language of his role, he believes that once he has discovered Truth he will be able to communicate it to others in words, although (significantly) at present, while promising to speak in "words and ways" true to his heart, he finds that speech "but ill / Expresses what [he] would convey" (1. 15, 428–29). "I am priest," he declares just on the point of departure (1. 801), and has no doubt that he will return as prophet.

In scene two he is no longer so assured that he is God's commissary. It may be that God enjoys his own role as puppeteer and "takes pleasure in confounding us" (2. 180). Surely this must be the answer, or else he is losing his sanity. "God! Thou art Mind!" he cries out like a Romantic visionary. "Unto the master-Mind / Mind should be precious. Spare my mind alone!" (2. 229–30). But what matter whether he has succeeded or not? He will still "reject / Single rewards," will "ask them in the lump" for "now 't is all or nothing"; he cannot "stop short of such / Full consummation" (2. 203–8).

Paracelsus admits that the text which he was to read is not so easily interpreted. No longer able to read unaided, he has come to ask the help of a Greek conjuror, whose first requirement is that he chronicle his life in a book. Speaking of his biography there set down as though it were a text to be interpreted, Paracelsus scorns the "uncouth recordings" and "blurred characters" in which he and others have written the accounts of themselves: "And yet those blottings chronicle a life— / A whole life, and my life" (2. 37–38). Reading over the text, he discovers how he has failed: he has scorned the vesture of truth, which he misconceived as falsehood. The "shows" of the world—life and death, light and shadow—he has read as

> bare receptacles,
> Or indices of truth to be wrung thence,
> Not ministers of sorrow or delight—
> A wondrous natural robe.
> (2. 156–60)

And having wasted his life in misreading, he finds it difficult to read at all here in the near-darkness where there is only light from the putrefying depths of self (2. 175–76). But still God could send light, here in this very city where Constantine was sent a luminous sign (2. 265–66). To Paracelsus too God could reveal outright the clue by which all phenomenal signs are to be read.

At this moment there comes "a voice from within"—the voice of Aprile, the complementary aspect of Paracelsus' personality. Where Paracelsus seemed to embody power in his relentless quest after knowledge, Aprile appears to be the embodiment of love. Where Paracelsus has disvalued the worth of the vestures of truth, Aprile has worshiped its robe, has, like Keats, loved beauty for what it is, not for what it means. To him the signs to be read are so lovely in themselves that he never tries to see beyond them. Overwhelmed and bewildered by the beauties of the phenomenal world, he has not had the strength to deal with them, replicate them in his art. But he has been like Paracelsus in that his too has been an all-or-nothing attitude. Because he could not capture all of life, he has set down none of it. Wishing to "love infinitely, and be loved" (2. 420), he has aspired to transmute all life into beautiful forms for the love of mankind, somehow overcoming the defects of "common speech," which was "useless to [his] ends" (2. 607a), and employing the "heart's language" (2. 560). Now at the end of his life, he recognizes that no one can overleap time to eternity but must work in the present with limited means and rude tools. "Yes; I see now—God is the PERFECT POET, / Who in his poem acts his own creations" (2. 648–49). No human can play the role God plays: he is both the playwright and the superstar.

The meeting of Paracelsus and Aprile is an encounter without dialogue, even though it is written as a colloquy: neither listens to the other. Aprile believes, in spite of all Paracelsus' disclaimers, that the man he addresses is the true poet who, taking advantage of time and opportunity, has achieved all that a master poet-dramatist could attain. Greeting him at the beginning as king, Aprile dies in his delusion that Paracelsus is the king of poets.

Like Paracelsus, Aprile had wished to assert his priority, his independence of tradition. What he learns, in his last moments, is his secondariness and dependency. The voice he hears is that of a chorus of poets who welcome him as their peer and who admit that theirs too has been a failure of attainment, poetry being a matter of "still beginning, ending never" (2. 324). Yet because he has aspired he can join them. But now convinced of his dependency, Aprile cannot accept the crown they offer: "Crown *me?* I am not one of you! / 'Tis he, the king, you seek" (2. 658–59). Only in acknowledging his dependency does Aprile attain to that love to which he aspired.

Paracelsus, still strongly imbued with a sense of power, cannot understand Aprile's message. And despite all that Aprile tells him, Paracelsus continues to regard himself as the lord and king on whom the feeble poet is to lean for support: "Lean thus, / And breathe my breath. I shall not lose one word / Of all your speech—one little word, Aprile" (2. 655-57). Paracelsus still insists on his own priority, believing that only by a beneficent exercise of power is he to love.

His misunderstanding of what Aprile tells him is curious. It is curious because Aprile never attributes his own failure to the fact that he did not recognize knowledge in his ideal. As Paracelsus formulates it, he believes that he and the poet are "halves of one dissever'd world" who must not part till Aprile the lover knows and he the knower loves (2. 634–37). Though perhaps complementary, they are only alike in their passion for ultimates. As personalities they are totally different and contrasting. It is all the more surprising, therefore, when Paracelsus decides to emulate Aprile, indeed assume his role. Abjuring the desire to know infinitely so as to seek infinite love, he is unheedful of Aprile's explanation that absolute love and beauty belong to God alone.

For five years Paracelsus tries to play Aprile's role. In scene three he has become in the eyes of the world "the wondrous Paracelsus—the dispenser / Of life, the commissary of Fate, the idol / Of princes" (3. 14–16). Yet according to the paragon himself it is his "proud fate / To lecture to as many thick-scull'd youths / As please to throng to the theatre each day" (3. 148–50). He has forced himself to play a role for which he is totally unsuited, and he can at present "put off / The wearisome vest of falsehood" only in the presence of his friend (3. 284–85). Yet this is "a rehearsal" (3. 301) for his future performance when, the theater crammed, "the zany of the show" will put off his "trappings" (3. 290–98). "I shall rejoice," Paracelsus says, "when my part in the farce is shuffled through, / And the curtain falls" (3. 591–92). Finally, he will reveal himself entirely and without costume to his uncomprehending audience; but that must wait: "*That* is the crowning operation claim'd / By the arch-demonstrator—heaven the hall, / And earth the audience" (3. 735–37). At present he is not sure what he is supposed to be about. God has given him no direction:

"I know as much of any will of His / As knows some dumb and tortur'd brute" (3. 517–18). In his direction of the play, God is much clearer as to what he does not want than what he does in fact desire (3. 599–602).

Paracelsus is unsuccessful as a professor because he cannot communicate his "truth"—that is, he will not accommodate himself to the requirements of teaching: "to possess was one thing—to display / Another" (3. 654–55). He is pleased to compare himself to his contemporary Martin Luther[16] as a fellow worker in the enterprise of bringing light to the world, but Luther succeeds where Paracelsus fails because he has learned the use of words, not only through his translation of the Bible into the vernacular—the "common speech" to which Aprile referred—but also by making it available in print. Festus begs Paracelsus that, since he cannot lecture successfully, he should take advantage of the newly invented printing press for the dissemination of "the precious lore / Obscured by [Paracelsus'] uncouth manner, or unfit / For raw beginnings" so that eventually what the professor would impart "shall be all-reveal'd" (3. 915–20). Parcelsus' reply is in effect an admission that he does not in fact have the proper language in which to set down his discoveries:

> I possess
> Two sorts of knowledge—one, vast, shadowy, hints
> Of the unbounded aim I once pursued—
> The other, many secrets, made my own
> While bent on nobler prize, and not a few
> First principles which may conduct to much:
> These last I offer to my followers here.
> Now bid me chronicle the first of these,
> My ancient study, and in effect you bid me
> Revert to the wild course I have abjured.
> And, for the principles, they are so simple . . .
>   I do not see
> But that my lectures serve indifferent well.
>   (3. 922–31, 939–40)

The first type of knowledge he can scarcely be said to possess because he cannot express it even to himself. The second he cannot make accessible to others. He has consequently resorted to outrageous displays of antics and bombast: "wild words" (3. 308), "foolish words" (3. 752), which even his devoted Festus finds incomprehensible (3. 496), hard to "interpret" (3. 544). Of these Browning says, in a note to the poem that was added in a later edition, "Bombast, his proper name, probably acquired from the characteristic phraseology of his lectures, that unlucky signification which it has ever since retained."

By the end of scene three, Paracelsus despairs not only of himself but of mankind in general. Yet still he perseveres in his belief that "man must be fed with angel's food" (3. 1014–15). The divine must be realized in the present. Casting off the role of Aprile, he says he will eventually return to his old search for absolute knowledge even though aware of the futility of the quest.

In scene four, the expected reaction against him having come, Paracelsus has left Basel. As long as he was the antic performer of "fantastic gambols leading to no end" (4. 85) he drew huge applauding audiences. But once he ceased to be a monologist and attempted to develop dialogue with his students—"a trust in them and a respect—a sort / Of sympathy for them" (4. 92–93)—they turned against him; they wanted only a show. Having tried to display the love that he believed Aprile enjoined upon him and having failed to do so, he will now reassert his power by returning to his old quest. It matters not "how the farce plays out, / So it be quickly play'd." The "rabble" are admonished to sit safely in "snug back-seats" so as to "leave a clear arena" for the brave actor about to perish for their sport: "Behold!" (4. 688–93).

The quest as Paracelsus now conceives it is correctly described as farce. For he will seek knowledge in every experience life has to offer, no matter how degraded. Recanting his old belief about the nature of the universe, he says that "mind is nothing but disease, / And natural health is ignorance" (4. 279–80). He now embraces the vestures of the world with a vengeance, besieging knowledge by grasping at any and all outward shows: "All helps—no one shall exclude the rest"

(4. 239). Throughout scene four, in expression of his new view, Paracelsus is drunk.

It is a bravura performance that the farceur gives in scene four, including a satirical lyric elegizing his past dreams ("Heap cassia, sandal-buds, and stripes") and a lyrical tale offered as a parable ("Over the sea our galleys went"). Much of what he says is by his own admission "cant," "petty subterfuges," a "frothy shower of words" (4. 627–28). More and more Paracelsus is drawn to the conclusion that language is but expression of a point of view, that truth cannot be encompassed in words. "We live and breathe deceiving and deceived" (4. 625). Words themselves are but vestures, not the thing itself; they "wrap, as tetter, morphew, furfair / Wrap the flesh" (4. 630–31). Indeed, some things cannot be put into words at all: for example, the notion of an afterlife, which Paracelsus finds himself unfit to clothe "in an intelligible dress of words" (4. 681).

Paracelsus had begun his quest in the belief that he not only would find absolute truth but also would forge a new language that could express that truth; that is, he would read phenomena and record his reading in a fully novel fashion. But his failure leads him increasingly to an understanding of the necessity of "all helps" (4. 239), both for the reading and the expression of it. This is suggested especially in the lyric that he presents as a parable (4. 440–527). Mariners come to an island that they believe to be untrod by other men. They set to work building shrines for their stone statues, and, when done, inhabitants from neighboring isles arrive to invite them to bring their "majestic forms" to the other isles that offer far more appropriate shrines already built. The point is that the mariners discover that others have been before them offering even better means for the enshrinement of truth than they. All that they leave behind is a pile of stones to be discovered by future explorers, who may read the "tracings faint" and who are thus made to realize that they are readers and writers in a tradition.[17] The priority that Paracelsus has previously claimed can be no more than a proud delusion. The way to knowledge is not "trackless," as in the beginning he believed, but covered with "tracings."

Paracelsus' acceptance of the idea of tradition and of the conventionality of language is underscored by his changing views on the nature of song. In the earlier parts of the poem, Paracelsus had held that poetry is esentially a private effusion. He speaks of Michal constantly in terms of her singing. He sees her as one who does "sing when all alone" (1. 642, 3. 36): if her song is heard at all, it is but overheard. Both Michal and Festus attempt to correct Paracelsus' false notion of her singing by pointing out that she does indeed sing to others (1. 642-44, 3. 37-38); but their words have no effect. Festus even ventures that lyric can be psychologically therapeutic insofar as it serves to relate the singer to the world outside himself (4. 546-47). Paracelsus' acceptance of this notion is suggested by the lyric "Heap cassia," which he sings to make fun of himself, and by the lyric "Over the sea our galleys went," which he employs to communicate his new understanding of tradition.

The result of Paracelsus' attempt to investigate all the vestures of life is tattered dress. Having earlier cultivated mind at the expense of body, he had grown prematurely old during the years between scenes one and two. Now having pleasured body to the extent of debauchery, he finds it no longer capable of sustaining mind. Yet as he speculated in the beginning, truth may emerge "in unused conjuncture" (1. 767). From the wreck of what he was, from a dislocation of the senses, he gains a new perspective. In scene five he hears the voices that Aprile also heard when dying, and he learns from them about science and philosophy what Aprile learned from them about poetry: namely, his inability or that of any man to probe "the inmost truth" and so "sink mankind / In uttermost despair" because they are left no more to do (5. 143-46). There will always be more to do and more to say; scientists and poets alike are always beginning, never ending, each providing in his end the point of departure for another. Each must try to find the sacred knowledge that Paracelsus quested for, and each must fail; yet the failure is success enough. It is the law of life that no man may preempt the race of its vitality by doing all there is to do or saying all there is to say.

As he prepares to reveal to Festus what he has learned from

the voices, he assumes again the role of the professor. "You are here to be instructed," he tells his friend (5. 460). But he must rise from his couch—"why I ne'er lectured thus" (5. 549)—and attire himself in all the trappings of the philosopher-king, which he has now become: "This couch shall be my throne: I bid this cell / Be consecrate; this wretched bed become / A shrine; for here God speaks to men through me!" (5. 555–58).

What Paracelsus unfolds in his magnificent final monologue is a philosophy of becoming. Life spirals upward, and history is the record of plateaus reached and ascents begun therefrom. From God all being emanates, all power proceeds. For his own joy God sets in motion the evolutionary process culminating in man. The process does not end there, however, for in man begins the fresh evolution of power and love that will in some far-off time result in the perfection of man. But since "progress is / The law of life" (5. 741–42), there will be a fresh development Godward, "in the eternal circle life pursues" (5. 776). There is no *telos* other than the striving itself.

Paracelsus replaces the notion of being with that of becoming as the essence of reality. Thus his Romantic quest for "full consummation" (2. 208) was misconceived: he could not find "the end" because in a state of becoming there is no such thing.[18] And even when he modified his pursuit after the meeting with Aprile, his conception of it remained faulty. He began with the desire for Godlike power, but he learned from Aprile the worth of love and what proportion love should hold with power: that is, that love should precede power, desiring power to set it free, and that under such circumstance new power would always mean a growing access of love (5. 856–59). But he failed to understand the dialectic of love and power as a dynamic process, characterized by temporary failure and regression as well as by success and progress. In a world of multitudinousness, the fertile abundance is constantly developing itself, by means of exhaustless energy, into new structures, or plateaus, of meaning. The present itself has "distinct and trembling beauty" when "seen / Beside its shadow" of the past (5. 828–30). Hence what seems hate is but a mask of love, evil but the temporary eclipse of good:

> To sympathize—be proud
> Of [mankind's] half reasons, faint aspirings, struggles
> Dimly for truth—their poorest fallacies,
> And prejudice, and fears, and cares, and doubts:
> All with a touch of nobleness, for all
> Their error, all ambitious, upward tending,
> Like plants in mines which never saw the sun,
> But dream of him, and guess where he may be,
> And do their best to climb and get to him.
> (5. 875–83)

This is the perspective that Paracelsus should have taken but did not. The philosophy of becoming that he now embraces holds that the phenomenal world, abundant chaos, is "upward tending" in ever higher and higher spirals. As we shall see, this philosophy forms the basis of all the early works.

As Paracelsus now reads the phenomena of the world, he speaks, with "the fore-finger pointing," "like one who traces in an open book / The matter he declares" (5. 531–33). He realizes that man writes himself into history, "imprints for ever / His presence on all lifeless things" (5. 718–19): the wind becomes "voices" of sorrow or gaiety, the pines transmit thoughts, the lily and the bird speak of things other than themselves—all help man "to ascertain his rank and final place" (5. 719–40). Such a reading of nature is part of man's self-creation as man, and "what thus collected / He shall achieve, shall be set down to him" (5. 766–67). Man thus can read only what he writes.

Embracing the doctrine of becoming, Paracelsus is led to a new theory of language. Like man's other faculties, attributes, and experiences, language is generative. Words evoke responses, which in turn act as stimuli; words are interanimating. Paracelsus regards this phenomenon in an evolutionary, developmental way: interanimation leads to new stages of linguistic ability where new things can be expressed. Words are not symbols mediating the noumenon and the phenomenon: they do not permit "vision," as he had thought; rather, they are signs that allow man to gain a larger grasp on himself and thus grow in understanding beyond present verbal constructs, "narrow creeds of right and wrong, which fade / Before unmeasur'd thirst for good" (5. 780–81). Hence Luther has led to a better understanding of Christianity, Erasmus to an appreciation of learning, Paracelsus to a new way of looking at the physical world.

As Paracelsus develops his linguistic theory, he shows that man deals with the world around him as language presents it to him. For language ties us to the world, especially language shaped as poetry. Poetry is the last defense of the mind against dream. "Speak on," Paracelsus says to Festus, "or I dream again. Speak on! / Some story, any thing . . . / I shall dream else. Speak on!" (5. 415–17). Festus' lyric of the gliding River Main as an image of both continuity and change reattaches Paracelsus to real life: "My heart! they loose my heart, those simple words; / Its darkness passes, which nought else could expel." Festus' song "broke through / A chaos of ugly images" (5. 446–47, 450–51). It is through language that "in man's self arise / August anticipations, symbols, types / Of a dim splendour ever on before" (5. 773–75). Man writes himself and his beliefs. To this extent "truth is within ourselves" as Paracelsus claimed at the beginning (1. 726). History, or philosophy, thus consists of restatements of what is already known, as in this poem, where scene five is a restatement in evolutionary terms of what is set down in scene one in metaphysical language.

Paracelsus is not, however, a logical positivist; he does not accept the permanent separation of the finite and the infinite. Language has its limitations in that it cannot speak of the noumenal. But man is granted spiritual intuition, which is nonverbal—

> a vast perception unexpress'd,
> Uncomprehended by our narrow thought,
> But somehow felt and known in every shift
> And change in the spirit.
> (5. 637–40)

No, spiritual insight cannot be expressed in words. That is why Paracelsus cannot tell Festus what he sees as he sets foot on the threshold of new and "boundless life" (5. 499–507).

And to the dying philosopher, this is as things should be. For the knowledge attained by Paracelsus in his final hour would, if granted earlier, have rendered his life meaningless. There would have been no more to do, for him or for others.

Though Paracelsus admits the misconception of his quest, he nevertheless is not guilty of false modesty about himself and his achievements. He insists on a starring role in the drama called *Paracelsus* right to the very end. He is a heroic redeemer "amid the half-form'd creatures round, / Whom [he] should save" (5. 784–85). They have rejected him and speak scornfully of him—and this is proper because the earth is never ready for its saviors—but this is only for a time: "I press God's lamp / Close to my breast—its splendour, soon or late, / Will pierce the gloom" (5. 900–902). Paracelsus will surely be a "star" forever. As he dies, the enlightened Festus, who had earlier in scene five already acclaimed him both a king and star, steps forward, like a chorus, to bring to an end the drama that the hero has just enacted and say: "And this was Paracelsus!"

At the close we see more than ever that Paracelsus' awareness of playing a role yields an ironic dimension to the poem that is the dramatization of his life, giving us as spectators two different and conflicting views of the action. For the protagonist's sense of role-playing does not permit us to view the poem or the hero other than ambiguously and paradoxically. As the actor, Paracelsus insists that "God speaks to men through me!" (5. 557), yet he also insists that man writes his own script. This, of course, is a contradiction, and Browning has been charged with the inconsistency as a defect in the poem.[19] But it is precisely the point of the poem that it presents two contradictory views of man and of language: a contradiction reflected in the very structure of the work.

It is frequently said that Browning turned to the dramatic mode for *Paracelsus* in reaction to the criticism made of the subjective, lyric nature of *Pauline*.[20] But it seems clear to me that he chose a dramatic model for his poem because he wanted to show his hero self-consciously playing a role in a play called *Paracelsus,* after himself. "And this was Paracelsus!" as Festus says in the last line, meaning this was the way that Paracelsus acted out his script. For the display of that life, Browning, naturally enough, chose the dramatic mode. He was at pains to insist in his prefatory remarks, as I have noted, that he had "endeavoured to write a poem, not a drama" and that the poem should not be judged by "the canons of the drama." But he did follow a dramatic model in having Paracelsus' life unfold in five parts, which he pointedly did not call acts. Its action is different from that of a five-act tragedy, however, in that there is a general falling action in the three middle parts. The imagery, reflecting the course of Paracelsus' quest, helps structure the poem. The abundant light imagery of scene one in which "Aureole" tells his plans is dimmed in scene two to that of a gulf illumined only from its own depths (2. 175–76), in three to that of a sky of "heavy darkness / Diluted; grey and clear without the stars" (3. 1032–33), in four to the near total darkness of the grave (4. 359). In part five the light returns in celestial brightness transfiguring the death bed/ tomb of the dying Paracelsus. The metaphor of plunging begins at the end of scene one with the hero's declaration "I plunge" (1. 832); is carried through two, where he has "sunk insensibly so deep" to "a dead gulf" (2. 80, 175); continues in three, where he compares himself to a "fallen prince" who has suffered "degradation" (3. 222, 783); drops to a nadir in four, where the protagonist declares, "I should be sad / To live contented after such a fall" (4. 416–17); and ends in five with his plunging to new perceptions in death from which he "shall emerge one day" (5. 500, 901).

Within the overall parabolic movement of the poem, there are two parallel sections separated by a middle. This is indicated by the titles of the five scenes:

1. Paracelsus Aspires   5. Paracelsus Attains

2. Paracelsus Attains   4. Paracelsus Aspires

3. Paracelsus

As an earlier critic has shown, the pattern is ironic, which is to say, initially false attainment follows true aspiration and ends with true attainment subsequent to false aspirations, scene three depicting the protagonist at rest, neither aspiring nor attaining.[21]

If we perceive the structure of the poem only in this way—that is, as full closure—I believe that we limit our appreciation of its ironic richness. Read only as the story of the protagonist's true attainment coming at the end of a life of ill-conceived aspiration and false attainment, the poem is an example of the irony of fate: the hero learns the truth of his quest only when it is too late to act on it. One point the poem makes over and over is that knowledge, which is power, is to be most valued when it can be displayed as love—that is, put to good use for oneself in the service of others. Ironically Paracelsus attains to an understanding of the role of power only when he is near death. But it is an equally important point of the poem that truth in the phenomenal world is a matter of changing apprehensions of it:

> so in man's self arise
> August anticipations, symbols, types
> Of a dim splendour ever on before,
> In the eternal circle life pursues.
> (5. 773–76)

Hence in this poem expounding the doctrine of becoming, which teaches that aspiration follows attainment, we are also invited to see its structure as circular:

1. Paracelsus Aspires
2. Paracelsus Attains   3. Paracelsus   5. Paracelsus Attains
4. Paracelsus Aspires

At the center there is the self—or, in a larger sense, the conglomerate self that is mankind—ever aspiring, attaining, aspiring, and so on. This structure is underscored by the pervasive imagery of expansion and contraction, beginning with Paracelsus' invitation to Festus and Michal to "come closer" and ending with his dying "hand in hand" with Festus-Aprile.

What are we then left with in this poem of two structures? Is it simply the irony of double vision, an undefining irony? I do not think so. For in the case of *Paracelsus,* unlike that of *Pauline,* we have still another perspective, indeed two more perspectives that modify and define the irony of the double perspective—those of the author and of history. Browning himself provides us with a note to the poem. "The liberties I have taken with my subject are very trifling; and the reader may slip the foregoing scenes between the leaves of any memoir he pleases, by way of commentary," he says, and then gives us his translation of an account of Paracelsus taken from the *Biographie Universelle,* together with his notes on that account. The point of his notes is to show us that, for all the liberties he *has* taken with the life of Paracelsus, the author has made use of a historical personage for his poem, that meaning is developed by reference to history rather than to consciousness.[22] By the note and its insistence on history, Browning modifies both the parabolic and circular structures to figure a spiral. The attainment of the protagonist in scene five is not merely an end in itself, nor is it merely a restatement of the quest articulated in scene one and thus a growth of consciousness. What Paracelsus the historical scientist attains is an advance for the race, a new stage in progress from which a new, more advanced beginning may be made. Questing is valuable not only for the quester but also for mankind in its ascent upward. Because of Paracelsus, "the father of modern chymistry" and the discoverer of "the circulation of the blood and the sanguification of the heart," and so on (as the notes relate), the world was changed: the past was modified and the future opened for still further evolutionary advance. Locating his poem in time—every scene is given a date—Browning seeks to define the irony that his double structures offer.

Yet in defining his irony he was not negating it. What we are left with in the end is the multitudinousness, the abundant chaos of life. Paracelsus was a magician as well as a scientist; what he discovered was wrapped in the most appalling vesture. Any system, the poet would have us see, is only an approximation—an "august anticipation"—that must ultimately be rejected so as to begin again. A philosophy which postulates that an ending is also a beginning is obviously paradoxical and ironic—a philosophy of contradictions. Browning's is consequently a philosophical irony that embraces both a creative and a de-creative activity.

The work of art informed by this philosophical irony moves back and forth between enthusiastic creation of a system or fiction and skeptical de-creation of it when as "truth" or mimesis it is subjected to scrutiny. In its dialectic, discontinuous movement, it reflects the fertile chaos of life-as-becoming. Browning was well aware that such a work is not easily understood. That is why in his prefatory remarks to *Paracelsus* he insisted "that a work like mine depends more immediately on the intelligence and sympathy of the reader for its success—indeed were my scenes stars it must be his co-operating fancy which, supplying all chasms, shall connect the scattered lights into one constellation—a Lyre or a Crown." In the work of ironic discontinuity, the reader must join in the process of creation. As we shall see, the demand is to be made more strongly in the works to follow.

Paracelsus is magnificent in conception. It suffers, however, from its length, although it is significantly shorter than Henry Taylor's dramatic poem *Philip van Artevelde,* which had taken the literary world by storm when it appeared the previous year. In style *Paracelsus* lacks the dramatic conciseness that was to become so characteristically Browningesque just a few years later. As for characters, neither Festus nor Michal is essential for the action, their function being, as I have said, to provide an audience to whom Paracelsus may reveal his thoughts and to serve as a stable moral center. Aprile is a mere device, though a necessary one; he is like a *deus ex machina,* but introduced not to resolve the problem as in Classical drama but to keep it going. It was to take several more years before Browning learned that he could dispense with all the customary accoutrements of drama in displaying the growth of the soul in dramatic poetry of lyrical intensity. *Paracelsus* proved, however, a *succès d'estime,* and for a number of years the title pages of Browning's new works bore the legend "By the Author of *Paracelsus.*"[23]

CHAPTER III
STRAFFORD

IT WAS TO BE EXPECTED THAT A POET WITH A marked gift for dramatic writing should turn to drama for the stage. In late 1835 Browning met the great Victorian actor-manager William Charles Macready, and they seemed to hit it off right away. When in 1836 the poet proposed a drama about Strafford, Macready leaped at the idea. During the autumn of 1836 and the winter of 1837, Browning worked on the project, revising it to meet many objections on the part of the actor, who grew increasingly fearful that the play would fail. Macready delayed production, "convinced that the play must be utterly condemned,"[1] and the author was so disheartened that he almost withdrew it. *Strafford* was, however, finally performed on 1 May 1837 and printed on the same day, the only one of his early volumes to appear at the expense of the publisher. It had a run of five performances.

It is not surprising that Macready or his audiences did not care for the play. For both were accustomed to a quite different kind of drama. Macready was worried chiefly by "the meanness of plot" and the lack of "dramatic power; character . . . having the [supposed] interest of action."[2] The audience likewise was perturbed by the lack of action. William Bell Scott's response to the play was typical:

> My admiration for *Paracelsus* was so great I determined to go and to applaud [the first performance of *Strafford*], without rhyme or reason; and so I did, in the front of the pit. From the first scene it became plain that applause was not the order. The speakers had every one of them orations to deliver, and no action of any kind to perform. The scene changed, another door opened, and another half-dozen gentlemen entered as long-winded as the last.[3]

Browning, however, was not interested in presenting the kind of action that his producer and audience expected. He was concerned with the development of the soul, with character—but not with character as an agent of plot. Already in *Paracelsus* he had aimed, as he said in the foreword, to focus on "the mood itself in its rise and progress" and to subordinate "the agency by which it is influenced and determined." Now, in writing a drama for the stage, he was again trying to show, as the preface relates, "Action in Character, rather than Character in Action"; which is to say, he was attempting a dramatic form that would retain the detachment and objectivity of drama yet that would also allow for the subjective action of the lyric. As Terry Otten says, Browning was seeking "to break down the barriers between lyric and dramatic form and discover a means of giving subjective matter objective expression."[4] In short, Browning wished to write ironic drama, a drama that originates in the incongruity of the reflexive activity of the self observed and observing.[5]

In his two previous works, Browning had investigated the local ironies of soul-making, the self in its development. The completion of *Paracelsus*, with its enunciation of the doctrine of becoming in scene five, provided Browning with a philosophical basis for his irony that permitted him to enlarge his conception of it. For once the poet accepted the idea that being is also becoming—that *a* is both *a* and not *a*—then the way was opened to the kind of irony that is to be seen not so much as a form of irony but as a way of presenting it—what one theorist calls "really the dramatization of irony."[6] Although the implications of such an ironic view had been set down by Friedrich Schlegel, it was an Englishman, who, borrowing from Hegel, most probably delineated for the young Browning the dramatic possibilities of irony as a cosmic view. Writing on the irony of Sophocles in 1833, Connop Thirlwall observed that in the *Antigone*, Sophocles impartially presented two equal and opposite points of view and, expanding on this, remarked that irony may reside in the attitude of an ironic observer or, more precisely, in the situation observed:

> There is always a slight cast of irony in the grave, calm, respectful attention impartially bestowed by an intelligent judge on two contending parties, who are pleading their causes before him with all the earnestness of deep conviction, and of excited feeling. What makes the contrast interesting is, that the right and the truth lie on

neither side exclusively: that there is no fraudulent purpose, no gross imbecility of intellect, on either: but both have plausible claims and specious reasons to alledge, though each is too much blinded by prejudice or passion to do justice to the views of his adversary. For here the irony lies not in the demeanor of the judge, but is deeply seated in the case itself, which seems to favour each of the litigants, but really eludes them both.

The most interesting debates or conflicts are not, Thirlwall writes, those in which evil is pitted against good. For

> this case . . . seems to carry its own final decision in itself. But the liveliest interest arises when by inevitable circumstances, characters, motives, and principles are brought into hostile collision, in which good and evil are so inextricably blended on each side, that we are compelled to give an equal share of our sympathy to each, while we perceive that no earthly power can reconcile them; that the strife must last until it is extinguished with at least one of the parties, and yet that this cannot happen without the sacrifice of something which we should wish to preserve.[7]

It was with such ironic possibilities in mind, whether gained from Thirlwall or not, that Browning sat down to write *Strafford*—"to freshen a jaded mind by diverting it to the healthy natures of a grand epoch," as he said in the preface to the play. Hence *Strafford* is important not only because it helps us chart Robert Browning's development but also because it may well be the first play in English consciously designed as a dramatization of irony.

Once we understand the ironic intent of the play, even surface ironies become almost immediately apparent. The characters are far from being "the healthy natures" of whom Browning spoke in the preface. At best Strafford and Pym are, like Paracelsus, monomaniacs. They are devoted, against all reason, to the furtherance of an idea—to the monarchial principle in the case of Strafford, to the parliamentary in the case of Pym. Yet if we investigate further, we find that what drives them, as well as Lady Carlisle, is not principle but love, in all three cases love frustrated.[8]

Postponing consideration of Carlisle for the moment, let us turn our attention to Strafford and Pym. In earlier life they had been friends who shared a dedication to the rights of Parliament; even now Strafford is susceptible to Pym's plea to return to his old friends. Yet somehow the King manages to captivate him, to seduce him away from his former friends. For even though he is fully cognizant of the King's waywardness and personal disloyalty, when Charles calls him "my Friend / of Friends" (1. 2. 241–42) Strafford vows, "I am yours— / Yours ever . . . / To the death, yours" (2. 2. 36–38). Hereafter, with the one brief exception in 3.3, in spite of every act of perfidy and disloyalty on Charles' part, Strafford remains utterly faithful to the King. Why? Because besottedly, like a romantic lover, he adores Charles, not the king but the man—"The man with the mild voice and mournful eyes" (2. 2. 292–93). It is this love that results in his death.

In the case of Pym there is a contrary movement. Where Strafford casts off notions of office in manifesting his love for the person, Pym puts aside the notion of love and friendship to serve the office. Pym declares continuing love for Wentworth (as he was known before becoming Earl of Strafford) in 1.1 and expresses hope that their former friendship might continue. In 1.2 Pym pleads with him to return to their old friendly ways and seems almost to succeed until the King appears and Wentworth lets Pym's hand drop. Though there is some expression of rekindled hope in 2.1, Pym increasingly sees that Strafford (as Wentworth has now become) devotes himself exclusively to Charles. Hereafter Pym, like a scorned lover, becomes in his own eyes "the chosen man that should destroy / This Strafford" (4. 2. 159–60) and the embodiment of the will of England who seeks "England's great revenge" (3. 1. 29). Only at the last "meeting," about which they have frequently talked and where their paths irrevocably diverge, does Pym speak again of his love for the doomed man: "I never loved but this man—David not / More Jonathan! Even thus, I love him now . . . " (5. 2. 287–88).

The dialectical movement of the antagonists shows that, in Thirlwall's words, "both have plausible claims and specious reasons to alledge, though each is too blinded by prejudice or passion to do justice to the views of his adversary." Both Strafford and Pym are led by belief in their causes to condone methods and actions of which they would otherwise disapprove. Strafford is loyal to a person whom he knows to be worthless and pursues a cause and courses of action that he knows to be futile. Pym places his faith in Strafford despite his former friend's known opposition to the parliamentary cause, and when it becomes plain that Strafford will support the king under all circumstances, he resorts to acts in total violation of parliamentary principles, including connivance with the king and collusion with the king's party. This means that the audience is faced with the paradox that the better man represents the worse cause.

The queen and courtiers are presented as pursuing their own self-interests, with no regard for the country at all. The parliamentarians, on the other hand, are shown in shifting attitudes. In the beginning they charge all the monarch's villainies to Strafford, although it is he who tries to mitigate the king's disgraceful actions with reference to Parliament. Vane, Rudyard, and Fiennes are the hotheads who wish to hound Wentworth from office, while Pym and Hampden advocate calm in consideration of a position to be taken with respect to Wentworth. In a reversal occurring in 4.2, Vane, Rudyard, and Fiennes become the moderates insisting upon fair treatment of Strafford, as Pym and Rudyard, pressing for a bill of attainder, declare, "We must make occasion serve" (173). The play leaves us in no doubt of the moral superiority of the parliamentary faction, even though it has a demagogue for its leader.

The dialectical movement of the antagonists in addition provides an ironic structure for the play much like that of *Paracelsus*, in which true aspiration leading to false attainment is followed by the reverse pattern. From the second act on, it is inevitable that the diverging paths of Pym and Strafford must cross again. "Keep tryst! the old appointment's made anew," says Pym. "Forget not we shall meet again!" And Strafford replies, "Pym, we shall meet again!" (2. 2. 154–55, 166). In act three Strafford submits to his antagonist as the embodiment of the will of England (3. 3. 96–97). But this proves not the true meeting, for Strafford discovers that he was "fool enough / To see the will of England in Pym's will" (4. 2. 74–75). He impeaches Pym, and far from there being a meeting of the two, the occasion is one in which Pym shrinks from, and quails before, Strafford (4. 2. 50, 59). To the parliamentarians, who demand that Pym bear Parliament's pardon to Strafford, Pym says: "Meet him? Strafford? / Have we to meet once more, then?" (4. 2. 186–87). And Strafford says in similar vien: "I would not look upon Pym's face again" (4. 2. 106).

Up to this point there has been an ironic reversal. Pym, the just man with a just cause, has grown in attitude and behavior to resemble the royalists, whose cause he detests and whose conduct he abominates—all because of his hate for Strafford. Even the king recognizes Pym's motives: "You think / Because you hate the Earl...(turn not away / We know you hate him)" (4. 3. 38–40). Strafford, on the other hand, grows in strength and dignity. Where in act one he was willing to perform any kind of deed for the sake of the king, no matter how much it offended conscience or common sense, in act four he marshals his energies for more apparently reasonable ends, even though on the king's behalf: "From this day begins / A new life, founded on a new belief / In Charles" (4. 2. 101–3). Strafford for the first time becomes in the eyes of the audience a partially sympathetic character in spite of the fact that his cause is shown to be less and less worthy and he himself a dupe. "We have all used that man," the king points out,

> As though he had been ours..with not a source
> Of happy thoughts except in us..and yet
> Strafford has children, and a home as well,
> Just as if we have never been!
> (4. 3. 44–47)

For the first time we learn that Strafford has a family and that Pym is, as the king says, "a solitary man / Wed to your cause—to England if you will!" (4. 3. 48–49). The claims of "family" will assert themselves in the last act.

Strafford's new life falsely founded on a new belief in the king leads only to the Tower. It is no doubt an intended comment on the two antagonists that Strafford is shown with his son and daughter whereas Pym's "England" is depicted as "a green and putrefying charnel" (5. 2. 325) devouring children. And it is this England to whom Pym would immediately "render up my charge" (5. 2. 280). For although this is the inevitable encounter, it is not to be the anticipated meeting. Pym foresees that he is to die soon after Strafford, and both agree that the tryst so long awaited will be better postponed till heaven (5. 2. 291–310). Yet at the end, when he thinks of Charles' fate at Pym's hands, Strafford begs that the king be spared: "No—not for England, now—not for Heaven, now . . . / *This* is the meeting....I'll love you well!" But Pym is relentless, and all the love sought from Strafford he now forgoes: "England—I am thine own!" Strafford's final line—"O God, I shall die first"—is full of ambiguities: after him will follow not only the king and Pym but also thousands of Englishmen killed in the Civil Wars. History—our knowledge of it, at any rate—forestalls closure.

Almost certainly the conflict between Pym and Strafford was the germ of the play: which is to say, the play was conceived as an ironic drama of character. It is of this, no doubt, that Browning speaks when he refers to *Strafford* as a play of "Action in Character, rather than Character in Action." Yet in *Strafford*, as in *Paracelsus*, the poet was not content to allow an undefined irony of movement and countermovement. He attempted to provide a stable center for his drama not only by reference to history—that is, to our historical knowledge of the outcome of the conflict between the two protagonists—but also by his injection of Lady Carlisle into the midst of the dialectical movement: like Festus in *Paracelsus* she would be the stable center from which meaning would derive. Pym and Strafford were the historical *données*: the portraits of them are, Browning said in the preface, "faithful." "My Carlisle, however, is purely imaginary." Why is this so? Because the dramatist initially conceived of his play as a struggle between, in Thirlwall's words, "two contending parties" in which "the right and the truth lie on neither side exclusively." Then came the afterthought that the play perhaps needed not only a conventional romantic interest but also a moral center.[9] If everyone in the play was to be fickle, self-serving, or blindly deceived, at least in Lady Carlisle there would be one "good" character who was faithful, selfless, and aware of the deceptions about her. What results, alas, is an incredible character.

Carlisle's love for Strafford is both selfless and hopeless. She loves a man who does not love her but instead loves another—the king. And she constantly hides from him all evidence of the king's duplicity so as to assure his love for Charles: "One must not lure him from a love like that! / Oh, let him love the King and die!" (2. 2. 243–44). To the last scene she keeps up this deception, pretending that it is the king and not she who plans Strafford's escape from the Tower. She speaks no more after Pym is discovered at the door of the prison, so that the last ninety-three lines are devoted to dialogue between the two antagonists, a fact that alone suggests her lack of centrality to the action of the play.

It is only by linking her to the major ironic theme of the play—deception—that Browning escapes making her totally extraneous. More than the other characters, she is aware of the discrepancy between things as they are and things as they seem. With her various pretenses concerning the king, Carlisle is conscious of playing a role. Indeed, she regards herself and others as actors in a play, a notion that, as we shall see, the other characters share. This self-consciousness on the part of the *dramatis personae* means that they become ironic observers and, as well, victims of irony to the extent that they doubt the meaningfulness of their actions in the drama.

At the beginning the Puritans fancy that Wentworth has turned Ireland "to a private stage" (1. 1. 41), has superseded other royalists "whose part is played" (1. 1. 151) and has tried to persuade Pym that "a patriot could not play a purer part / Than follow in his track" (1. 1. 115–16, as the passage reads in the 1863 revision). Strafford does indeed play a role, but not the one the Puritans envision. He perceives that the king wears a mask (2. 2. 123) to hide his real self and that in order to save the monarchy he too must do likewise. Thus when members of the parliamentary party arrive just at the moment that Strafford discovers the king's double dealings, Strafford immediately drops to his knee before Charles in a gesture of hurried but loyal farewell. As Lady Carlisle says, "there's a masque on foot" (2. 2. 260).

In this play within a play, conspirators teach their henchmen to recite to others "all we set down" with "not a word missed" and "just as we drilled" (3. 8, 21). Strafford is to be kept "in play," ignorant of the real circumstances (3. 2. 126). As in a theater the king and his party witness the impeachment proceedings against Strafford from a screened box, which "admits of such a partial glimpse" and whose "close curtain / Must hide so much" (4. 1. 17–26). Their judgment of the trial is that is "was amusing in its way / Only too much of it..the Earl withdrew / In time!" (5. 1. 17–19). At the end Strafford wonders whether history will declare the chief part in this masque to have been played by an actor named "the Patriot Pym, or the Apostate Strafford" (5. 2. 57).

The characters' sense of being observers and victims in a play is underscored by their reiterated belief that they are but puppets pulled by a master puppeteer. Pym and the Presbyterians feel, as good Calvinists should, that their actions are predestined. More than once Pym speaks of his fated course and of himself as "the chosen man" (4. 2. 159). Yet the royalists too also ascribe their actions to fate. Strafford says, "There's fate in it—I give all here quite up" (2. 2. 195). And the king feels, "I am in a net.. / I cannot move!" (4. 3. 82–83). But of course there is really no question of the irony of fate at all: there is only the irony of falsely believing oneself trapped by a fateful irony: in actuality the characters are free to do as they choose.[10]

The actors in the masque are also very much aware of the superfluity of words enveloping the action. The opening scene, for example, is devoted to those who "will speak out" (36) and those who say there has been "talk enough" (263). The Puritan who appears and reappears like a character in *Hellzapoppin* is forever quoting Scripture. What is needed is that "word grow deed" (243). The next scene shows Wentworth discovering the machinations of the royalist party, who have "decried" his service (53) without ever uttering a "precise charge" (39) because they "eschew plain-speaking" (141). Wentworth believes that "one decisive word" on his part will put matters straight; surely the king "mistrusts . . . their prattle" (146). Pym argues however that even though Wentworth's letters to Charles "were the movingest" (159) and that the messages from the Scots were "words moving in their way," Wentworth can be sure that the king pays no attention to the words of either (162–63).

Act two again presents parallel scenes. The first shows the parliamentarians once more awash in a welter of words and divided in aim, until Pym brings news that Strafford will now be forced to take their part. Scene two shows Strafford reproaching the king for his duplicity but finally consenting to serve Charles in a new way. Lady Carlisle tries to convince Strafford that his enemies at court will again seduce the king, but Strafford does not want to hear: "In no case tell me what they do!" Having warned him, Carlisle will be silent and allow Strafford to continue in his illusion.

In the remaining acts Strafford is impeached on trumped-up charges, to which he responds with countercharges. When the trial threatens to expose the machinations of the Puritans, Pym brings in a bill of attainder, which even his followers recognize as a "hideous mass / Of half-borne out assertions—dubious hints / . . . distortions—aye, / And wild inventions" (4. 2. 129–32). Never denying this, Pym justifies himself by claiming that "the great word went from England to my soul" (4. 3. 99). In his last moments Strafford, wanting "to hear the sound of my own tongue" (5. 2. 83), begs Pym to spare the king, while Pym waits to hear "if England shall declare her will to me" (5. 2. 353).

The characters not only see themselves as actors in a play whose words alone convey the action but also regard themselves and their circumstances as part of a text to be interpreted. The parliamentary party are ever reading, or about to read, reports. Pym charges the king with attempting "to turn the record's last and bloody leaf" so as to record a new "entry" on a "new page" (1. 1. 153–59). Strafford conceives of himself as a figure in a romance in which "we shall die gloriously—as the book says" (2. 2. 169–81). The text of every proposal is carefully scrutinized by both Puritans and royalists. It is a set of notes that seals Strafford's fate (4. 1. 65). Only time and fame, "the busy scribe," will provide the "curious glosses, subtle notices, / Ingenious clearings-up one fain would see" (5. 2. 52–55).

Because words are only signs and not the thing itself,

because men use words to rationalize their actions, the text that is life and living can never be interpreted in a wholly satisfactory way. One speaks truly only when one has nothing to hide, from oneself as well as from others. In the phenomenal world this never happens. Language remains a deceptive veil through which it is impossible fully to penetrate.

Yet though deceptive, language is the means by which the characters realize themselves—that is, advance themselves in soul-making. In this play, far more clearly then in *Pauline* or *Paracelsus*, Browning represents language itself, speech, as an activity—as the active, formative force of the mind in the process of self-articulation. Full of asides, interjections, half-completed statements, interruptions, the dialogue is characterized by numerous semantic breaks that offer possibilities for extension of meaning. Let us take for example the following colloquy between Strafford and Lady Carlisle near the end of act two, when Strafford has just discovered the full selfishness and faithlessness of the king and Carlisle realizes the extent of his foolish love for Charles:

> CARLISLE. The King!—
> What way to save him from the King?
> My soul..
> That lent from its own store the charmed disguise
> That clothes the King..he shall behold my soul!
> Strafford...(I shall speak best if you'll not gaze
> Upon me.)...You would perish, too! So sure!...
> Could you but know what 'tis to bear, my Strafford,
> One Image stamped within you, turning blank
> The else imperial brilliance of your mind,—
> A weakness, but most precious,—like a flaw
> I' the diamond which should shape forth some sweet face
> Yet to create, and meanwhile treasured there
> Lest Nature lose her gracious thought for ever!...
> STRAFFORD. When could it be?...no!...yet...
> was it the day
> We waited in the anteroom, till Holland

> Should leave the presence-chamber?
> CARLISLE. What?
> STRAFFORD. —That I
> Described to you my love for Charles?
> CARLISLE. (*Aside.*) Ah, no—
> One must not lure him from a love like that?
> Oh, let him love the King and die! 'Tis past....
> I shall not serve him worse for that one brief
> And passionate hope..silent for ever now!
> (2. 2. 225–46)

This staccato conversation reveals the degree of repression that enables each character to progress until he becomes "the Apostate Strafford" and she the selfless, untelling lover. Strafford seems to know what she is getting at, but then with that resolute "no!" he returns to the king, while she with her "What?" delays understanding him until she decides to say as an aside what evidently she was about to declare to him openly.

The dramatic irony here is easily discernible. A higher irony, however, resides in the fact that such exchanges, which are the building-blocks of the drama of "Action in Character," do not produce dialogue. As Browning here conceives language, it is not only an instrument of soul-making but, as we have seen, a means of deception, of oneself or others. *Strafford* might well have as its motto Paracelsus' statement "We live and breathe deceiving and deceived" (4. 625).

Though there is much to admire about *Strafford*, I find it difficult to like as a play. First, the dialogue is often stiff or florid. And even when most interesting, as in the passage just discussed, the semantic gaps and blank linguistic moments, which become part of the meaning of the play, are not appropriate to "the healthy natures of a grand epoch." Only modern subject matter can accommodate such modern dramatic use of language. Even Beckett and Pinter would find it near impossible to apply their techniques to a tragedy about the Civil Wars. Second, there is no character who can serve as a pole of sympathy to pull the audience into the action. It might be objected that this is the whole point, that it is a play without a hero. But even were this to be granted, there would still be something additional to say: that any such work must have characters of sufficient interest in themselves to offset their villainies, imbecilities, or insipidities. And this is not true of Strafford or Pym or Lady Carlisle, all of whom remain pretty much what they were at the beginning. If there is tragedy in this "Historical Tragedy" (as Browning subtitled it), it is the tragedy of the people of England, who are made to suffer from the conflict of wills between the royalists and the parliamentarians, which, but for Strafford and Pym as they are here represented, might have been averted. But this is the tragedy of history and not of the play *Strafford*.

CHAPTER IV
SORDELLO

BROWNING SEEMS TO HAVE WORKED ON *Sordello* for seven years, from 1833 to 1840. Both *Paracelsus* and *Strafford* appear to have been diversions from the composition of what he envisioned as his *magnum opus*. In a sense they, as well as *Pauline,* are building blocks for the long work and thus share a symbiotic relationship to it: they serve as glosses on, and are glossed by, *Sordello.* They are what is called in the note to *Pauline* "sketches" of the "genre" of the longer work. *Sordello* is, however, written in a more radically ironic mode; and before proceeding to examination of the poem itself, I should like to outline briefly the aesthetic context of the peculiar kind of irony called Romantic Irony.[1]

The chief theorist of Romantic Irony, as well as of philosophical irony, was Friedrich Schlegel,[2] who insisted that the work of art represent the ontological process of becoming. The artist begins, objectively and mimetically, with the creation of a fiction or system; but then he questions it as an accurate representation of the chaos of change and in the act of doing so soon discovers that it is but a mere subjective construct of his own making, an inadequate and fragmentary exposition of infinite becoming, from which he recoils. Through reflection the artist is able to withdraw from his work, and then through irony he soars above it to hover between an enthusiastic self-creation and a skeptical self-negation, thereby escaping an imprisoning immanence and realizing self-transcendence. Hence, says Schlegel, artistic irony "is, as it were, the demonstration of infinity, of the universality, of the feeling for the universe."[3]

As a representation of ontological becoming, ironic art—what Schlegel called Romantic poetry or *Universalpoesie*—takes all forms, modes, styles, and genres for its expression. Using fragments, differing perspectives, critical comments, disruptions of cause and effect, confessional interpolations, it mirrors the fertile chaos of life itself. Such poetry requires, furthermore, that its creator rise above the self that elaborates the fiction in which he is imaged to present his audience with another self, an aesthetic self hovering between the order of being and the chaos of becoming. Outwardly this poetry will resemble an arabesque, a fantastic interlacing of diverse and disparate elements, and will make the same impression as that created by the harlequin figure in comedia dell' arte, who both controls the plot and mocks the play, or by the parabasis of Greek comedy in which the author's spokesman interrupts the action of the play to address the audience directly on matters of concern to the author. Such poetry (which may be in prose or verse) "should portray itself with each of its portrayals; everywhere and at the same time, it should be poetry and the poetry of poetry" (*Athenaeum* Fragment No. 238).

The poet bears the same relation to his poem as God does to his creation. Each may be said to be both *in* and *out* the creation, immanent *and* transcendent. Just as God's purpose, according to orthodox Protestant theology, is to show forth his power and love in the cosmos, so the poet wishes to reveal his own microcosmic splendor, his own artistic power and love in relation to his literary work.[4] In each case irony is involved. For what appears as complete objectivity on the part of God and the artist toward their creations is in fact and purpose merely a vehicle for something very personal and objective—namely, as a revelation of the personalities behind the creations. This state of Godlike self-division and self-consciousness that the poet enjoys is central to the whole concept of Romantic Irony.[5]

I do not know how directly familiar Browning was with Schlegel, Tieck, and other theorists and practitioners of Romantic Irony. He studied German at the University of London; and his teacher, Ludwig von Mühlenfels, introduced him to modern German writers.[6] Subsequently his "literary father," W. J. Fox, introduced him to German biblical scholarship.[7] Moreover, his admiration of, and friendship with, Carlyle kept him abreast of recent trends in modern German literature.[8] The poet himself said, in 1842, that he read German "pretty well" and "tolerably" (Domett, pp. 49, 52). Mrs. Orr claimed, however, that Browning did not know German directly, "his bond of union with German philosophy" being "but the natural tendencies of his own mind": "He resembles Hegel, Fichte, or Schelling, as the case may be, by the purely creative impulse which has met their thought . . . (*Handbook*, p. 4). Yet whatever his direct knowledge, Browning was able to keep in touch with German culture. *Paracelsus* is but the first of his works with a German setting and German characters.

Sordello is one of the chief examples of Romantic Irony in nineteenth-century English literature.[9] How Browning came to cast *Sordello* in this difficult mode can perhaps best be understood by tracing its growth over the seven years of its composition.

The history of the genesis and composition of *Sordello* is, however, involved and depends on speculation in reconstructing it. Most commentators believe that there were four stages in the writing and thus four different versions of the poem. According to DeVane's scheme (*Handbook,* pp. 72–85), the initial version, largely the subject matter of the printed first two books, traces the development of the young Sordello as a poet. This first stage, which includes little historical background, was interrupted by the writing of *Paracelsus,* which usurped much of its theme and method of developing it. The second period of composition presumably began after the completion of *Paracelsus.* In the preface to *Strafford,* Browning says that prior to writing the play he "had for some time been engaged in a Poem of a very different nature"; and in the advertisement there is the announcement "Nearly ready. Sordello, in Six Books." Then in July 1837 appeared a long poem by Mrs. W. Busk entitled *Sordello* on the same subject and somewhat in the same manner. Browning now felt it incumbent upon him to revise his poem, which apparently was almost ready for publication and which in this second version developed the post-Goito period of Sordello's life by treating of his passionate love for Palma and his military exploits in medieval Italy.

The third version seems to have developed the historical background in great detail. Harriet Martineau recorded in her diary for 23 December 1837: "Browning called. 'Sordello' will soon be done now. Denies himself preface and notes. He must choose between being historian or poet. Cannot split interest. I advised him to let the poem tell its own tale" (DeVane, *Handbook*, p. 78). Finding himself at an impasse, Browning decided, as he wrote to a friend, to visit Italy "to finish my poem among the scenes it describes" (Orr, *Life*, p. 95). In Italy he experienced the kind of "conversion" described in the last part of book three of the completed *Sordello*: feeling intensely for the plight of suffering humanity he views in Venice, he comes to realize that he does not require chiefs and bards and princesses as the subjects of his poem but will henceforth champion ordinary men and women.

With redirected aim he began the final stage of composition upon his return home. This fourth version introduces most of the material of the last three books: Salinguerra, Sordello's hidden relationship to him, the struggle between Guelf and Ghibellin and Sordello's championing of the Guelf cause as the cause of the people. It was published in March 1840, at the expense of the poet's father.

If this reconstruction in meagerest outline of the composition of *Sordello* is anywhere near accurate, we see that when he sat down to begin the writing of the final version Browning was faced with fragments from three prior versions, each conflicting with, and often contradicting, the other. Not only were aims and intentions at war with each other but also the conception of characters and their roles was vastly changed—Palma, for example, who was earlier the romantic heroine and was now to be displaced by female waifs in Saint Mark's Square in Venice. The material was plainly intractable. Some of Browning's earlier difficulty is indicated in the preface to *Strafford,* where he states that he had undertaken the play out of "eagerness to freshen a jaded mind." And this was in April 1837! What must his attitude toward his poem have been in the second half of 1838 when he had revised his intentions at least twice since? How, he must have asked himself, could all this inchoate mass of material be somehow transformed and transmuted into a harmonious union? The answer is that it could not be. And once Browning accepted this as the answer, he sat down and wrote the approximately 5,800 lines of rhyming iambic pentameter couplets with such dispatch that he seems to have almost concluded it in 1839 while also working on other projects.

As he looked back on *Paracelsus*, he doubtless reflected on the doctrine of becoming enunciated in the last scene, and it occurred to him that in a state of becoming the principle of non-contradiction is not applicable. For anything can be both itself and not itself at any specific moment, it being in process of becoming something else. This meant that he could include all the different versions of *Sordello*. Why, for instance, could not Palma be both "passion's votaress" (5. 998) and the instigator of Sordello's turn to social action? Why could not Sordello himself be both poet-dreamer and political activist?

But presuming he was bold enough to write a poem composed of such disparate and contradictory material, how could he organize it? Such unity as it had lay only in his experience of it. This being true, he would have to step into his work so as to show not only that it was *his* poem but also that it was his experience of his poem.

> Who will, may hear Sordello's story told:
> *His* story? Who believes *me* shall behold
> The man, pursue his fortunes to the end
> Like *me*; . . .
> Only believe *me*.
> (1. 1–4, 10; italics added)

But what kind of poem would it be, what its genre? All conventional forms and genres would be but restrictions and obstructions. What was needed was some means of reproducing the infiniteness of life and also of penetrating to the very heart of the individual, some way of cramming in everything so that the work could be a mirror of the surrounding world yet also express the reflection of the poet upon the objects he represents. In effect it would have to be what Friedrich Schlegel called *Universalpoesie:*

> Its mission is not merely to reunite all separate genres of poetry and to put poetry in touch with philosophy and rhetoric. It will,

and should, now mingle and now amalgamate poetry and prose, genius and criticism, the poetry of art and the poetry of nature, render poetry living and social, and life and society poetic, poetize wit, fill and saturate the forms of art with solid cultural material of every kind, and inspire them with vibrations of humor. It embraces everything poetic, from the greatest system of art which, in turn, includes many systems, down to the sigh, the kiss, which the musing child breathes forth in artless song. It can lose itself in what it represents to such a degreee that one might think its one and only goal were the characterization of poetic individuals of every type; and yet no form has thus far arisen appropriate to expressing the author's mind so perfectly, so that artists who just wanted to write ... have by coincidence described themselves. [This] poetry alone can, like the epic, become a mirror of the entire surrounding world, a picture of its age. And, it too can soar, free from all real and ideal interests, on the wings of poetic reflection, midway between the work and the artist. It can even exponentiate this reflection and multiply it as in an endless series of mirrors.... Other types of poetry are completed and can now be entirely analyzed. [This new] type of poetry is still becoming; indeed, its peculiar essence is that it is always becoming and that it can never be completed.... [As] its first law it recognizes that the arbitrariness of the poet endures no law above himself. [This] genre of poetry is the only one which is more than a genre, and which is, as it were poetry itself.... *(Athaeneum* Fragment No. 116)

As for mode, since the poet was to be present in the poem it could not be purely dramatic as he might prefer and as was his previous practice.

> Never . . .
> Of my own choice had this [method] . . .
> served to tell
> A story I could body forth so well
> By making speak, myself kept out of view
> The very man as he was wont to do,
> And leaving you to say the rest for him. . . .
> (1. 11–17)

No, it could not be purely dramatic. Since it was to recount the fortunes of Sordello, it would have to be some form of fictional narrative. But any conventional form of verse narrative—the verse romance in the manner of Scott, for example—would not serve because it did not permit the open presence of the writer and of his response to his work. No, it would have to be something more nearly like the novel, already in the 1830s the most popular form of literature.[10] But the novels of the period were not adequate models. What was needed was something more nearly like the *roman*, which the German critics spoke so highly of—an "arabesque" permitting both "objectivity *and* subjectivity," "symmetry *and* chaos," something that was an "artistically arranged confusion," a "charming symmetry of contradictions."[11] And where might an exemplar of this be found? In *Don Quixote*, which the Germans praised so highly and which Browning himself knew intimately:[12] in it there is a pretense of historical objectivity that the author destroys upon the slightest occasion by interrupting the narrative with reflections upon himself, his work, his readers, and the society of his day. Yes, why not "a Quixotic attempt"?[13]

>   for as the friendless people's friend
>   [Don Quixote]
>   Spied from his hill-top once, despite the din
>   And dust of multitudes, Pentapolin
>   Named o' the Naked Arm, I single out
>   Sordello. . . .
>   (1. 4–8)

Having arrived at such decisions concerning his work, Browning was now willing to embrace a more thoroughgoing irony than that manifested in *Strafford*. Adopting an irony that Schlegel characterized as permanent parabasis—which, it will be recalled, is the stepping forward of a chorus or actor to break the dramatic illusion and speak directly to the audience—Browning undertook a mode of composition that confounds and deconstructs the narrative order and determinable meaning that it pretends to offer.[14] It was an ideal mode for one who wished to be both "objective" and "subjective."

The manner of narration has proved puzzling to most commentators on the poem, mainly because, not perceiving its essential ironic nature, they have tried to fit it into one particular kind of generic mould. *Sordello* is not merely a novel or a puppet show or a diorama:[15] it is all these things and more. In fact, the narrator at the beginning draws our attention to his several stances for the presentation of his story. First, as an illusionist, with his repeated command "appear, / Verona!" Then as a painter (or tailor?) who "chalk[s] broadly on each vesture's hem / The wearer's quality" (1. 28–29). Then as a clown–stage-manager in commedia dell' arte who "take[s] his stand / Motley on back and pointing-pole in hand / Beside them" (1. 29–31). Then as storyteller to an imaginary audience: "I face ye, friends, / Summoned together . . . / To hear the story I propose to tell" (1. 31–34). Such a variety of narrative poses is necessary for one who would be among "setters-forth of unexampled themes, / Makers of quite new men" (1. 26–27).

Whatever his pose, the narrator is not simply a fictional presence distinct from the poet: he is that, but he is the poet also.[16] Browning exploits the perpetual discrepancy in narrative between author and narrator and, as we shall see, between narrator and character in indirect discourse for his own personal ends. Browning actually appears recognizably in the poem in book two when he refers to his own May birthdate (296–97), and in book three when he speaks of himself musing on palace steps in Venice (676–77) and finishes with apostrophes to Walter Savage Landor and Fanny Haworth (950–74).[17] Yet there is never any assurance that the narrator speaks with the full authority of the poet; indeed, the ambiguity as to the exact degree of identity between the poet's empirical self and his aesthetic self, the narrator, is carefully maintained throughout.

Browning does this for at least two reasons. He had chosen as the protagonist of his work a historical figure—Sordello, the poet troubadour of the thirteenth-century—and proposed an imaginative reconstruction of his life—not as in the case of *Paracelsus*, where the historical figure is little rooted in Renaissance soil, but this time a protagonist surrounded by a background so rich in historical detail that he would seem to have stepped forth from some late medieval chronicle, "the very man as he was wont to do" (1. 16). His narrative would be presented as if it were fact. Yet the more he worked on the poem, the more he discovered that "the very man" was irrecoverable. At best he could produce only an approximation of the historical Sordello: not "the very man" but one "of quite new men" (1. 27). He would then have to admit the difficulty of presenting the poem as if it were history. To put it another way, given his announced intention, he would have to admit to the difficulty of writing the poem—and this is where his narrator's role becomes important. We discover this early in the work. For the narrator has some trouble even getting his story started. "I single out / Sordello" he says, soon thereafter to beg his audience: "Only believe me. Ye believe?" Then "Appears / Verona." But Verona does not appear at all; what occurs are some reasons for telling his story in such and such a manner. Then a second time comes the command "appear, / Verona!" (59–60), which proves to be another false start. Finally, on the third try, "appears / Verona" (77–78), but Sordello does not enter till line 328, whereupon Verona disappears, to be followed by a flashback to Sordello's youth in Goito: "I would do this! if I should falter now" (373). This flashback lasts for some 2,000 lines, when "appears Verona!" (3. 261), soon to be followed by a digression lasting till the close of book three and the promise that "you shall hear Sordello's story told." This faltering manner of narration continues to the last book, where, for example, the narrator says, "One word to end!" (6. 589) and then continues for nearly three hundred lines. In sum, the narrator haltingly unwinds not only the story he seeks to tell but also the means by which he seeks to tell it. Thus the metapoetry, the continual commentary on the poem's own means and ends, is almost inextricable from the actual presentation. It is the narrator's role to be the metapoet and hence to leave the poet free for higher things.

But this is only partially true. For in the process of writing the poem, the poet discovers that, in art at any rate, ends and means are inseparable, the process part of the product, the metapoetry inextricably interwound with the poetry. This is the discovery related, as we shall see, in book three, when having got his narrator ready at last to tell Sordello's story, the poet finds that the narrator-distinct-from-poet cannot proceed:

ends and means, narrator and poet have to be brought into clearer (if not closer) relationship.

The examination of his art begins playfully enough when the narrator asks his audience for their approval of what has been accomplished thus far: "Nor slight too much my rhymes—'that spring, dispread, / Dispart, disperse, lingering overhead / Like an escape of angels'" (593–95), using the same words to characterize his own verse as those used earlier to characterize Sordello's earliest "dream performances" (1. 881–83). But no, his verse is more than "angelic": it is more like a "transcendental platan" of pyrotechnical brilliance written by an "archimage" for the amusement of his audience from whom he is totally "apart" (595–607). But no again: he is, rather, like a god who comes and goes in his creation. Hence he will "entrance" his audience and godlike depart from his work, with the intention of later "returning into it without a break / I' the consciousness." Thus the narrator leaves the poem to become the poet: "They [his audience] sleep, and I awake / O'er the lagune [at Venice]" (607–15).

Only in those older, unselfconscious works of art where the poet believes himself achieving all there is to be achieved are the singer and his song one: there is no need for a narrator who is other than the poet. But in more modern and ambitious works where the self-conscious poet aims for more than can be achieved, there is always some indication that the poet possesses more energy and personality than can be encompassed by the work itself. It is in such poems as these that the question of the relationship between the poet and his narrator and, further, between the poet and his audience arises. With works like the former, the audience is totally satisfied by the completeness of the work itself; in the case of the latter, the audience asks the poet for more, for "another lay" into which he compresses "his whole life's business" (3. 616–51).

But alas, such works are but "dream-performances that will / Be never more than dream" (3. 623–24). For the poet is like a sailor who pulls into harbor and tells his story to those on shore. He manages to enthrall his audience, but he also keeps them constantly mindful that he is the narrator, that he and his story are not one:

> on we went
> Till...may that beetle (shake your cap) attest
> The springing of a land-wind from the West!

Then the sailor departs: "we and you / Part company: no other may pursue / Eastward your voyage, be informed what fate / Intends" (3. 652–75). No, the self-conscious poet remains eternally faced with the irony that the teller of the tale is different from the person who lived the tale, even though that person be the teller himself. Self-conscious narrative, in other words, is linear and does not admit of that "compression" which allows the poem, the poet, and the narrator to be totally one.

Engrossed by his speculations, the poet asks why he should continue in such vein, why get on with his narrative when it will not yield what he wants from it. As he muses thus on a palace step in Venice, his eye is caught by a group of picturesque market girls and he is led to ask for the oppressed ones of the world what these girls now have—youth, strength, and health—opportunity, in a word, rather than the full physical and spiritual attainment that, utopia-minded, he had wished for them in England (3. 676–721). And this new social awareness on his part leads him to consider his art in much the same way: he cannot at once achieve artistic perfection—the full compression that earlier he had lamented being unable to attain—but he does possess the opportunity to work toward it. His art is like a machine in the process of being built and not to be despised because it has not yet been completed, although he may have to endure opprobrium and epithets flung at him. He will simply have to tolerate a narrative in which there remains some distance between himself and his narrator. So occupied, he will strive to impart the gift of seeing to his audience; and though admitting to the impossibility of revivifying the historical Sordello, "the very man as he was wont to do," he now in a more confident mood returns to his neglected auditors to say: "and therefore have I moulded, made anew / A Man, delivered to be turned and tried, / Be angry with or pleased at" (934–36). Thereafter, in the last three books, the narrative proceeds less haltingly and with little of the uneasiness about the narrator's role reflected in books one through three.

Having accepted parabasis as a necessary condition of his narrative and having come to terms with the necessary lack of congruity between poet and narrator, Browning was left with the problem of the poet-narrator's relationship to his protagonist. It doubtless occurred to the poet that if his relationship to his narrator was dialogic, there was perhaps no better way of proceeding than to make the relationship of the poet-narrator to the protagonist a dialogic one also. As we shall see, this mode of procedure, which becomes a structural principle, gives rise to theme and theme in turns plays into structure.

In the first book, which traces Sordello's growth to consciousness during his early years at Goito, the world is experienced from Sordello's point of view. Placing us at Goito, the narrator invites us

> Pass within:
> A maze of corridors . . . ,
> Dusk winding-stairs, dim galleries got past,
> You gain the inmost chambers . . .
> (1. 389–92),

the invitation being not only into the castle but also into Sordello's mind. The boy does not speak, but the narrator relates what happened to him and how he responded to each experience as a child would: "On each full-fraught / Discovery brooding, blind at first to aught / Beyond its beauty" (1. 483–85); "he never could remember when / He dwelt not at Goito" (1. 604–6). At the same time, the narrator does not speak on the child's behalf but adds some comment (frequently sarcastic) on certain aspects of the boy's development:

> up and down
> Runs arrowy fire, while earthly forms combine
> To throb the arrowy secret; a touch divine—
> And the scaled eyeball owns the mystic rod:
> Visibly through his garden walketh God.
> (1. 580–84)

> Fool, who spied the mark
> Of leprosy upon him . . . ?
> (1. 567–68)

Such remarks are addressed not only to the audience but to Sordello as well, as though the narrator were attempting to tug the boy into consciousness of the world about him and to an awareness of where during the formative stages of his life he went wrong.[18] As an adolescent wrapped up in himself and living in a dream world, Sordello is allowed to speak in his own voice to express his hopes of being emperor and Apollo: "though I must abide / With dreams now, I may find a thorough vent / For all myself" (1. 832–34). At the end of book one occurs the event that, "breaking on Sordello's mixed content / Opened, like any flash that cures the blind, / The veritable business of mankind" (998–1000).

Sordello now a man, the narrator enters more directly into dialogue with him, sliding back and forth between the second and third person, as he projects the protagonist's thoughts by means of indirect discourse—"presently / He will be there—the proper You, at length." Or he addresses Sordello directly:

> Dear monarch, I beseech,
> Notice how lamentably wide a breach
> Is here! discovering this . . .
> So much the better for you.
> (2. 415–20)

More and more Sordello takes on a separate life of his own.

The nature of the relationship between the narrator and the protagonist is, in the first three books especially, deliberately obfuscated, however, by the syntax and the punctuation, or lack of it, as in the following passage chosen at random:

>   Lacks
> The crowd perceptions? painfully, it tacks
> Together thoughts Sordello, needing such
> Has rent perception into: it's [sic] to clutch
> And reconstruct—his office to diffuse,

> Destroy: as difficult obtain a Muse
> In short, as be Apollo. For the rest,
> E'en if some wondrous vehicle exprest
> The whole dream, what impertinence in me
> So to express it, who myself can be
> The dream! nor, on the other hand, are those,
> I sing to over-likely to suppose
> A higher than the highest I present
> Now, and they praise already: be content
> Both parties, rather: they with the old verse,
> And I with the old praise—far go, fare worse!
> (2. 596–610)

In books two and three, the more Sordello takes on a life of his own and the more he is allowed to speak for himself, the more he is merged into the narrator.

Yet in the last two books, there is a growing separation of the two. The narrator addresses him more often and more directly by name, as in the beginning of book five; and in the last book he apostrophizes, "Ah my Sordello, I this once befriend / And speak for you" (6. 590–91), as though he had not been doing that all the time. In the end the separation between narrator and protagonist is so great that the narrator loses sympathy for his hero and, in apparent perfect detachment from him, sums up Sordello thus: "a sorry farce / Such life is after all" (6. 849–50).

Now this dialogic mode of procedure suggests how the poet-narrator uses his protagonist and indeed the poem itself. By means of a persona, he traces something like his own development and then, having got to a certain point of self-knowledge and thus of a certain superiority over his material, he effectively separates himself from his hero, as in fact Browning had attempted to do in *Pauline*. In other words, he uses Sordello as a whipping boy, ascribing to his protagonist faults he discerns within himself. Here as elsewhere in the poem, there is that spiraling of "artistic reflection and beautiful self-mirroring" that Schlegel found so characteristic of Romantic Irony (*Athenaeum* Fragment No. 238).

The youthful years of both Sordello and the speaker of *Pau-*

line are remarkably similar, and Betty Miller correctly notes the resemblances between them and their creator.[19] It appears that Browning, in his first version of *Sordello* at any rate, wished to rework the material of the earlier poem, this time however focusing mainly on the youth's development as a poet. The speaker of *Pauline* had, of course, represented himself as a poet but had shown fairly limited interest in the poet's chief tool—language. As Browning's own interest in language and language theory grew—a concern strongly reflected, as we have seen, in *Paracelsus* and *Strafford*—the poet began to focus increasingly on that one subject.

The *Pauline* poet had hoped to become a world redeemer with words, like the Sun-treader, whose "words . . . seemed / A key to a new world" (414–15). Apparently he reckoned that if he had the right aspirations for mankind, then the words to move them would magically come unsought for, as to "one who has a right" (1014). As we noted, the *Pauline* poet fails because his "words are wild and weak" (904).

In *Sordello*, Browning again deals with one who would be a Shelleyan (but acknowledged) legislator of mankind. This time, however, the boy-who-would-be-bard is located at a point of cultural crisis where, willy-nilly, he must address himself to the question of language. "Born just now— / With the new century—beside the glow / And efflorescence out of barbarism" (1. 569–71), Sordello is faced with forging a new language for Italy out of the late Latin vernacular: "he slow rewrought / That Language, welding words into the crude / Mass from the new speech round him" (2. 575–77).

Growing up in the isolation of Goito, he lives mainly in fancy. Soon discovering that all external beauties take on value only insofar as he responds to them, Sordello projects himself into the phenomena of the world not only to endow them with life but also to confirm his own consciousness of himself as a personality. In addition, the more life he experiences in this imaginative manner, the greater "soul" he becomes; the more the self sends forth itself to attack and overcome the not-self, the larger self it becomes. Such a nature stands in constant need of something to work its will upon and challenges all life to elicit and enlarge itself; such a nature fancies itself capable of growing to any height and, further, showing men with "more bounded wills" how they may follow. Thus believing itself "equal to all," such a nature is subject to thinking, like Aprile, the labor too large for life's scope or attempting, like Paracelsus, "to display completely here / The mastery another life should learn, / Thrusting in time eternity's concern" (1. 523–66). Belonging to this second class, Sordello looks around for the proper role by which to display his gifts and, after impersonation of, among others, the poet Eglamor and the emperor Frederick, he ultimately selects Apollo, as concentrating all excellence. Sordello might have continued living in fancy—though "restlessly at rest" because "hardly avail / Fancies to soothe him" (1. 966–67)—had he not one day wandered by accident farther away from Goito than usual and come upon a court of love near Mantua.

In the song contest Eglamor sings a song of Apollo, and Sordello, finding that he knows the song better, takes up Eglamor's names and time and place and reworks them into "the true lay with the true end" (2. 82). As "word made leap / Out word; rhyme—rhyme," so that "the lay could barely keep / Pace with the action visibly rushing past" (2. 85–87), Sordello learns that language is generative: "a discovery grew / Out of it all!" (2. 124–25). This is our first clue that the poet's-narrator's theory of language is based upon imagination, emotion, and reflexivity instead of upon the Cartesian concept of language as logically formed and clearly constructed.

Now chief minstrel in Mantua, Sordello faces up to his new role. He must "think now," whereas "hitherto / He had perceived" (2. 123–24). At Goito he had become aware of the world by perception, meaning abstract perception or idea or character as well as visual perception pure and simple. And during his Goito years, he dimly recognized that his "perceptions strange" (1. 629) must find "a thorough vent," "an instrument," a "body" for their expression if his soul were ever to "obtain its whole / Desire some day" (1. 833–37). In Mantua he soon discovers that pure lyric, "that happy vehicle" by which he had won acclaim, was not an adequate vehicle for expression of himself. Turning to other modes, mainly the allegorical, he strives to find the proper means, but with no satisfaction. Then he turns to an examination of his province's form of the Latin language:

> He left imagining, to try the stuff
> That held the imaged thing and, let it writhe
> Never so fiercely, scarce allowed a tithe
> To reach the light—his Language. . . . he sought
> The cause, conceived a cure, and slow re-wrought
> That Language, welding words into the crude
> Mass from the new speech round him, till a rude
> Armour was hammered out. . . .
> (2. 570–77)

With a new language at his command, he next attempts the dramatic mode, but again fails to do what he most wants: to create and to have so recognized by his audience something that is both expressive of himself and simultaneously distinct from himself. Sordello wants a vehicle embodying both "perception" and "thought." Perception, as we have noted, is abstract and inchoate, a flow of psychic energy. Thought, on the other hand, is rational cognition, the mind dealing analytically with phenomena and proceeding syllogistically from origins to goals. Sordello discovers that although language can express thought, it cannot, in his hands at least, be made to exhibit perception. The "armour" of language simply disintegrates, "because perceptions whole, like that he sought / To clothe, reject so pure a work of thought / As language." Language is the means by which perception moves to thought—hence "Thought may take Perception's place"—but it cannot re-present the perception that thought has usurped. Between the conception and the creation falls the shadow. Language is linear, susceptible to analysis of its parts, whereas perception, more nearly temporal than spatial, does not admit dissection. Language is the "mere presentment" of perception, "of the Whole / By Parts, the Simultaneous and the Sole / By the Successive and the Many" (2. 588–95). Ironically, language, the medium of poetry, can only express that which is least "poetic."

Unable to find the "wondrous vehicle" to manifest "the whole dream," "to become Apollo" (2. 601–3), Sordello decides that he had best give up poetry altogether. Anyway, "what impertinence in me" deficiently to express the dream "who myself can be / The dream!" (2. 603–5). Sung melodies are sweet, but those unsung are sweeter still. Sordello returns to Goito, where

>   back rushed the dream, enwrapt
> Him wholly. 'Twas Apollo now they lapped
> Those mountains, not a pettish minstrel meant
> To wear his soul away in discontent. . . .
>   (2. 959–62)

In his refuge at Goito, Sordello stoically accepts the fact that because he has been unable to forge a language unique to his own expressive need, his must be the language of silence. But he is restless because he still retains will and the need to manifest it. Then almost miraculously appears the opportunity when Palma summons him to Verona and a life of action. Having, as he believes, exhausted the resources of language, Sordello, like Rimbaud six centuries later, turns to deeds. Not language now but acts will be the "body" his soul requires.

As a would-be man of action, he comes to realize that "Thought is the soul of act" (5. 567), unexpressed perceptions having no part to play in the world:

> 'Tis knowledge whither such perceptions tend,
> They lose themselves in that, means to an end,
> The Many Old producing some One New
> A Last unlike the First.
>   (5. 433–46)

Ultimately language is a social enterprise, the mind in the world. Those like Salinguerra and Naddo who are buckled to the world speak easily, but Sordello, ever mindful of himself as distinct from the rest of the world, speaks with difficulty. Only once, when "quite forgetting for the one time / Himself," does speech come easily for him (5. 468–69). Only an other can make an individual aware of his linguistic potential by drawing words out of him.

This recognition of the essential dialogic nature of language leads Sordello on to a theory of poetry as a dialogic art, about which I shall have more to say later. In the type of poetry that Sordello foresees, there is a dialogic interchange between the poet and his audience: "Yourselves effect what I was fain before / Effect, what I supplied yourselves suggest, / What I leave bare yourselves can now invest." This is a poetry of nonstatement. As Sordello had earlier discovered, a statement can delude by inadequately representing the utterer of that statement. A word, however, does not lie. And it is a poetry of words and not of statements that Sordello envisions: the language of his art of interchange being "brother's speech"—"half-words," no "explicit details," calling things by "half-names," speech "where an accent's change gives each / The other's soul" (5. 622–37). Sordello realizes that poetry must of course be language and must function somewhat like discourse, but it need be "no speech to understand / By former audience" (5. 637–38), need not in fact be even rational or reasonable.

This language of suggestiveness and spareness will permit an art in which more can be said than ever before in so compressed a space and time. Always, however, perception will require the mediation of thought, the whole must yield to the parts, the simultaneous must suffer transformation into the linear if they are to find verbal expression.[20] Language can never describe consciousness, which is primarily averbal. Even in poetry there can never be metaphors whose first terms are inexpressible. The poet must simply accept this as a condition of his art, "stoop contented to express / No tithe of what's to say—the vehicle / Never sufficient" (5. 652–54). As we first noted in *Paracelsus*, for Browning language can never express the truth, which, in a state of becoming, is ever in advance of any formulation of it.

Some of Sordello's thoughts on language are amplifications of the brief reflections on the matter in the personal digression in book three. The poet-narrator comes to understand language in other than Cartesian terms: that is, not merely as an expression of mental and emotional content of which a speaker is consciously aware. Men rationalize, justify, apologize for themselves and their actions, but in doing so they reveal more about themselves and their motives than they intend (3. 787–802). By its failure as mimesis, the "betrayal" of language becomes a dramatic narrative device. Furthermore, language can be its own stimulus: men can come to believe in what they say just because they are speaking. The dramatic possibilities of these discoveries are unfolded in Sordello's long, casuistical interior monologue in book six, in which he considers accepting the badge flung on him by Salinguerra. The essential dialogic nature of language is at the heart of both the poet-narrator's and Sordello's linguistic theory.

Their thoughts on language, of course, govern in part their aesthetic theory. If language is indeed a social enterprise, then all notions of the poet as a Romantic bard must be called into question. As we noted in an earlier chapter, John Stuart Mill carried Romantic ideas of poetry to their logical conclusion when, in his essay "What is Poetry?" published in the *Monthly Repository* for January 1833, he said that all poetry worthy of the name is lyric in mode, the singer singing to himself. "All poetry is of the nature of soliloquy," he remarked; "eloquence is *heard*; poetry is *over*heard. Eloquence supposes an audience; the peculiarity of poetry appears to us to lie in the poet's utter unconsciousness of a listener." As we saw, Browning examined such ideas in *Pauline* and *Paracelsus*, yet although Pauline's lover and Paracelsus do speak to someone, with the exception of the encounter with Aprile, who actually is not listened to, the auditors merely provide the dramatic occasion; there is no interchange, no true dialogue. And even in *Strafford* the characters' speech is very little conformed by the audience or the setting. This was why William Bell Scott found that the speakers had only orations to deliver. However, as Browning looked further into the nature of language, he became increasingly aware of the extent to which the human being is a linguistic animal: how character is, to no small degree, the product of language. In his work on *Sordello*, he was concerned to investigate the question more profoundly.

From his acquaintance with Italian literature of the early

Renaissance and from his wide reading of English and French poets of the sixteenth and seventeenth centuries—Ronsard, Donne, Butler[21]—Browning was aware of how the old poetic tradition had socialized the poet. As Walter Ong observes, this tradition associated with rhetoric "had kept the poet engaged, struggling, not only with an audience but with other poets as well. . . . Contest, ceremonial polemic, was a constitutive element in the noetic organization of the old preromantic rhetorical world and of the poetic this world enfolded."[22] These earlier poets seemed to know instinctively what Browning had but recently discovered—namely, that language is a social enterprise. Would it be possible to return poetry to its dialogic inheritance?[23] To pursue the matter there could be no better way than to take for his subject a troubadour, a poet in constant contact with his audience and other poets. Such a choice would certainly prove a means for the working out of that very vexing modern problem—the relationship between the artist and his audience. It was to be the way that Wagner chose only a few years later, in *Tannhaüser* and *Die Meistersinger*.

For his protagonist Browning selected the historical poet-troubadour known mainly as the precursor of Dante. He aimed to reclaim the figure from the "hateful surge" and the "abysmal past" (1. 19) and also "disentwine" the "herald-star" from Dante's "consummate orb" (1. 350–61), thus deriving his hero from two different sources—history and imagination—and thereby allowing for a dialectical interplay from the very beginning. We soon see this reflected in Sordello during the Goito years: he lives physically in the world but mentally and emotionally in fancy, a luminous presence in a numinous world. Sordello is, however, of such disposition that he cannot belong to what he worships but must refer all qualities back to himself: "So homage other souls direct / Without, turns inward" and, requiring grist for his mill as well as confirmation of the process, he "must ever live before a crowd" (1. 535–36, 746). The crowds on whom Sordello is to work his will are necessarily all imaginary—and being imaginary they are no more or no less than reflections of himself and thus unable to be affected by his will.

At the court of love, he stands up after Eglamor finishes his song and "taking the other's names and time and place / For his" (2. 83–84), is enabled to excel. This is a dialogue by contest—the *tenson* (at which the historical Sordello outstripped his contemporaries) being an example of it—and it is the first instance of dialogue of any kind that he has experienced. Yet the immediate result of this is to encourage the notion that he is different from, and indeed superior to, other men. As the reincarnation of Apollo, he would be the heroic redeemer of other men. But as to the means by which he will do this, no matter: "Himself, inactive, yet is greater far / Than such as act, each stooping to his star, / Acquiring then his function" (2. 381–83). At this stage all dialogue has ceased: what he should be drawing from others, he would have them draw from him; yet since he does not love, such love as others should have in him does not exist.

In time Sordello settles on song—"Song, not Deeds, / (For we get tired)"—as the "channel to dispense / His own volition" (2. 440–44). Although he is proclaimed a bard, song itself soon becomes a sore annoyance because, singing not to communicate the joy of song itself but to have an effect, he finds that his audience does not respond as he would have them do. Although he loves the crowd's applause, he is nevertheless aware that they do not understand his intentions, caring only for the product and not the maker of it:

> he found that every time
> He gained applause by any given rhyme
> His auditory recognised no jot
> As he intended, and, mistaking not
> Him for his meanest hero, ne'er was dunce
> Sufficient to believe him—All at once.
> His Will...conceive it caring for his Will!
> (2. 621–27)

There is no interchange between him and his audience at all.

It is at just this time, however, that Sordello is most regarded as a bard. Having assumed the bardic crown of Eglamor, he is universally applauded but most of all by the critic-friend Naddo, who assures him that he is "true bard"

(2. 497). When Sordello begins to doubt his vocation, Naddo reassures him that as "a bard, a bard past doubt" (2. 788), he should cast aside all notions of introducing philosophic problems into his verse. Speak to the common heart, Naddo says, and hide all that sense of power that urges poetic genius to special ardor: "True bards believe / Us able to achieve what they achieve— / That is, just nothing." Poetry makes nothing happen. "The knowledge that you are a bard / Must constitute your prime, nay sole, reward!" (2. 815–20).

Sordello is not comforted by such prattle. How, he ponders, can a young poet, having lived at far remove from the crowd and thus with little knowledge of it, arrive at sufficiently accurate knowledge of others so as to satisfy the demand of an audience—which wants to see its own image in art—and still maintain a solid and evolving sense of self? How make congruent an actual (as opposed to an imagined) crowd, one in whom the poet lives and moves and has his being, and an actual (as opposed to an imagined) self? How, in other words, to make man and bard one? The question is aesthetic and psychological but not, at this point in Sordello's life, moral. Finding no answer, "the complete Sordello, Man and Bard," is "sundered in twain" (2. 690, 657) and, "foreswearing bard-craft" (2. 703), he soon returns to Goito, where, no longer Apollo, he continues to puzzle over the dilemma "to need become all natures yet retain / The law of one's own nature—to remain / Oneself, yet yearn . . . " (3. 39–41).

From Goito he is rescued by Naddo, who, "leaning over the lost bard's shoulder" (3. 223), tells Sordello that he must leave his treasured refuge for the gauds and pomps of the city. Arriving in Verona, he resolves to become the people's champion and take an active part in political events, thereupon ceasing to be a poet, "one round / Of life . . . quite accomplished" (3. 563–64), and leaving us with the impression that the problem of the poet-audience relationship admits no solution.

In book five we learn just how Sordello went wrong. First, he aimed to be a perfect poet—and there is no such thing: it was madness to believe he could be Apollo. Poetry is, like everything else, always in a state of becoming, new poets filling the voids left by their predecessors, Sordellos replacing Eglamors. Second, Sordello's idea of himself as half man and half bard was erroneous. A poet is part of mankind, "nor one half may evade / The other half: our friends are half of you" (5. 252–53). His fate being bound up with others, he must join with them to help the advancement of what formerly he had called "the crowd" toward an unrepressed and happy life. This means that he must shunt aside forever the idea of the poet as bard, one separated from his audience.

The opportunity to act on this new knowledge is soon granted. "Since talking is your trade," cries an inner voice, persuade Salinguerra to act on the people's behalf (5. 300–301). His argument fails, however, because, putting his feelings into his speech as something apart from himself, he is too self-conscious and too aware of trying to make an effect. Recognizing his failure, Sordello sinks into despair. He is soon roused by Salinguerra's slighting reference to poets and poetry and rises to their defense, speaking as unselfconsciously as he had sung when besting Eglamor. As Sordello responds vigorously, he is aware of contest, of being watched and judged: "round those three the People formed a ring" to watch Sordello proved their lord "ere they exact / Amends for that lord's defalcation" (5. 456, 466–67). It is he that has failed, not poetry, and his failure is primarily owing to two reasons. First, he worked with inherited forms, by which he could only copy nature, not shape it. Mimesis in art is but a means to an end, the end being enlargement and extension of "essence," of soul. Second, he had been at a monologic remove from his audience. Had he given his soul real sway, he, already embodying the life of the multitude, would have engaged in a true dialogic relationship and made himself part of the crowd, living in and with them. Had he done this, he would have attained a poetic power to be transmitted to a succeeding age and to be transcended by new poets. In the last analysis, it was the moral (and thus dialogic) aspect of art that he overlooked. He is now no longer merely willing to feed his own individuality but, instead, willing to contribute his part to mankind, whom, incidentally, he no longer refers to as "the crowd."

Looking back on his mistakes, Sordello discerns an evolutionary scheme in the history of poetry and foresees a new kind of poetry embodying the dialogic process in a new way. Indeed, Sordello views literary history as increasing dialogue between the poet and his audience, or, perhaps more exactly, as the increasing role of the audience in the creation of the poem, the exercise of what in the preface to *Paracelsus* is called their "co-operating fancy." In the beginning mankind's deeds rose successively to the birth of song. Song in turn produced deeds and then "acts . . . for the mind" (5. 575). Next came poetry of a more sophisticated sort, that of the "epoist,"[24] in which the poet displays men and women by exaggerating their good and bad qualities. This perfected, "Next age—what's to do?" The dramatist, or "analyst," shows without exaggeration how men and women act in circumstances provided for them. Lastly, the "synthetist" turns to display of man's inner life. Each of those three phases of poetic art involves an increasing role for the audience to play—Sordello, in fact, refers to his run-through of literary history as a "masque"—so that in the art of the synthetist, poetry advances to full-fledged dialogue. Acting on the principle of complementarity, the poet casts "external things away" and "yourselves effect what I was fain before / Effect, what I supplied yourselves suggest, / What I leave bare yourselves can now invest." Talking "as brothers talk"—in "brother's speech, . . . where an accent's change gives each / The other's soul"—the poet and his audience proceed by "a single touch more" or "a touch less" to effect an "all-transmuting" art (5. 584–650), in which they together more or less play the same role.

No longer is there any talk of "the bard" or "the crowd" but only of "brothers." Tracing the history of poetry from the lyric through epic and drama, Sordello speaks of the poet's role in making his audience see life as lived apparently and really. Not once is there mention of any one poet's priority. To Sordello poetry is dialogue not only between the poet and his audience but also between him and his peers, who are "brothers" as well. All poets are engaged in the corporate enterprise of the ultimate unveiling of "the last of mysteries"—man's inmost life—focusing on man in time, not on the disclosure of divinity or on man in eternity. They work "stage by stage" in the advance:

> Today
> Takes in account the work of Yesterday—
> Has not the world a Past now, its adept
> Consults ere he dispense with or accept
> New aids? . . .
>   ends
> Accomplished turn to means: my art intends
> New structure from the ancient.
>   (5. 627–31, 641–43)

The brotherhood continues thus to work until, in their display of man and his psyche, they reach the stage where they "divest / Mind of e'en Thought, and, lo, God's unexpressed / Will dawns above us" (5. 575–77). But this will occur only at the great unfolding of the Apocalypse because in time the poet "must stoop contented to express / No tithe of what's to say" (5. 652–53). A poetics of dialogue can hardly go further.

Sordello's aesthetic theory is reflective of the poet-narrator's expressed in book three. At the beginning of the personal digression, the narrator discards all non-evolutionary views of poetry and with them any notion of poetic enclosure. Only in art like Eglamor's is there to be found formal completeness. For Eglamor believed himself accomplishing all that a singer could accomplish: he fully embodied himself in his art so that singer and song were one. Eglamor is, in Schiller's terms, a "naïve" poet who, representing the sensuous surface of life, "flees the heart that seeks him, the longing that wishes to embrace him. . . . The object possesses him utterly . . . ; he stands behind his work; he is himself the work, and the work is himself; a man must be no longer worthy of the work, or be incapable of mastering it, or be tired of it, even to ask after its author."[25] In book one the poet-narrator had spoken of this type in almost the same terms:

> A need to blend with each external charm,
> Bury themselves, the whole heart wide and warm,

> In something not themselves; they would belong
> To what they worship.
>
> (1. 507–10)

Such a poet is "objective."

The other type of poet is, in Schiller's terms again, "reflective." It

> eagerly looks, too,
> On beauty, but . . .
> Proclaims each new revealment born a twin
> With a distinctest consciousness within
> Referring still the quality, now first
> Revealed, to their own soul.
>
> (1. 523–28)

This "subjective" type cannot be fully embodied in art, always having something left over and giving the audience "proof" that "the singer's proper life" exists underneath his song, that the song itself is but an episode in the poet's life (3. 622–30). For such a poet formal closure—"completeness"—is out of the question, because more is suggested than can ever be produced. For such a poet there is always an imbalance between himself and his forms.

This is not at this point a consoling notion for the narrator, who reveals himself to be, like his Sordello, a poet of this second sort. He had set out to write a long poem, and if formal closure was more or less impossible for such as he, how was he ever to proceed to an appointed end? He had traced Sordello's first thirty years in a flashback and had now got his hero to the point where he could act in the present. But what action? And how? Browning himself, as we saw earlier, had worked himself into an impasse and had decided to visit Italy "to finish my poem among the scenes it describes" (Orr, *Life*, p. 88). Musing on a step in Venice, he asks in the poem, "Who's adorable / Enough reclaim a—...be a queen to me?" (3. 679–81). It is, as he had said on behalf of Sordello, "as difficult obtain a Muse / . . . as be Apollo" (2. 600–601).

Looking for a queen, a muse of incompleteness and fragmentariness, he asks, why not take that *contadina* with the brown cheek? What "if I make / A queen of her, continue for her sake / Sordello's story?" (3. 689–91). Whereupon a "sad disheveled ghost," presumably the muse of the first part of the poem, comes "to pluck at me and point" and in effect says, "Get on with the show." To which the poet-narrator also in effect replies, "This is more or less part of the show," as his muse is transformed before his very eyes. Previously, under inspiration of his old muse, he had sought perfection for mankind. "At home we dizen scholars, chiefs and kings"—Paracelsus, Strafford, the young Sordello—"But in this magic weather hardly clings / The old garb gracefully" (3. 719–23). Life is variegated, like Venice itself, made up of good and evil, healthy and sick, wealthy and poor. Hence he does not ask for perfection for mankind, only for so much happiness as possible, and hence he turns to a different muse. No longer a queen, this new muse is a poor waif of trembling thin lips and tear-shot eyes—"into one face / The many faces crowd"—whom he loves far more than "she I looked should foot Life's temple floor" in the preceding parts of the poem:

> for I regret
> Little that she, whose early foot was set
> Forth as she'd plant it on a pedestal,
> Now . . . seems to fall
> Towards me.
> (3. 749–77)

Instead of awesome and distant, the new muse is more like a friend with whom there is a reciprocal relationship of service. The muse is no longer a goddess, and the poet is no longer a bard.

No, mankind is not to be despised even in its most seemingly depraved aspects, each having an idea of good that he uses to justify his seeming evil. This recognition of the mixture of good and evil in the world is but "a slight advance" (804) in the understanding of men, but at least it is better than what is offered by so-called bards from their poetic heights, who promise more than they deliver. Bards glibly talk of founts in the desert, "while awkwardly enough your Moses smites / The rock though he forego his Promised Land" (826–27).

Bards talk grandly of "office" without knowledge of what the term means. As the narrator understands it, "office" simply means doing what one is able to do to aid the human enterprise of living decently. Each is a cog in a machine, less valuable in itself than for what it can do. Poets "simply experiment / Each on the other's power" in building a "complex gin" of poetry, reaching completion of it at last and then watching it be dismantled by the next age. At present "this of ours [is] yet in probation" and "the scope of the whole engine's to be proved" (3. 837–54). The "office" of poets neither blind nor dumb has been, is, and will be of three separate kinds: the worst say they have seen; the better tell what it was they saw; the best impart the gift of seeing—apparently the lyric, narrative (epic), and dramatic modes. Having given this synoptic view of literary history and having offered examples of each, the poet-narrator speaks of yet a fourth kind of poetry. This type asks the audience to advance, "and having seen too what I saw, be bold / Enough encounter what I do behold / (That's sure) but you must take on trust!" (3. 912–15). This seems to be the art of the synthetist spoken of in greater detail in book five. At this point in the writing of his poem, however, Browning had not fully worked out the details of a poetics of dialogue, and only later did he realize or admit that the poet who casts off externals and makes "Natures, váried now, so decompose / That...Why, he writes *Sordello*" (5. 617–19).[26]

Having spoken at some length about poetic theory, the poet-narrator now draws back hurriedly from appearing "bardic." After all, he had just been attacking bards and here he was seeming to talk like one. As Griffin and Minchin report, Browning "had a horror, carried almost to excess, of assuming anything like a bardic pose" (p. 286). Why burden anyone with reflections on the function of the poet? Quite rightly the crowd dispenses praise on Salinguerras in preference to Sordellos. These former may not see a great deal, but they turn their bit of vision into action. They at least do something without a lot of palaver. But that is the way the world is: only in heaven will it be possible to see and act on that sight. Meanwhile, he who sees and causes others to see—"the Maker-see"[27]—does have a mighty role to play: to keep before men an awareness of Heaven's gifts.

Accepting the fact that for a "probational work" like the one he is engaged in there can be no sense of completeness such as "bards" achieve, the poet-narrator now feels free to present his poem as process rather than product: "The scope of the whole engine's to be proved" (849). What the result will be he does not know.

Assuming that the digression in book three is a reliable account of Browning's own thoughts and attitudes during his first Italian journey, let us again take note of some of the problems and decisions he faced upon returning home to complete *Sordello*. First, his subject matter was changed. Where formerly Sordello was portrayed as knight and bard, he now was to be shown as a man of the people. Second, the change in subject meant a change in treatment. After apparently patterning his poem on an epic model, he now realized that epic or grand romance would not serve to depict the people's champion. The style, the mode, even the genre would have to be reconsidered. Third, his own ideas about his art had shifted. Poetry, he had come more and more to realize, means neither singing to oneself nor delivering divine commandments. It is dialogue and process, not ukase and product. Yet, being a linguistic entity, it does come to an end and yield a product. And as for dialogue, the poet, possessing profound insight and the ability to tell what he sees, is different from ordinary men, who, furthermore, are mostly uninterested in what the poet has to say. We see this reflected in the two metaphors at the end of book three: Hercules sacrificed upon an altar, Saint John departing for Patmos. If *Sordello* were to be a reflection, it would also be a revelation. With, then, a changed subject matter and the consequent necessity to change style, plus an altered attitude toward his art, Browning decided, as we noticed at the beginning of this chapter, to step into the poem himself to present this disparate and contradictory material. He would "dance" as "Metaphysic Poet" (3. 829) and, employing a radical ironic mode, make it impossible to tell the dancer from the dance. He would be both narrator and hero, and at the same time neither.

In later years also Browning would refer to *Sordello* as a "metaphysical" poem.[28] By this I understand him to mean a correlation in the poem between various attributes and activities of man's spiritual and physical life. Perhaps the most evident of these is the implied correspondence between soul's body and artist's form. Just as artistic form is never adequate to enclose the artist's psychic energy, so is the physical body an imperfect manifestation of the soul. This disparity between aspiration and achievement is both a limitation and an opportunity—and this is precisely what Sordello never learns to accept and why in those parts of the poem dealing specifically with him there is an alternating imagery of contraction and expansion. When seeking a "body," "vent," "instrument," "vehicle," or "machine," he feels contracted and restrained; only as "soul" living in "dream" and "fancy" does he expand: upon returning to Goito, for example, "Back rushed the dream . . . heart and brain / Swelled; he expanded to himself again" (2. 959, 963–64).

Pleasant as the dream is, it is not, however, satisfying. Expansion and flight are exhilarating, but eventually one longs for firm ground. "Tis Joy when so much Soul is wreaked in Time." (6. 493). Lovers of beauty like Sordello are "blind at first to aught / Beyond its beauty," but eventually "exceeding love / Becomes an aching weight" and

> they are fain invest
> The lifeless thing with life from their own soul
> Availing it to purpose, to control,
> To dwell distinct and have peculiar joy
> And separate interests.
> (1. 484–94)

It is, however, this "purpose" that Sordello lacks: he "loves not, nor possesses One / Idea that, star-like over, lures him on / To its exclusive purpose" (2. 396–97). And having no purposeful idea or center within himself, he must discover it in others. As Friedrich Schlegel says,

> An artist is he who has his center within himself. He who lacks this must choose a particular leader and mediator outside of himself, not forever, however, but only at first. For man cannot exist without a living center, and if he does not have it within himself, he may seek it only in a human being. Only a human being and his center can stimulate and awaken that of another. (*Athenaeum* Fragment No. 45)

Possessed of a nineteenth-century sensibility (although dressed in medieval garb), Sordello quite naturally turns his fancy to thoughts of love. As we have noted, Browning in earlier works was concerned to work out for himself the meaning of human love. In *Pauline* the speaker had believed himself redeemed by romantic love. In *Paracelsus* it is domestic love (between Festus and Michal) that is pure and ennobling, although the protagonist does not experience it. In *Strafford* love is shown as a kind of madness. In the writing of *Sordello*, Browning was still working out his idea about love between men and women, and his changing thoughts on the subject are reflected in the poem, especially in the characterization of Palma.

In the beginning Sordello knows only the stone maidens of the font, who are his inspiration to high thoughts and the objects of his erotic fantasies. In adolescence "his votaries / Sunk to respectful distance" (1. 928–29) to be replaced by one who was to be Daphne to his Apollo—Palma. But he has seen her only at a distance, and only "conspicuous in his world / Of dreams sate Palma" (1. 947–48). One day, wandering fancifully in pursuit of Palma, he finds his dreams come true when he enters the court of love presided over by her. He sings and she awards him the prize—"Unbound a scarf and laid it heavily / Upon him, her neck's warmth and all" (2. 104–5)—whereupon he falls into a deep swoon. Although appointed Palma's chief minstrel, he apparently continues to see her only from afar, if at all. In Mantua he is unable without a muse to hammer out a tenable aesthetic and so returns to Goito, where he throws his minstrel's crown into the font upheld by the caryatides. Having discovered neither a human love nor a human inspiration for his song, he once more embraces the silent stone maidens and gives up song altogether because he has no idea or controlling purpose for his song. Unhappy and restless at Goito, pining subconsciously to mix with the world, he nevertheless can think of nowhere to go and nothing to do. He retains will but lacks the means for its exercise.

Then comes a summons from Palma to join her at Verona. Telling Sordello her story "with a coy fastidious grace / Like the bird's flutter ere it fix and feed," she says she too has had a need similar to his. At Goito she also had lived in dream, hers being of an "out-soul" that would lure from her her "force" and direct it and make it grow. This other was to determine for her every law of life; this other was to be nothing less than the incarnation ("corporeal shape") of Divine Will. He for God, she for God in him. This instrument of Deity remained to be found till the song contest, when she knew then and there that Sordello, the boy from Goito whom she had already set her heart upon, was the one. She was sure of him, moreover, because "Men's acknowledgment / Sanctioned her own" (3. 306–58). She like Sordello must "ascertain / If others judge their claims not urged in vain" (1. 742–43). Only unpropitious circumstances had prevented her from proclaiming her love for this "Fomalhaut" (3. 430), a star associated with Venus, the planet of love.

All this sounds like a medieval, mystical view of love, and the high-blown sentiments expressed in semireligious language have convinced a number of commentators of the true nobility of Palma's soul.[29] Yet if we look closer, we discern that what she wants from Sordello is for him to be, as Porter and Clarke put it, "an instrument of her ambition,"[30] Palma wishing to hold the same power that Adelaide, her stepmother, held. Telling Sordello her plans and how he can help her fulfill them, she asks "if I have misconceived / Your destiny, too readily believed / The Kaiser's cause your own" (3. 549–51).

Sordello does not reply. Up to this point he had barely heard of Guelfs and Ghibellins, much less known the difference between them. He ponders all night and then, never questioning his ability as a politician or warrior,

resolves to be
Gatevein of this heart's blood of Lombardy,

Soul to their body—have their aggregate
Of souls and bodies, and so conquer fate.

At last he has found the body for his soul, the means for self-display. No question of social good, merely self-fulfillment—this is the only concern "while our Sordello drank / The wisdom of that golden Palma" (3. 555–61, 585–86). As the allusion to Brennus following suggests (3. 588–92), all that glitters is not gold.

Some indication of the nature of Palma's love for Sordello may be guessed from the fact that she knows the secret of Sordello's birth but does not reveal it until Salinguerra throws the imperial badge around Sordello's neck. It is indeed fortuitous that the much-needed out-soul, whom for years she has seen at a distance, is acclaimed only after her discovery of his noble birth. Just as Adelaide feared a son of Salinguerra because he might be like his father in prowess, so does Palma—who "would blend / With this magnific spirit [Adelaide] to the end" (5. 800–801)—want as her champion (and spouse) the son of her father's chief general and adviser. And her disclosure of the mystery of Sordello's parentage has the (desired) effect of Salinguerra's insisting, "But only let Sordello Palma wed" (5. 932) so as to recoup the losses of her family.

And then the narrator does a very strange thing. After recounting Salinguerra's plans for dominion over Italy, he interrupts to say parenthetically:

> (Strange that...such confessions so should hap
> To Palma Dante spoke with in the clear
> Amorous silence of the Swooning-sphere,
> Cunizza, as he called her! Never ask
> Of Palma more! She sate, knowing her task
> Was done, the labour of it—for success
> Concerned not Palma, passion's votaress.)
> (5. 992–98)

In *Paradiso* (9. 25–36) Dante depicts Cunizza, whose amours, especially with Sordello, were notorious, but whose later life is said to be adequate recompense for her sins. She was indeed "passion's votaress." But Palma (as Browning renames her)? Surely more connivance than passion in her case. From all that has gone before, we have every reason to believe that success concerned her a great deal. Are we then to believe that Palma is transformed by her love for Sordello? But "never ask / Of Palma more!" She is to be dropped from the story just as we are invited to see her in a different light. Yet as it turns out, she is not dropped at all; at least the narrator will have more to say and suggest about her.

In book six the narrator repeats his observation that natures like Sordello, lacking a center, need a controlling purpose to be supplied by something outside themselves: "a transcendent all-embracing sense / Demanding only outward influence, / A soul, in Palma's phase, above his soul" (6. 39–41). Sordello, alas, has never found it, or accepted it when offered. He has been one of those who shied away from "the food / That's offered them." Certainly "a Palma's Love" would not "equal prove / To swaying all Sordello," but this does not mean that there is no "Love meet for such a Strength" as he possesses (6. 85–92).

In his interior monologue in book six, Sordello tries to justify his unwillingness to accept what has been offered by way of love. If, say, he had embraced Palma as a worthy "Love," "influence," "moon," "out-soul," he would have been settling for something less than the best imaginable and that would have meant debasement of his own soul. Where then "descry the Love" that shall be sufficient to affect "all Sordello" (6. 585)? The narrator supplies an answer, but for this we shall wait. The point to be made here is that Palma's love does not prove redemptive.

As we have seen, the narrator appears to have changed his mind about Palma during the course of the poem, altering his characterization of her from an ambitious politician (or power-behind-the-throne) to a romantic lover, who as her last passionate act "prest / In one great kiss her lips upon his [Sordello's] breast" (6. 619–20). He does this, I believe, because after his Venetian experience he comes to a more informed awareness of the need for love and sympathy in human life.

In his own life Browning, even prior to 1838, had been working out the proper relationship of power and love. I say this because we have watched him in *Paracelsus* examining the temptations of the aspiring intellect (Paracelsus) and the yearning heart (Aprile), both seeking to overcome all limitations and live in the infinite, only in the end recognizing that knowledge (power) and love must join forces for effective realization of either.[31] Now in *Sordello,* after his visit to Venice, he investigates the will that would manifest its infinite energy in the deployment of all its resources and how this involves both a concept of power and a concept of love. To do this, he decided to make Palma more nearly representative of love while characterizing Salinguerra as the figure of power, each having a claim on the hero who would not only manifest his energy but would also compel men to recognize him as their superior and master.

It is a mistake to view Salinguerra as the representative of crude, brutal power. If he were only that, he would not be the attractive character that he so obviously is to the narrator.[32] Salinguerra is one of those people who can both speak and act with confidence not because they are witlessly single-minded but because they are so firmly rooted in the world: "why, men must twine / Somehow with something," he says (4. 778–79). It is perhaps no small indication of the narrator's liking for Salinguerra that he is permitted to speak at much greater length and to be far more fully characterized than Palma. Like the Wife of Bath, Salinguerra has had the world in his time and enjoyed it all, and at age sixty looks younger than Sordello at thirty.

In the first half of the poem, Salinguerra hardly appears. Called "easy-natured soldier" (2. 1014) and speaking in "noble accents" (3. 548), he is but a presence in the background. Though there is occasional use of the words "strength" and "power," they are nearly always associated with grace and beauty, Sordello believing that song will be the means by which he will exert his power. When Sordello decides to make society the instrument for manifesting his will, the words are used in a political or military sense and come to be closely connected with Salinguerra.

Sordello's difficulties in being a man of action are roughly the same as those he had in being a poet: where he tried to manifest himself fully in words, he now wishes to do the same with deeds: "to display completely here / The mastery another life should learn, / Thrusting in time eternity's concern" (1. 564–66).[33] Sordello wishes to ally himself with the good and serve mankind. But what is the good and what service should he undertake? The Guelfs and the Ghibellins, the chief political parties, are no guide. "If a Cause remained / Intact, distinct from these, and fate ordained, / . . . that Cause for me?" (4. 950–52). Where he could imagine verbalization of a whole perception only to discover his medium of language incapable of rendering it, he now finds that he can imagine a perfect society—a new Rome—only to discover that he has no means for realizing his vision: there is no more possibility of building it "all at once" than of saying it "all at once." Rome was not built in a day.

Given the power to take on Salinguerra's strength, Sordello is left in a quandary as to what to do. Making the decision becomes an impossible burden for him. Others who made pretense to strength not half his own had succeeded in various pursuits, while he had not, because they had some inner "core" or submitted to "some moon" drawing them on. In short, they had a "function" (5. 57–60) because they had a purpose.[34] Neither Palma nor Salinguerra would prove equal to swaying *all* Sordello, but the strength and love they offered would have provided at least a partial sense of purpose. But no, he could embrace neither because neither was sufficient "moon" to "match his sea" (6. 89–93):

> Since
> One object viewed diversely may evince
> Beauty and ugliness—this way attract,
> That way repel, why gloze upon the fact?
> Why must a single of the sides be right?
> Who bids choose this and leave its opposite?

Where is the "abstract Right" (6. 441–47)? Where are the power and love that will sanction life in the finite world?

Retiring to an upper room, Sordello ponders what he should do—and being Sordello he can do nothing. Taking one course of action is the denial of the validity of all others: "The real way seemed made up of all the ways"; thus "why must a single . . . be right?" (6. 36, 445). Sordello's fault in this as in other possible endeavors is that he is unwilling to adopt a limited course of action. For to be valid it must yield immediate satisfaction and perfect results. Why sully truth by working with only a flint of truth? Why "brutalize" soul by enclosing it within a restraining body? Why yield eternity for the "single sphere—Time" (6. 575, 555).

Finding no answer to the questions, Sordello has it supplied by the narrator. "Ah my Sordello," he says

>   I this once befriend
> And speak for you: A Power above him still
> Which, utterly incomprehensible,
> Is out of rivalry, which thus he can
> Love, tho' unloving all conceived by Man—
> What need! And of—none the minutest duct
> To that out-Nature, nought that would instruct
> And so let rivalry begin to live—
> But of a Power its representative
> Who, being for authority the same,
> Communication different, should claim
> A course the first chose and this last revealed—
> This Human clear, as that Divine concealed—
> The utter need!
>   (6. 590–603)

It is the Incarnation of Christ that serves as the pattern for him who seeks to understand how energy and power find satisfactory manifestation in the phenomenal world, or, to use Sordello's terms, how soul is embodied with meaning and purpose. What the narrator means, among other things, is that any effort to achieve a perfectly incarnate soul is nothing more or less than "an insane impulse" (3. 27), this being a power reserved to God alone. Yet the Incarnation can serve as a pattern for self-realization, as Sordello apparently discovers in his dying moment, his eyes being like a "spent swimmer's if he spies / Help from above in his extreme despair" (6. 616–17).

With his power God created the world, and with his love he embodied himself in human form, not abhorring the Virgin's womb, so as to reveal a divine plan for creation. If God can condescend to time and matter, find the joy that comes "when so much Soul is wreaked in Time on Matter," surely it is hubris for anyone, artist or politician, to "let the Soul attempt sublime / Matter beyond its scheme." No, let the artist or politician take God's act as a model for his own and so "fit to the finite his infinity" (6. 493–99). The soul must supplement the body's fragility with its power of infinitely adapting itself to temporary conditions. True adaptation is not utter embodiment; but "true works" will, like the Incarnation, reflect the passion and the power and the knowledge "far / Transcending these, majestic as they are" (3. 622–28) and will, as Sordello desired, "oblige . . . recognise / The Hid by the Revealed" (3. 570–71).

It is to the Myth of the Incarnation that all elements in the poem have been leading. I am not prepared to argue that Browning accepted the orthodox Christian doctrine of the Incarnation—in fact, the passage cited above makes no mention of Christ at all—but I do feel safe in saying that he, like Schlegel and other Romantic Ironists before him, embraced it as a mythic pattern, a model of organization for his life as artist. The obsessive subject matter of his first three published works—the sense of the infinite power of the imagination and the concern to channel it—is surely reflective of the poet's own struggle to fit imagination, which he felt to be boundless, to the quotidian world, which he knew only too well to be limited. Power, knowledge, love he believed himself to possess in abundance, even in superfluity. What he needed was "some point / Whereto those wandering rays should all converge" (*Paracelsus*, 5. 690–91). Although Paracelsus is granted a vision of progress, he nevertheless dies before understanding how power and love—Paracelsus and Aprile—might effectively combine so that "dim fragments" can "be united in some wondrous whole" (5. 686–87). All he can hope for is that in the dim future men will "shape forth a third, / And better temper'd spirit, warn'd by both" (5. 886–87). But this hope for an evolved humanity resulting in what Tennyson in *In Memoriam* called "the Christ that is to be" was like Sordello's vision of a new Rome. What was lacking was some authority or sanction giving impulse and impetus to progress: a recognition of a Power beyond all human power that even the most imaginative of men with their extraordinary sense of power cannot hope to rival and that has created the world purposefully. Ah yes, "what need!" But how know this Power? Never except through revelation.[35] And what form could revelation take so as to be made accessible to men? Only human form—human form "representative" of Power and having its "authority": "This Human clear, as that Divine concealed." Ah yes, "the utter need!"

When Browning arrived at this conclusion, we cannot know. Presumably it was after his return home from Venice that he induced the Incarnation from his own personal need. That it was not orthodoxly Christian, or even Christian at all, may be inferred from the metaphor that follows the passage devoted to it:

> as says
> Old fable, the two doves were sent two ways
> About the world—where in the midst they met
> Tho' on a shifting waste of sand, men set
> Jove's temple.
> (6. 605–9)[36]

The Incarnation also provided for Browning the perfect paradigm for his conception of the poet. We have frequently noted his growing dissatisfaction with the Romantic concept of the poet as bard. The notion of the poet as prophet living on a mountaintop and singing, mostly to himself, under divine inspiration did not fit Browning's idea of poetry as dialogue. But the poet as God living among the creatures he had created, giving and drawing sustenance from them—this was more nearly congruous with his own understanding of the poet's role—at least better fitted his own experience of himself as poet. His almost expressed aim had been to be both "subjective" and "objective," not sequentially but simultaneously. The Incarnation offered the pattern by which the creator could be both in and out of his creation, immanent and transcendent. In addition, the Incarnation was the perfect expression (and explanation) of the irony Browning felt drawn by and had displayed, as we witnessed in *Strafford*. In the Mystery of the Incarnation was the supreme irony: what appears as complete objectivity on God's part is in fact a vehicle for something very personal and subjective—namely, the revelation of Personality behind creation. For one who wished to display the irony that occurs when the poem "oblige[s] . . . recognise / The Hid by the Revealed" (3. 570–71), the Incarnation was the perfect paradigm.

On the human level this irony involves nothing less than an attitude of the self before the problem of existence; it is the taking of a philosophical position on the fundamental question of the relationship of the self and the world. It presents itself as the negation of the "serious" or "objective" character of the external world and, correlatively, as an affirmation of the creative omnipotence of the thinking subject. But this affirmation is only provisional; for Romantic Irony, which is always dynamic, does not allow the self to come to a stop at a single point but causes it to travel incessantly between the infinite and the finite, the determined and the undetermined. Irony is not, as Thomas Mann observed in *Doctor Faustus*, a matter of either/or but of both/and; or as V. Jankélévitch says, it is not "neutrum, mais utrumque."[37] It is a balance of dialectical movement. If the movement stops, then irony disappears and with it the possibility of a comprehension of external and internal reality. If the world is denied, then madness reigns and one is plunged into an imagined universe; if, in turn, the soul or spirit is denied, then one is left with a mechanistic world from which values, especially artistic ones, are forever banished. Irony is therefore what Jankélévitch calls "the drunkenness of transcendental subjectivity," although it must be added that the liberty of irony is exercised by leaving phenomenal reality with the view of a return to it.[38]

It was this dialectic movement between the infinite and the finite, this hovering between the real and the ideal that the

Incarnation symbolized. And it was Browning's acceptance of the Myth that allowed him to become the radically ironic poet who, as noted in the beginning of this chapter, could bring together in one poem the disparate elements that make up *Sordello*. Browning had found the "moon" for his "sea" apparently in the process of writing the poem, and "this once" he could speak for Sordello because he at last knew what to say on his protagonist's behalf.

Earlier I mentioned how the dialogic mode of procedure in *Sordello* becomes a structural principle and how this gives rise to theme and how theme in turn plays back into structure. We have already noticed the dialogic mode and theme in reference to the poet, the narrator, and the protagonist. As we saw, the irony that Browning adopted does not allow the signified to be the end of discourse; on the contrary, it is the return of the sense of the signified—first understood directly and then ironically and indirectly—to the signifier that provides the value of the discourse, that of an aesthetic act.[39] Romantic Irony, in other words, does not permit conclusion: it forms a cycle of contradictory senses perpetually defying the principle of noncontradiction. Where Romantic Irony is concerned, a thing is simultaneously that which it is and that which it is not; it affirms simultaneously the nullity of the work that it supports and inspires and the transcendent value of that work.[40]

Let us see how these observations may be applied to the structure of *Sordello*. Upon first acquaintance the poem seems to lack unity: there appear to be two main parts separated by the personal digression. The first part is circular. It begins with the present, soon retreats to the past, finally returns to the present. The time span is thirty years; the locations are Goito, Mantua, Verona; the emphasis is on narrative and concrete detail even though the subject matter is largely focused on the protagonist's inner life. The narrator refers to this first half as the first "round" of Sordello's life (3. 563). The introduction to the chronological narrative in the first part, which deals with the suffering caryatides bearing the burden of the font at Goito (1. 389–427), is paralleled by an introduction to part two, which is again concerned with caryatides, but these "up and doing" (4. 138–69). The second part is horizontally linear. The time span is three days; the focus is on abstract discussion and psychological exploration of motive. The narrator brings the tale to an end with Sordello's death and the events ensuing from Sordello's inability to act.

This is the apparent structure of the poem. Upon closer inspection we find that the division into two parts may be more apparent than real. If we look upon *Sordello* as a poem cast in the epic mold, as the narrator almost says it is (1. 360–73), then we see that it opens *in medias res* with present action and then switches to a long flashback to explain how the present moment of crisis is reached. The present is condensed in time and concentrated in locality—the short stay in Verona being transitional—in contrast to the retrospective part, which is diffused in time and setting.[41] Regarded in this way, the poem may be represented by a straight line interrupted only by the personal digression in book three, which we might call a variation on the traditional epic invocation to the muse.

Or if we view the poem in terms of growth of the protagonist's moral consciousness, we can represent it by a rising diagonal. In Goito the self is idealized and aggrandized; in Mantua it is alternately arrogant and despairing; in Verona the self enters into a state of relationship, although this is limited to one person; in Ferrara the self is transcended through moral sympathy and ends in "triumph" over "extreme despair" (6. 615, 617). This, then, is a comedy in the Dantean sense—a progress from despair to bliss.

If we look at the poem in terms of Sordello's actual accomplishments, we must figure it as a circle. The narrator will allow no prize to Sordello at all; on the contrary, he castigates Sordello vigorously for all the things he did not do both as a poet and as a political leader (6. 756–69, 829–51). Sordello's body is returned to Goito and buried "within that cold font-tomb" (6. 632) wherein his mother is buried and by which the boy had sat many an evening. In effect, Sordello is returned to the womb: there has been no birth at all. That is why after Sordello's death the figure of the circle and the idea of return frequently occur in the last 260 lines of book six and why the last line ("Who would has heard Sordello's story told") repeats, except for the tense of the verb, the opening line of the poem.

Sordello does, then, possess a unified structure, to be figured as either linear or circular, according to how we view Sordello's life. The story of Sordello is not, however, the final subject of the poem; rather, it is the poet and his efforts to write a poem. The narrator suggests this when he relates how, a week earlier, an old priest had told him that Alberic's skeleton had been recently brought to light after six centuries and also, apparently quite superfluously, that June is the month for carding off the first cocoons that the silkworms make. This is, says the narrator, "a double news, / Nor he nor I could tell the worthier. Choose!" (6. 795-96). Which is the more important—the present or the past, an unearthed piece of history or the act of fabrication, the seer or the fashioner? We must choose. If we let ourselves, with our "co-operating fancy," be guided by the ending of the poem, we must choose both.

For the ending returns us to the playful irony that almost seems to vanish in books five and six and in effect cancels what had appeared likely to become the center of the poem, a philosophical-moral center. Sordello's apparent "triumph" in discovering the power and love of which the narrator spoke as needful promised victory of meaning over irony. But this is true only if we read the narrator's befriending speech (6. 590-603) as the last word, as so many commentators do. "Is there no more to say?" the narrator asks (6. 819). Of course there is, as there always is in Browning. Here as in *Paracelsus* the poet makes an appeal to history for an additional perspective, a final word, on his subject. But in this poem history, when divorced from legend, is unyielding: its word is at best equivocal and paradoxical. Sordello was a failure but also a small success. He did not achieve what he should have achieved, but nevertheless lives on, through a small snatch of his verse, among the glorious company of poets. But the last word does not belong to history. The last word belongs to the poet, who, turning to his audience, insists in effect that the imaginative *donnée* of his poem is Romantic Irony, which ends in a spiraling self-consciousness and forgoes meaning for metaphysical and aesthetic play.

We may perhaps best see how Romantic Irony is informative of the structure and also the style of *Sordello* if we note how the poem reflects Browning's attempt to destroy the conventional responses to, and prefabricated interpretations of, language that use of an inherited poetical vehicle entails: "my art intends / New structure from the ancient" (5. 642–43). The Romantic Age took form at a time when printing had become almost the sole means for the storing and dissemination of knowledge. Print had reduced sound to surface and hearing to vision, knowledge being tied not to spoken words but to texts. This new economy inevitably affected ideas about poetry, and during the late eighteenth century, it was clearly understood that a poem was a text, something separated from the lived world.[42] As we have already seen, Browning wanted poetry to be something more than a text having a peculiar life of its own, separate and distinct from the poet. He wanted to move closer to the reader (or auditor). And to do this he had to transcend the limitations of print, which means that he had to circumvent the contrivances of print to enclose everything within its bounds. In short, Browning, though using print, attempted to achieve immediacy by dialogue. This is why *Sordello* is addressed to an audience to whom the poet responds during the course of the poem.

To subvert the linear and sequential nature of a text, Browning organized *Sordello* to give it the effect of being spatially nonsequential. He sought to concentrate its entire length, almost 6,000 lines, into a single moment of simultaneous perception filtered through the eye of the narrator. The style of the verse itself he also contrived to yield this effect. The systematic derangement of tense, the shifting point of view, the absence (in 1840) of quotation marks, the frequent ambiguity of referent, the elliptical and involuted syntax—all contribute to the effect of simultaneity. The diction is highly colored, ranging from the grotesque to the delicately beautiful, and the rhythm varies from lyric mellifluency to halting, stammering speech—these too giving the impression of everything going on at the same time. Browning aimed to hold "the imaged thing" (2. 571) in abeyance until all elements were brought before the reader and the entire style-meaning could be perceived as a whole, simultaneously. Like his Sordello, he would say it "all at once" (2. 626).

But while simultaneity is pursued, linearity is emphasized by other means: book-by-book progression of the story, realistic and historically accurate details, explained motives, symmetrical division into two parts, rhymed couplets. Thus the ambition to say it "all at once" receives its check—and this not unconsciously or unwillingly on the poet's part.[43] For Browning was highly skeptical about both the ability of his audience to interpret correctly and his own ability, given the resources of language, to express himself rightly. But to ensure at least a certain availability of meaning, he has to yield to some of the demands of a printed text. In brief, the poem is carefully structured, the basic organization being logically sequential. Yet it seems disorganized and formless, the effect of the whole being one of unreality, of fantasy rather than history.[44]

This arabesque—Schlegel's "artistically arranged confusion" with its "charming symmetry of contradictions"—is, then, Browning's attempt at a poem that is both text and speech, embodied in print and constrained by linearity but defying the rules of grammar and the expectations of logic. *Sordello* exemplifies how Romantic Irony cannot accommodate itself to anything that seeks to limit it, how it wishes to be everywhere, to be all or not to be, and how the ironist must be a comedian or buffoon who makes sport of himself, his reader, and his work. As Friedrich Schlegel observed, in truly ironic works "there lives a real transcendental buffoonery. Their interior is permeated by the mood which surveys everything and rises above everything limited, even above the poet's own art, virtue, and genius; and their exterior form by the histrionic style of an ordinary good Italian buffo" (*Lyceum* Fragment No. 42). In such works everything is jest and yet seriousness, artless openness and yet deep dissimulation. The kind of irony informing *Sordello* is that which "contains and incites a feeling of the insoluble conflict of the absolute and the relative, of the impossibility and necessity of total communication" (*Lyceum* Fragment No. 108). Hence in *Sordello*, Browning tries to say it "all at once" with the ironist's full recognition of the impossibility of such utterance. It is Sordello's tragedy that he never learned to be an ironist.

If, as Aprile discovered, only God is the perfect poet, then no mortal, even though he mimics God's creative act and God's ability to be both immanent and transcendent, can be "a whole and perfect Poet" (5. 116, in the revised *Sordello*). As the ghostly voice of his fellow poets tells Sordello, the collective poet surpasses what the individual poet can do. The song started by a predecessor is carried on by a present singer, whose works in turn will be furthered (and modified) by a future poet till "time's mid-night / Concluding" (5. 103–18). It is the irony of incomplete completion—the work that is offered as a finished product yet that is but a stage in an ongoing process—that ultimately dictated Browning's decision to cast *Sordello* as an offering to, and a dialogue with, his poetic predecessors.

Speaking of his disappointment concerning the reception of his poetry, the poet tells his audience, mainly of the dead summoned from both heaven and hell, that he regards them as his "lovers" who have been tempted to return "to see how their successors fare." They are a brotherhood, sitting each by each and "striving to look as living as he can." During this performance the poet will occasionally peep forth to see whether they are asleep or approve of what he is doing. But he dismisses one spirit, who in the 1863 headnotes is identified as Shelley, because the consciousness of his presence would make the other poets seem nearer and more formidable and the narrator's task therefore more presumptuous. The narrator feels, in other words, that he must define his own difference as a poet and not be overly encumbered by the burden of the past.

As we have seen, something of this same situation occurs in *Pauline*, where the speaker invokes Shelley–Sun-treader, and in *Paracelsus*, where Aprile hears a voice of poetic attainment and where Paracelsus encounters Galen in hallucination. In each case a present figure comes to terms with a past one. As Herbert Tucker points out, "in his forerunner the secondary figure meets a double to whom he must defer, and emerges from the meeting with a distinguishing, sometimes chastening difference which strengthens his individuality."[45]

This is more or less what happens in Sordello's encounter with Eglamor, although Sordello tends to regard the older poet at first as "imbecile" and his "opposite" (2. 135–95). Eglamor is, as noted earlier, a formalist poet, one of fixity and enclosure (2. 204–06; 3. 619–20), who completely identifies himself—his whole meaning and purpose—with his art and who when shown the inadequacy of his formally faultless art, unenviously passes his crown on to Sordello, kisses his hand, and dies. Sordello then is chastened: hearing Eglamor's ode once more, he learned from it "how to live in weakness as in strength" and recognized Eglamor's just claim to fame (2. 280–90): Eglamor is simply a different kind of poet from Sordello, although it was Eglamor who, in book one, was the younger poet's inspiration. Just as Sordello begins to define his difference from Eglamor, so does Browning continue in book three to examine his own relationship with his poetic predecessors under the guise of talking about Sordello and Eglamor (615–75).

The poet-narrator turns to his audience of poets again in book three in a discussion of bards, who are said to offer more than they can deliver and who finally are less valuable to mankind than the present poet-narrator. "Presumptuous!" cries out one of his audience. But the poet-narrator replies that it is some of his brother poets who magnify the office of the poet. For the poet aims not only at wide vision, as bards insist, but also at effecting right action, the full realization of which can never be attained on earth. It is true that the poet-narrator does not do what he would like to do. But has his audience done any better? Poetry is, as we have seen, like a complex engine constantly set up and dismantled when its function is completed, each individual poet but adding his part to the making of the machine. It is, in short, a corporate enterprise carried on by a company of poets. After addressing two of them directly, he then turns to his larger audience to ask that they not misconceive his "portraiture" or "undervalue its adornments quaint," because what may seem merely devilish may prove a transcendent vision (986–88). In fact, like Saint John, they may find it a portrait of themselves.

The idea of tradition among the fraternity of poets is developed in book five where Sordello addresses Salinguerra on the progress of poetry. Tracing the advance from the epoist to the dramatist-analyst to the synthetist, he speaks in greater detail about the "complex gin" that poets as a brotherhood are always engaged in making and dismantling. Browning seems to have gained from Friedrich Schlegel many of his notions about synthetist art. Schlegel says:

> The analytical writer observes the reader as he is; accordingly, he makes his calculation, sets his machine to make the appropriate effect on him. The synthetic writer constructs and creates his own reader; he does not imagine him as resting and dead, but lively and advancing toward him. He makes that which he had invented gradually take shape before the reader's eyes, or he tempts him to do the inventing for himself. He does not want to make a particular effect on him, but rather enters into a solemn relationship of innermost symphilosophy or sympoetry. (*Lyceum* Fragment No. 112)

> Perhaps a completely new epoch of sciences and arts would arise, if symphilosophy and sympoetry became so universal and intimate that it would no longer be unusual if several characters who complement each other would produce common works. Sometimes one can scarcely resist the idea that two minds might actually belong together like separate halves, and that only in union could they be what they might be. (*Athenaeum* Fragment No. 125)

In the past the poet and his audience or the poet and his predecessors were hardly "brothers" because of a lack of full appreciation of the past or of a poetic tradition. But now with awareness of a rich and copious past, the poet does not elaborate on those forms of previous ages but instead reduces and so transforms them:

>   a single touch more may enhance,
> A touch less turn to insignificance
> Those structure's symmetry the Past has strewed
> Your world with, once so bare: . . .
>   need was then expand,
> Expatiate. . . .

Hence the present poet joins the brotherhood of poets, not shoving them aside or ignoring them or being immobilized by the necessity to compete with them but making use of them, building on them:

> my art intends
> New structure from the ancient: as they changed
> The spoils of every clime at Venice, . . .
> till their Dome
> From earth's reputed consummations razed
> A seal the all-transmuting Triad blazed
> Above.
>
> (5. 627–51)

Having, under the mask of Sordello, worked out to his satisfaction his own differences as a poet from Shelley and other poetic predecessors and thus liberated himself from the burden of the past, the poet-narrator can now proceed to a better appreciation of his inheritance. That is why he changes his mind about Eglamor, who in books two and three stands as a rival to be bested. Eglamor at the end of book six becomes "the face I waited for" in "the golden courts": "despite ill-reports, / Disuse, some wear of years, that face retained / Its joyous look of love." And as the poet-narrator spirals upward in his art, there is "ever that face there," the last admitted to the golden realms of poetry, who, concerned that those ascending will not find "perfect triumph," nevertheless "wish thee well, impend / Thy frank delight at their exclusive track, / That upturned fervid face and hair put back!" (6. 798–818). The passage is difficult to interpret because of the syntax and ambiguity of pronominal reference, but the narrator and Eglamor seem to blend to the point where Eglamor is not only an inspiration but a brother in the spiraling flight of "gyres of life and light / More and more gorgeous."

Turning to his audience, the poet-narrator says, "friends, / Wake up; the ghost's gone." Ghosts—not only Sordello's but also the "sad disheveled ghost" (3. 696) that is his muse—are said to be either fair or foul according to the odor they leave behind. Is it Satan's brimstone or the perfume of Saint John's Patmos that they smell? The rose may be sweet but it has no lingering smell. The musk-pod on the other hand has an enduring pungnecy and strength—just like the poem they have heard. It has not been easy and the burden has been put on them, but "who would has heard Sordello's story told." *Fratres, avete atque valete.* Tomorrow, on to engines new.

It is said of *Sordello* as of *Pauline* that, stung by criticism of it, Browning abandoned this particular style of writing and moved on to another more accessible to his readers.[46] One wonders, however, how he could have continued in the *Sordello* vein. For it is the perfect vehicle for what he wanted to do. And Browning being Browning, he had no intention, especially during these early years, of remaining at work on the same cog of the engine that is poetry. As Ezra Pound observed, "Hang it all, there can be but one *Sordello!*"[47]

The poem is remarkable for its amazing architecture, only some aspects of which I have been able to mention. Though appearing to most readers as chaotic, it is one of the most carefully constructed poems in the English language. Almost no event and almost no utterance is without parallel elsewhere in the poem. Structure and theme are perfectly fused, one giving rise to the other that in turn informs the first so that this one may illuminate the other and so on *ad infinitum*. *Sordello* is a beautiful, endless mirroring of itself, like that box of Quaker Oats which Aldous Huxley has Philip Quarles allude to in chapter 22 of *Point Counter Point.*

In verse style as in theme and structure, there is also the constant process of reflection. This running-together is perhaps most evident in the passages in which the narrator speaks for Sordello in indirect discourse, but it exists in many other passages as well. For example, this passage following Palma's kissing the dead (or dying) Sordello:

> By this the hermit-bee has stopped
> His day's toil at Goito—the new cropped
> Dead vine-leaf answers, now 'tis eve, he bit,
> Twirled so, and filed all day—the mansion's fit
> God counseled for; as easy guess the word
> That passed betwixt them and become the third
> To the soft small unfrighted bee, as tax

> Him with one fault—so no remembrance racks
> Of the stone maidens and the font of stone
> He, creeping thro' the crevice, leaves alone.
> (6. 621–30)

The bee and Sordello and Palma are all fused, not only in ambiguous pronouns but also in suggestive actions. In addition, the rhyme—and thus the pause at the end of the line—causes a line to be read first one way and then, when the reader goes on to the next line, in another.[48] This is what we may call the ironic style.

Subsumed under it is the "Metaphysical," "witty" style:

> Deeds let escape are never to be done:
> Leaf-fall and grass-spring for the year, but us—
> Oh forfeit I unalterably thus
> My chance? nor two lives wait me, this to spend
> Learning save that?
> (3. 94–98)

and the ur-Hopkins style:

> Down the field-path, Sordello, by thorn-rows
> Alive with lamp-flies, swimming spots of fire
> And dew, outlining the black cypress' spire
> She waits you at, Elys, who heard you first
> Woo her the snow-month—ah, but ere she durst
> Answer 'twas April! Linden-flower-time-long
> Her eyes were on the ground.
> (3. 104–10)

To the verse style of *Sordello* may be applied the epithet *impressionist,* a term that I use in preference to Browning's own word *synthetist* as being more generally understandable.[49] The purpose of impressionism in language as in visual art is to sketch in the intuitive moment and nature intermediate between the reality and its apprehension as an idea; impressionism attempts, in a word, to render perception. As Browning noted in book two, the self does not apprehend experience as a series of discrete entities like the words of a sentence but in an immediate and comprehensive way. Perception reaches us whole, before the analytic machinery of language resolves it into a series. Impressionism aims to make us as viewers or hearers aware of the experience at the moment of its generation, before the artificial control of percept and concept has set in.[50] It is this impressionistic style that gives much of the effect of simultaneity and wholeness in *Sordello*.

Whatever we call it, it is a highly personal style. The style of his first two published works is generally a Romantic style and not very distinctive. The style of *Strafford* is more experimental but still not characteristically Browningesque. With *Sordello*, however, we know we are reading Browning. He has found his proper voice at last, for though later poems modify to some degree the style of *Sordello*, they are still recognizably kin to it. No one can say that it is easy, but it is far more penetrable than it is generally made out to be. Indeed, *Sordello* deserves a fate far better than that which it has suffered even until this day.

CHAPTER V
PIPPA PASSES
AND
KING VICTOR AND KING CHARLES

CRITICAL RESPONSE TO *SORDELLO* WAS ALMOST universally condemnatory. Browning felt himself pelted with "cabbage stump after potato-paring" *(New Letters,* p. 18). In an effort to redeem his reputation, he wished to publish, as soon as possible, three plays that he had been working on and put aside to complete *Sordello.* At the suggestion of Edward Moxon, the publisher of *Sordello,* he decided to approach the public in a different way: printing his works not in boards but in a series of inexpensive pamphlets, priced at sixpence or a shilling (the last two, longer pamphlets selling at two shillings), the cost of publication to be borne by the poet's father. The series was entitled *Bells and Pomegranates,* a name that proved for most readers a pure mystification until the author, at the urging of Elizabeth Barrett, explained in the last number that it was meant "to indicate an endeavour towards something like an alternation, or mixture, of music with discoursing, sound with sense, poetry with thought." In all there were eight pamphlets—seven plays (two in the final number) and two collections of shorter poems—extending from April 1841 to April 1846.

The initial number was *Pippa Passes,* We know nothing about its composition. The poem seems to reflect memories of Browning's visit to Italy in 1838, and in all likelihood was written after the completion of *Sordello* in the spring of 1839. It will be recalled that in book three of *Sordello* the poet witnesses in Saint Mark's Square some market girls come to the city from the area around Venice, even "from our delicious Asolo" (683), that his heart goes out to them, and that he reorients the poem he is writing to serve them as symbols of suffering humanity. He had, in short, been touched by them. Browning, however, was always suspicious not only of others' but also of his own feelings and motives; and he must have wondered, as he looked back upon the experience, what its true nature was, what being "touched" means. Is it simply sentimentality, the inflation of the emotions to match the pathos of the scene? Does one in fact ascribe values to the "toucher" that are not really there, "invest / The lifeless thing with life from [one's] own soul" (*Sordello,* 1. 490–91)? Was it anything more than pretense? Moreover, such questions might be posed not only about the nature of love but also about the nature of poetry. What does it mean to say that poetry has an effect, such as both Sordello and the poet-narrator of the long poem wish it to have? It was questions like these that Browning wished to investigate in his next work.

Fresh from the Italian background of *Sordello,* Browning decided to set his new poem again in Northeastern Italy, not however during the early Renaissance but during the contemporary period, the very time of the personal digression in *Sordello,* book three. Furthermore, he would investigate the problem from the reverse situation—that is, not so much from the point of view of the one "touched" as from that of the one "touching." Mrs. Sutherland Orr reports that Browning was walking alone in a wood "when the image flashed upon him of some one walking thus alone through life; one apparently too obscure to leave a trace of his or her passage, yet exercising a lasting though unconscious influence at every step of it; and the image shaped itself into the little silk-winder of Asolo, Felippa, or Pippa" (Orr, *Handbook,* p. 55).

Such an image and such a situation would almost inevitably suggest the role of the poet with respect to his audience and, in Browning's case, would have brought to mind his own career as one who had consciously decided to define his own poetic gift as different and distinct from that of his immediate predecessors. What if he had become the kind of poet that J. S. Mill wanted all poets to be, a singer overheard? What if this "little silk-winder of Asolo" were to sing and her songs were to be overheard by various people?[1] The basic conception of the poem dictated a fragmentary structure of various points of view, and it could only produce ironic results.

Pippa's songs are overheard by eight people whom she

falsely presumes to be the happiest inhabitants of Asolo. Four of them interpret her song as having some special significance for themselves individually. As in *Paracelsus* there is again a poetry of moments with no pretense of a continuous narrative, an understanding of the poem depending upon the reader's "co-operating fancy." Like *Strafford* it is cast in the form of a drama, but one to be read and not enacted upon the stage.[2]

On her annual holiday from the silk mill, Pippa rises early in expectation of living the day fully by pretending to participate in the life of others. Her speech is packed with brilliant, sensuous images of nature, each following another with great rapidity and seemingly little development, like the sun that "boils, pure gold" and "overflowed the world" (Intro., 1–12.)[3] Hers is a Keatsian world of living and growing things, each observed in its minutest and most detailed aspects: the exotic lily "ruddy as a nipple, / Plump as the flesh bunch on some Turk bird's poll" that she guards "from weevil and chafer." In this world there is no human other than Pippa, who is "queen of thee, floweret" (Intro., 90–100). Insofar as persons exist in this contracted sphere, it is only in fancy, as she begins her holiday by going

> down the grass path gray with dew,
> 'Neath the pine-wood, blind with boughs,
> Where the swallow never flew
> As yet, nor cicale dared carouse:
> No, dared carouse.
>
> (Intro., 209–14)

Pippa is, in short, a Romantic nature poet whose song, like that of the cicada, is heard only from afar and in no direct relation to humankind.

Pippa's only mode of utterance is lyric, unlike that of other characters in the poem. As she moves in the varied human world, she "carouses" with pimps, prostitutes, hired assassins, paid informers, murderers, debauched students, adulterous lovers, newlyweds, worldly clergymen; and she is as untouched by them as the cicada would be. Insofar as she enters their world at all, it is unknowingly or fancifully.[4] Absolutely untouched by the real world, she comes away from it confirmed in her preconception that those who have heard her song are Asolo's happiest ones.

Yet instinctively Pippa realizes at the end of her day that fancy is not adequate to sustain life. The holiday, which was to invigorate her for the coming year, is past. And she: "what am I?—tired of fooling!" (4. 291, 293). In addition, the natural world that she delights in is also insufficient to support human needs—even, in fact, to support itself: the bee, the mouse, the grub—they "wile winter away"; but the firefly, the hedge-shrew, the log worm—how fare they (4. 239–44)? What Pippa really wants is dialogue and relationship, to "approach all these / I only fancied being . . . , so as to touch them, . . . move them . . . some slight way" (4. 340–42). As Sordello discovered, nature and fancy "hardly avail . . . to soothe" *(Sordello,* 1. 966–67). The fancy cannot cheat so well. Like the young Keats, the lyricist must forgo make-believe—pretenses about men and nature—for the agony and strife of human hearts if he is ever to be anything more than the idle singer of an empty day. He must in short cease to hold the notion of being a "bard."

The psychic necessity of dialogue and relationship is further exemplified in all four episodes of the poem. Like Pippa each of the protagonists is caught in a web of illusions of his own making and each sees himself as playing a role in life's drama. Pippa perceives herself as "Pippa," frequently speaking of herself by this name in the third person. She never alludes to herself as Felippa, but only as Pippa the poor, loving, singing silk-winding girl, one of God's puppets whose service ranks the same as others' and whose only amusement is pretending to be someone else. It is a kind of Shirley Temple role, although at fourteen, roughly the same age as Phene and Luigi, she is a bit old for the part.

In the first episode, "Morning," Sebald casts himself in the role of Romantic Lover, a man of grand passion, for which the world is well lost. He has killed Ottima's old husband more or less for an idea—an idea of reckless passion. If he has to suffer for it, at least he will have lived splendidly. "One must be venturous and fortunate— / What is one young for else?" (1. 136–

37). Yet the "recompense" has not been adequate: he cannot escape the guilt and the shame, not so much out of moral outrage as out of aesthetic disgust. A *crime passionel* is surely excusable and perhaps even commendable. But this!

> to have eaten Luca's bread—have worn
> His clothes, have felt his money swell my purse—
> Why, I was starving when I used to call. . . .
>   He gave me
> Life—nothing less.
>   (1. 140–42, 146–47)

Lovers in romances do not act this way. No, this role has been played badly. "Let us throw off / This mask. . . . Let's out / With all of it!" (1. 40–42).

Ottima, however, would continue the play. "Best never speak of it," she says in allusion to the hideousness of the crime. Sebald nevertheless wants to "speak again and yet again of it." He will rise above mere "cant" and, in the new role of one who boldly speaks the truth, will eschew all euphemisms and say, "I am his cut-throat, you are—." But he is not quite sure about the new parts to be played by Ottima and himself: "But am I not his cut-throat? What are you?" (1. 52, 57). Ottima still insists on the old script and continues as Isolde to his Tristan. Her words of passion have their effect. He who had wished to talk plainly of the murder "till words cease to be more than words" (1. 44), now whipped up to feverish state, pleads to Ottima to speak "less vehemently." But at this moment of passionate intensity, she aims to confirm him in the old role: "Crown me your queen, your spirit's arbitress, / Magnificent in sin. Say that!" He begins to repeat her words and has just come to "Magnificent" when Pippa passes by.

Like nearly everyone else in the drama, Sebald has difficulty with language, not only getting his own words right but interpreting those of others. For when Pippa sings her lyric about order in the Great Chain of Being,

> The year's at the spring,
> And day's at the morn:

> Morning's at seven;
> The hill-side's dew pearled:
> The lark's on the wing,
> The snail's on the thorn;
> God's in his heaven—
> All's right with the world!
>
> (1. 221–28),

Sebald turns on Ottima to say, "I hate, hate—curse you! God's in his heaven" (1. 269). All passion spent, Sebald throws off the mask of Romantic Lover and, almost as if addressing an audience assembled to witness the play, speaks of Ottima in the third person: even her hair that "seemed to have a sort of life in it, / Drops a dead web" (1. 257–59, 246–47). Isolde the queen is shown to be merely Vivien the enchantress. The magic web—romantic love—of La Belle Dame sans Merci has held him in thrall, and now released, by Pippa's song, he is free—free to commit another murder, the killing of himself.

The failure of dialogue and true relationship between Sebald and Ottima is suggested throughout the episode by the fact that both consciously play roles: they speak to each other as they presume characters in those roles should speak. Then when Sebald is disillusioned in his part, he speaks not to Ottima but of her. "Speak to me—not of me!" she says more than once (1. 247, 250). Sebald's resort to monologue is but the final indication of the lack of dialogue in their relationship all along. Ultimately it is emblematic of an inner vacuity that demands role-playing.

Sebald, as I have said, conceives of himself as the Romantic Lover, with love as his religion and the Beloved as "my spirit's arbitress" (1. 219). When he fails to sustain that role, he is totally undone: his sense of self decomposes, as his final speech with its images of disintegrating consciousness indicates. The idea of God and of punishment of himself for God's sake is all he has to cling to. And this new idea gives him a new role—the Penitent and Punisher of Vice. Pippa's song, then, does not stimulate him to a love of God but to playing a new role that has no moral or religious content. I know of no other work of such brevity that examines so fully and so well the psychology of romantic love.

In the second episode, "Noon," it is also a self-conceived role that prevents Jules from realization of a relationship of dialogue and interchange. Where Sebald had sought redemption in romantic love, Jules seeks it in art. He has a vision of himself as the artist in quest of ideal beauty, "the human Archetype" (2. 86). Having little hope of ever finding his ideal in real life, he has worshiped perfect works of art, like Canova's statue of Psyche. Then he discovers Phene, whom he perceives as the living embodiment of this ideal—*a tableau vivant*, as it were, of Canova's pure white marble form. Where previously he had lived in art, he would now make her his ground of being: "Nay, look ever / That one way till I change, grow you," he says; "I could / Change into you, beloved!" (2. 8–10). He would establish his selfhood by becoming Phene.

Jules's perception of Phene's splendid qualities of both body and soul is based on illusion. For Phene is not what she seems. Some of his fellow art students have played a cruel trick on him, writing beautiful letters to him in her name. Before they marry, Jules knows her only by sight and through the letters supposedly hers. He proposes marriage and Phene agrees, on the condition that there be no conversation between them till after the wedding ceremony. All is as in a play: everything is arranged, even the script, as we shall see, being written by someone else.

As the episode opens, Jules declares his eternal devotion and then proceeds to talk for 115 lines. Occasionally he interrupts himself to suggest that Phene speak, for the *first* time in his presence (2. 13, 24); but she has no chance to make a murmur because he will not hush up. This is the Nuptial Monologue (as he sees it), and it must proceed at a stately pace and touch on profound themes. Phene, however, is not loath to remain silent because she wishes to stay "where your voice has lifted me," transported by words "above the world" (2. 124, 129). She would, if she could, play the role that Jules has foisted on her and enjoy forever the words that he speaks, like the hero in a tragedy by Racine. For it is speech that sustains the illusion, as Ottima, too, well knew. But now she must speak, and it is the words of others that she must repeat, doggerel which declares that Love has pitched his tent in the place of excrement.

Jules's immediate inclination is to disavow Phene and seek revenge from the perpetrators of the malicious hoax. But then Pippa comes passing by, singing a song of a page's love for a queen who lived in Asolo long age. And immediately Jules is moved to forgo revenge and to love Phene in a new way. This comes about through a strange application of Pippa's song to himself. For the song of an inferior's love for a great and scornful lady stimulates Jules to identify himself with the queen: "I find myself queen here it seems!" (2. 287). Why should one always play the page's part? Having discovered Phene not perfect, he will mold her as he had shaped marble, "evoke a soul" from the raw materials that she presents: "This new soul is mine" (2. 299–300).[5] He will, in other words, assume a new role, that of Pygmalion. He will take Phene off to "some unsuspected isle in far off seas" (2. 327) and, free from all corrupting societal influences, possess her utterly as he molds her anew. Once again, in a very brief space, Browning portrays the master-slave relationship that love can engender and sustain.

The failure of dialogue is, of course, emblematic of a general breakdown of human relationships in modern life. Jules, like Sebald, never transcends his own subjectivity; he sees the other simply as an object, an object to be possessed and used to confirm his sense of self. If upon first glance it seems that Jules and Ottima are cast (or cast themselves) in very different roles, the difference is more apparent than real. The fact is that the first two episodes are complementary, portraying contrasting panels of lovers using each other pretty much to the same effect. We see this in the way that the second episode picks up where the first left off. Sebald is dying at the end of the first, and the second begins with Jules saying, "Do not die, Phene." Sebald is the "slave" who must be held in thrall by his queen, and Ottima is the queen who must rule; Jules is the "queen" who governs the "page," and Phene is the willing subject. Both Ottima and Jules exert their dominion through words, words that confirm themselves and their subjects in the roles in which they cast themselves. In both cases it is the drama of what they call love that provides them with, and indeed sanctions, their roles.

In the third episode, "Evening," we are presented with another kind of love, of parent and child, also characterized by a lack of dialogue.[6] Luigi has made up his mind to play the role of Martyr in the fight for Italian freedom. His mother tries to dissuade him from carrying out his plan, but to no effect; for whatever reasonable objections she poses, he brushes them aside as though rational action were of no import, the emotion and the passionate intensity being all. Tell me, she says, what good the assassination of the Austrian emperor will do the Italian cause. But Luigi can give no answer because, like Sordello, he has not the foggiest idea about politics. Her words to him are like the wind, the imagery of which, along with the imagery of light, dominates the episode. He himself hears only echoes of his own voice (3. 1–15, 159).

Like the lovers in the preceding episodes, Luigi finds a lack of meaning in modern life; but where they turned to love and art for salvation, he flirts with the idea of political martyrdom. Ideally he would have lived in a time of queens and knights and heroes. But since he is confined to the colorless present, the assassination of the emperor is an action worthy of the heroic self he would be. And so he makes up a little drama and gives himself a starring role. He envisions himself in "handsome dress" for the occasion—"White satin here to set off my black hair"—and "in I shall march" straight past the guards: "I have rehearsed it all" (3. 104–11). And watching him in spirit will be the glorious company of political martyrs as he kills the tyrant and cries out, "Italy, Italy, my Italy! / You're free, you're free" (3. 120–21). No opera could be grander.

And then of course he will be captured and put to death. For the drama to be acted out rightly there must be no escape—"to wish that even would spoil all!" Yes, "the dying is best part of it" (3. 64–65). If there are crowns yet to be won in this late age, it will be through martyrdom for the cause of country. *Dulce et decorum est pro patria mori*! Love of mother country is surely nobler than love of one's own parent.

His mother, who is given no name and is referred to both by Luigi and the author by the name of her parental role, points out to him that this kind of patriotism is "the easiest virtue for a selfish man / To acquire" (3. 125–26). As she continues her attempt to dissuade him from this fatal undertaking, Pippa passes by singing of a good king of ages long ago who was preserved from attack by a python. Luigi applies the words to himself and, strangely enough, instead of deciding against the assassination, as the sense of Pippa's song would seem to suggest, rushes out bidding his mother, "Farewell, farewell—how could I stay?"

Luigi's misapplication of Pippa's song seems a little less peculiar when we recall that he is so swept up in his fancy of political martyrdom that everything he sees and hears not only reminds him of his proposed act but also confirms him in it. At the beginning of the episode, the echo in the turret seems to cry out the name of a leader of the revolt that established the Roman republic, the wallflowers overhead seem to be men and women urging the death of the emperor (3. 6–15). Moreover, his mother's mention of the morning star evokes this observation:

> "I am the bright and morning-star," God saith—
> And, "such an one I give the morning-star!"
> The gift of the morning-star—have I God's gift
> Of the morning-star?
>
> (3. 148–51)

For one who can interpret natural phenomena in such a way, it is perhaps not so curious that he should misunderstand the import of Pippa's lyric. In short, Luigi is a monomaniac, a kind of Don Quixote who lives entirely in fancy and gives his life meaning by playing a role; and he disregards everything that does not minister to that mania.

The following episode, "Night," begins with the bishop saying, "I desire life now," in contrast to the conclusion of episode three, where Luigi wills his own death. Again there seems to be a question of altruism—namely, the Monsignor's gaining for the Church some of his family's ill-gotten wealth. But unlike Luigi the Monsignor speaks coolly, with great self-possession. He knows who he is: he has his role as bishop and is confident in it. As Pippa says, he carries an "exalted air" (4. 275). The only "queen" he acknowledges is the Queen of Heaven (4. 109–10). He is, in brief, "the Monsignor," who is given no name, only the title, while the intendant, a slippery fellow, is given not only a name but also many aliases.

So long as he is in control, he speaks easily, the way a bishop should. Yet from the beginning there is a slight suggestion that things are not quite right about this churchman. Being a Sicilian, he is not at home in northern Italy and thus suffers from even the mild weather of this first January day. He has a cough that interferes with conversation—"if my cough would but allow me to speak!" (4. 128–29). Even when he is in control of things, there is something slightly amiss. And then when he ceases to command the situation, he loses his self-possession entirely.

Although he has detained the intendant so as to converse with him, there is never any idea on the Monsignor's part that there will be dialogue: he is master here! Indeed, if dialogue were to occur, the Monsignor would no longer be in control of the situation. If there are facts that Maffeo may wish to reveal, even these he knows already. The Monsignor believes that the Intendant has murdered his niece Felippa (Pippa) so that she could not inherit the family estate. "But I want you to confess quietly, and save me raising my voice," he says. "Why, man, do I not know the old story?" The intendant had not, however, murdered the child at all but has saved her as a means of plaguing the Monsignor, who otherwise would receive the money for himself or the Church. "So old a story, and tell it no better?" he responds, even sarcastically repeating the bishop's liturgical "howsoever, wheresoever, and whensoever" of the previous speech. "Liar!" shouts the Monsignor, for the first time showing emotion (4. 165–79). He is now no longer the bishop but the pawn. Passively he listens to the intendant's plans for doing away with Pippa, uttering no demur and seemingly offering assent (4. 205–9). Then Pippa passes by, singing of an early appreciation of the music of nature and an imminent understanding of the harmony of the spheres when "suddenly God took me" (4. 233).

At this the Monsignor springs up and calls for his people in the outer hall. "Gag this villain," he says, to hush up unsettling words; "he dares—I know not half he dares—but remove him—quick." Just briefly before so suave and well-spoken, the Monsignor becomes inarticulate. He has almost ceased to be "the Monsignor," and now to recapture the role he must resort to the proper language of that role: "*Misere mei, Domine*! quick, I say!" The episode ends, like the one preceding, with Pippa's song serving to recall the hearer of it to a sense of personal identity with his chosen role.[7]

In the end each of the protagonists in the four episodes is left alone with his self-conceived role. In the little dramas enacted, the speakers are never at a loss for words, employing language to satisfy their own psychological needs. Browning had already investigated this irony earlier, but what is new in *Pippa Passes* is that here Browning goes further to show that men also filter the language of others to fit their requirements; that is, they hear what they want to hear. We have already noted how each of the persons who acts on Pippa's lyrics either misinterprets them or wrenches and contorts them to make the words mean what they want them to mean. One of the basic themes of *Pippa Passes* is, then, the problem of interpretation of language.

Another theme, to which it is closely allied, is the problem of perspective. As Paracelsus observed, "We live and breathe deceiving and deceived" (*Paracelsus*, 4. 625), not only because we fit ourselves into categories but also because of the locus of our perception. Things are never as they seem. In *Pippa Passes* the characters in the four episodes are not the happy and enviable people whom the little girl from the silk mills would impersonate; all is not right with the world; Pippa has indeed "touched" many lives on this day which, at its close, she believes to have passed uneventfully; Pippa in fact is not a mere working girl but the heiress to a considerable fortune. Most appearances have no reality at all—and this not only because mankind are willfully purblind. The fact is that their vision is necessarily bounded by their locations: various angles of vision yield varying reports of things observed. A work of perspectivist art like *Pippa Passes*, which employs points of view to transcend point of view, must therefore be ironic in mode and circular in structure.

We see this most clearly perhaps in the attitudes of the various characters concerning free will and determinism, to which, of course, the idea of enslavement is closely bound. Pippa thinks of herself in the main as determined, almost in the Marxist sense. She has but one free day a year, and so she must take full advantage of this day, which itself is partly determined and partly free:

> Day, if I waste a wavelet of thee,
> Aught of my twelve-hours' treasure—
> One of thy gazes, one of thy glances,
> (Grants thou art bound to, gifts above measure,)
> One of thy choices, one of thy chances,
> (Tasks God imposed thee, freaks at thy pleasure,)
> Day, if I waste such labour or leisure
> Shame betide Asolo, mischief to me!
> (Intro., 13–20)

Others, however—"happy tribes"—are prepared to take or let pass indifferently what the day offers: "Day, 'tis but Pippa thou ill-usest / If thou prove sullen" (Intro., 30–31). This day can be of no great importance to Sebald, Jules, Luigi, or the Monsignor, for theirs is a different lot. God has so ordained it; men are but "God's puppets," working "but as God wills." And this is a consolation because "all service ranks the same with God" and hence "there is no last or first" (Intro., 190–95). The idea of fate and arbitrariness becomes a major theme of the poem and is closely connected with the concept of power that Browning had addressed himself to directly in *Paracelsus* and *Sordello*. As Pippa says, there is not "one deed / Power shall fall short in or exceed" (Intro., 200–201).

Pippa, who is to have such importance in the lives of a number of people, is portrayed, like one of the Fates, as engaged in "silk-winding, coil on coil" (Intro., 71). Sebald sees himself caught in a web of Ottima's hair (1. 247). Jules, finding himself the victim of an evil prank, believes that "all's chance here" (2. 250). Bluphocks, the satanic figure always hovering in the background, adopts a philosophy of *carpe diem* because all is predestined, he (punningly) having "renounced all bishops save Bishop Beveridge," the Calvinist divine. His other allusions are, moreover, mainly to determinism—for example, Rabelais's Panurge consulting Hertrippa. When his mother urges him to mistrust his own sentiments, Luigi argues that "heaven / Accords with me," that he has "God's gift" (3. 73, 150). The Monsignor—"I, the bishop"—also holds that "my glory springs from another source" (4. 109–11).

The characters see themselves in terms of a power relationship, which the narrative underscores time and again. Let us note how everybody is subject to the domination of someone else: Pippa's life is controlled by Luca, her employer; Luca has been killed by Sebald; Sebald is enslaved by his "queen," Ottima; Phene is exploited by the students to get at Jules, who, the victim of his fellow art students, will nevertheless 'mold" Phene; Luigi is manipulated by political schemers; Bluphocks is paid by the intendant; the street girls are whores in the employ of Bluphocks; the intendant is at the mercy of the Monsignor, who almost becomes the intendent's accomplice and thus subject to blackmail; the Monsignor is governed by the pope; Pippa is alive only because the intendant has plans to use her as an instrument against the Monsignor. Indeed there is a Chain of Being, but not the one Pippa sings of when she passes outside Ottima's house. This is not a chain of love but a chain of power: everyone is the puppet of someone else. Hence, in a meaning quite opposite to that intended, Pippa's final words are right: "All service is the same with God— / Whose puppets, best and worst, / Are we......"

What then are we to make of all this? Is it the final meaning of *Pippa Passes* that human beings are but the playthings of a God who uses them presumably only for his own amusement?[8] The answer must be, as to like questions posed about *Sordello*, both yes and no. For here again we are dealing with a work of Romantic Irony that does not allow the signified to be the end of discourse. Hovering above the work there is the figure of the poet, to whom the sense of the signified returns. Pippa unknowingly describes the process and indeed the whole structure of the poem when in the beginning she speaks of the sunbeam hitting the water in a basin: a splash breaks it up into bits that are sent "wheeling and counterwheeling, / Reeling crippled beyond healing" till they "grow together on the ceiling." How does this happen? "That will task your wits," demand exercise of the co-operating fancy in joining together the fragments supplied by the author. Meantime, "where settles himself the cripple?" (Intro., 77–82, 87).

Each of the four episodes is apparently a discrete entity, their only connection being Pippa, who is ignorant of the content of each and who touches each one in a very tangential but nonetheless important way. Between the episodes there are three interludes of "talk by the way," which is "by the way" only in the geographic sense. But there is upon nearer inspection a much closer relationship of the dramatic fragments than at first was evident. It is an interconnectedness not only of theme but also of imagery and circumstance, only a few of which I shall mention.

The ironically named heartsease that Pippa picks in Ottima's garden is set next to the lily in Pippa's room in the epilogue and is suggestive not only of the (unknown) richness of the day's adventures but also of how perception, understanding, is limited to a point of view. Pippa commands the lily to wake up and note how this new plant has a flower thrice as large, thrice as spotted, and containing thrice the pollen while the leaves and parts "that witness / The old proportions and their fitness / Here remain, unchanged, unmoved now." Suppose, she says, that there is a king of the flowers who holds "a girl-show" in his bowers:

> "Look ye, buds, this growth of ours,"
> Says he, "Zanze from the Brenta,
> I have made her gorge polenta
> Till both cheeks are near as bouncing
> As her...name there's no pronouncing!
> See this heightened colour too—
> For she swilled Breganze wine

> Till her nose turned deep carmine—
> 'Twas but white when wild she grew!
> And only by this Zanze's eyes
> Of which we could not change the size,
> The magnitude of what's achieved
> Elsewhere may be perceived!"
>
> (4. 307–19)

The heartsease and the lily also contribute to the dominant imagery of the poem, the colors red and black or dark and light.

In somewhat similar fashion Jules's new profession as a painter is alluded to by the Monsignor in the fourth episode. The murdered Luca is surely "That old...somebody I know" referred to by the third girl in "talk by the way" between episodes three and four (3. 233). Bluphocks is the author of the verse Phene recites, the informer on Luigi, the pimp of the three girls of the street, the would-be seducer of Pippa.[9] Similar imagery and circumstances are woven into the fabric of the poem.

In a number of ways, the structure of the poem calls attention to the work as an artifice. What could be more obviously artificial or contrived than the fact that Pippa just happens by at the crucial moment in the lives of eight people and that her singing, which they just happen to overhear, provokes four of them to action of greatest importance for their own lives and for the lives of the others? What could be more artificially circumstantial than that the intended victim of episode four is the one whose song stimulates one co-conspirator, who is also her uncle, to reverse his momentary inclination to permit her to be done away with?

The reasons for this, I think, are twofold, First, Browning is concerned to show that, whether we realize it or not, society is a fabric. As Dickens demonstrates in his novels, so much happens to us of which we are totally unaware, and yet these circumstances unbeknown to ourselves can be of tremendous significance to us personally and to society at large. From the social, moral standpoint we must make connections, engage in dialogue, join the radiant "cripples" into a healthy whole.

When, for instance, the poor girls of Asolo are unable to find work to feed and clothe themselves, they turn to prostitution and criminal intrigue. Love, to use Browning's term, demands that we be responsible. That is the moral import of the circular structure that encloses the society of Asolo on this New Year's Day pregnant with possibilities for good and thus shows that "all service ranks the same."

Secondly, Browning has the poem call attention to itself in order to show that any plan is but a convenience and a fiction. Although love may call for the making of connections, power does not permit us to know what connections to make, not least because we are not free to act as we would. In the case of Pippa, for example, she cannot know what is going on inside the buildings that she passes by nor can she have any idea as to the effect her songs will have. To blame Pippa for being other than poor Pippa, the little girl from the silk mills of Asolo, would be absurd, because given her circumstances she can be no other. And the same observation of the other characters in the poem may to a great degree likewise be aptly made. Men are indeed what Pippa calls them: God's puppets, caught in a cycle of recurrence, one year of toil following the next.

Which view is correct? Is man free or determined? The answer that *Pippa Passes* makes is both. And it is the ironic nature of the poem that allows the two views to be alike true. For only God can know whether men are puppets or not—and men, of course, can never get to know what God knows.[10] As readers we have an overview of the events of this New Year's Day in Asolo—we have, as it were, the world in microcosm—and yet we ultimately know little more than any of the characters in the poem about God's ways. What more we do know is that, from the evidence of the poem itself, the ways of God are inscrutable and can be neither explained nor justified. That is the ironic import of the circular structure that shows that there is nothing more to be known.[11] Not for nothing is the poem entitled *Pippa Passes*: like Pippa we pass unknowingly through most of life.

The Romantic Irony of *Pippa Passes* is thus more strongly pronounced than that of *Paracelsus*, *Strafford*, or even

Sordello. Where *Paracelsus* had Festus and *Strafford* had Lady Carlisle as chorus-figures to guide us and where *Sordello* had a narrator to speak on behalf of the protagonist, there is no guide at all to our interpretations of the actions of *Pippa Passes*. The author provides us with no more clues to right interpretation than God does for the inhabitants of Asolo on this New Year's Day. Like them we have only the Janus face on this first day of January. *Pippa Passes* is, I believe, the only one of the longer works of Browning's early career that metaphysically is characterized by an undefining irony.

Pippa is a highly experimental work, combining as it does the lyric, dramatic, and narrative modes in verse and prose. Unhampered by the demands of the stage, Browning was able to write a drama that allowed full play to his ironic imagination. A number of commentators have seen it mainly as a transitional work that looks back to the so-called lyricism of *Pauline* and *Paracelsus* and, in its concentration on the fragmentary scene, looks forward to the dramatic monologue.[12] I myself see it as a further development of *Paracelsus*, which as we have noted is a series of lyric moments treated dramatically, and of *Strafford*, Browning's first play and first dramatization of irony. It represents an advance on the two preceding works in that the moments are more fully concentrated and dramatized than in *Paracelsus* and the protagonists' decisions to act in a certain way more clearly focused than in *Strafford*. *Pippa Passes* is a fully lyrical drama—that is, one in which the drama is brought into being by song, not only Pippa's but also that of the other characters as well, who express themselves with lyrical intensity and thereby heighten their fears and longings that Pippa's songs only further enhance and strengthen. It is song that evokes the crucial decision in each scene (the resulting action from which is not dramatized) and song that moves the narrative from morning to night.

Even though we are left with an undefining irony concerning the metaphysics of the poem, it is, I believe, nonetheless clear that insofar as Browning's aesthetic position is concerned there is a definite meaning to be gained. For the poet has contrived his poem to show that ultimately poetry is a social enterprise. Poetry is power.[13] It has an effect whether the poet intends it or not. And though he sing to himself and be accidentally overheard, as Mill and other aesthetic theorists of the 1820s and 30s insisted he should be, he still through the power of his verse can move his audience, for good or ill—and for this he must take responsibility. He must also demonstrate that love which develops through dialogue. A lyric poet, in other words, must also be dramatic. Otherwise he remains, like Pippa, at a monologic remove from his listeners, exercising power over them but abnegating his obligation to love them and hence help them advance in the business of soul-making. There is more than one way to "touch" an audience.

The second number of *Bells and Pomegranates* was published in March 1842. It seems to have been conceived, and perhaps composed, almost five years earlier. Writing to Miss Haworth in August 1837, Browning said that he was about to begin completion of *Sordello* "and to begin thinking a Tragedy (an Historical one . . .)" (Orr, *Life*, p. 103). This new play was almost certainly *King Victor and King Charles*, which Macready had in hand by 5 September 1839, when he recorded in his diary the following passage: "Read Browning's play on Victor, King of Sardinia—it turned out to be a *great mistake*. I called Browning into my room and most explicitly told him so . . . " (*Diaries*, 2: 23). Although advertised at the end of the *Sordello* volume as being "Nearly Ready," it presumably was published subsequent to *Pippa Passes*, which apparently was written later, because he wished to put forward his best work as the first number of his new series.[14]

King Victor and King Charles bears close resemblance to *Strafford*. It also is a drama on a historical subject[15] intended for stage production and concerned with the idea of kingship and the idealization of the man who is king. As we shall see, Charles holds the same illusion with respect to King Victor as Strafford does with respect to King Charles. It is, however, a less accessible play than *Strafford*: even more than Browning's first drama, it is largely a matter of oration rather than action, of events alluded to instead of represented; and its basic themes are barely discoverable upon repeated rereading and would hardly be discernible at all from presentation in the theater. Macready was right to term it a great mistake insofar as its suitability for the stage is concerned.

In structure it is different from *Strafford*, which follows the conventional five-act pattern established by the Elizabethans. *King Victor and King Charles* is in two divisions—"First Year, 1730.—King Victor" and "Second Year, 1731.—King Charles"—which are in turn divided into two parts. The parallel division of *King Victor and King Charles* is, however, to a certain degree reminiscent of the structure of *Strafford*, in which Browning used parallel scenes (the first two acts) and parallel acts (three and four). But where the structure of *Strafford* properly suggests that the two parties and indeed the two chief politicians are on the same level, the parallel structure of *King Victor and King Charles* does not accurately reflect the content of the drama. For it is not the aim of the play to show that Victor and Charles are to be judged equally: Victor is nothing less than the villain of the piece, whereas Charles, though seriously flawed, elicits our sympathy and, whether heroic or not, is clearly preferable to Victor.[16] Yet the structure suggests that we should view the two kings as though, to paraphrase Thirlwall's words quoted earlier, they were two contending parties with good and evil so intermixed that we are compelled to give each an equal share of sympathy.

Part one of "King Victor" ends with Charles in despair because he believes his father is about to force him to resign his claim to the throne, and with his reliance on his wife Polyxena. Part two shows Charles not deposed but crowned as king and Charles's turning away from Polyxena, who sees through the old king's ruse to retire and then reappear to reclaim the throne when Charles will have solved certain problems. The first part of "King Charles" depicts the return of Victor and the refusal of Charles to yield the crown. Part two deals with Charles's giving the crown to his father without a struggle and with the reunion of feeling between Charles and Polyxena when Charles admits that he too saw through his father's trick. The play ends with the death of Victor, presumably from an access of sentiment too strong for his old heart, when he learns that Charles is not to insist on keeping the crown as he had feared. *King Victor and King Charles* is thus made up of a series of reversals that, quite contrary to expectation, lead to the typical ending of early Victorian domestic drama—the husband and wife fully rejoined as one and the father and the son reconciled at the moment of death. It is as though Browning wished to carry further the ironic aims of *Strafford* but retreated almost at the last moment, presumably for the sake of success in the theater, to bring his work to a close with a situation more properly suited to a play by Bulwer or Knowles.

Like *Strafford*—and *Pippa Passes* too, as we have just noted—*King Victor and King Charles* portrays the ironies of love and to a certain extent explores the dialectic of love and power examined in *Sordello*. As the play opens, Charles expresses his need for Polyxena in his uncertain situation. Although the crown prince, he is treated contemptuously by his father, the prime minister, and the king's mistress. What bothers him most, however, is not his mistreatment but the fact that he does not enjoy his father's love. He insists on retelling Polyxena the whole story, apparently for the hundredth time, as she keeps saying, "You have told me," "I know." His parents (his mother has since died) openly discussed his "insignificance" in front of him, but he bore all because "Victor was my father in spite of that" (1. 1. 59, 63). So he suffered, but less, because he was soon married to Polyxena, who served partially to take the place of his father.

During the interview when Victor reveals that he is abdicating, Charles rehearses how in the past he has borne his father's hate and insults but now in resigning the throne, "you insult yourself, and I remember / What I believed you, what you really are / And cannot bear it" (1. 2. 170–73). Charles cannot conceive of his father other than in a position of power and of himself as other than subordinate.

It is an ideal of his father as the embodiment of power that exercises such control over the son.[17] Being weak himself, he idolizes the strong. It is something resembling his father's strength that draws him to Polyxena, who Charles believes could be king more easily than he (1. 1. 140–44), and upon whose strength he depends for support (1. 1. 175–78). She in fact tells him how he must act (1. 1. 157, 289), and so dependent is he upon her that he is fearful of taking any action without her direction. She is his "queen," as was Ottima to Sebald.

Although loath to accept the crown and thus ostensibly be placed in a more powerful position than his father, Charles finally does so when his father commands it. Charles well knows that Victor is engaging in a charade. But he does not give voice to this; instead he turns away from his wife at the end of "King Victor" when she begs Victor to retake the crown now rather than later. Dismissing all suggestions of trickery, Charles will guard his ideal of his father.[18]

Charles surprisingly proves a good and efficient ruler. Even D'Ormea, the prime minister inherited from Victor, is won over from political chicanery to true statesmanship by his monarch's example. Charles does it all, however, mainly for his father's benefit—that is, to clear Victor's name from obloquy (2. 1. 55–67). No sooner does he redress his people's grievances and appease justly angered Spain and Austria than he is presented with the news that Victor is returning to reclaim the throne. Although D'Ormea has good evidence of Victor's intentions, Charles categorically refuses to believe it and charges his minister with misbehavior for his own ends. In addition, Charles turns pleadingly to his wife to ask that she also refute the charges against Victor (2. 1. 136–40). Charles can deal only with those, including his wife, who support him in his illusion concerning his father.

Only when Charles is willing to confess that it is his father's power and not his love for the man—which, to be sure, he had identified with power—that compels him is he able to face up to the truth of what his father is—"One that's false— / False—from the head's crown to the foot's sole, false!" Victor returns to take the throne not out of any regard for his people but for the sake of power, to undo all Charles's good works, "restore the past—prevent the future" (2. 2. 226–32). But if he has to suffer defeat, Charles says, "The best is that I knew it in my heart / From the beginning, and expected this, / And hated you, Polyxena, because you saw thro' him . . . " (2. 2. 233–35). It was only a willed delusion all along: his father did not and does not love him; and he has hated anyone who wished to dispel the illusion.

It is at this point apparent, if indeed it has not been for some time, that Browning's main interest in the play is the psychological examination of Charles's character. Charles is revealed as one who, deprived of parental love from early youth, will do anything to win his father's approval. Weak himself, he loves his father's power: "What would I give for one imperious tone / Of the old sort!" (2. 1. 235-36). Yet it seems that Browning's root conception of the drama was of the conflict between love and duty, and only with great difficulty does he manage to point this up in the closing moments of the play. Were the manuscript extant and were we able to examine it, I think it would show Browning at some pains to force the work into shape. It was, after all, almost five years between conception and publication of the play.

The conflict between love and duty is highlighted in Polyxena's admonition to Charles, whom in an oration of twenty-seven lines she addresses not as her husband but as king:

> King Charles? Pause you upon this strip of time
> Allotted you out of eternity!
> Crowns are from God—in his name you hold yours.
> Your life's no least thing, were it fit your life
> Should be adjured along with rule; but now,
> Keep both! Your duty is to live and rule—
> You, who would vulgarly look fine enough
> In the world's eye deserting your soul's charge—
> Ay, you would have men's tongues—this Rivoli
> Would be illumined—while, as 'tis, no doubt,
> Something of stain will ever rest on you—
> No one will rightly know why you refused
> To abdicate—they'll talk of deeds you could
> Have done, no doubt,—nor do I much expect
> Future achievements will blot out the past,
> Envelop it in haze—nor shall we two
> Be happy any more; 'twill be, I feel,
> Only in moments that the duty's seen

> As palpably as now—the months, the years
> Of painful indistinctness are to come—
> While daily must we tread the palace rooms
> Pregnant with memories of the past—your eye
> May turn to mine and find no comfort there
> Through fancies that beset me as yourself—
> Of other courses with far other issues
> We might have taken this great night—such bear
> As I will bear! What matters happiness?
> Duty! There's man's one moment—this is yours!
> (2. 2. 253–80)

The speech is excellent in its austere dignity, but it seems better suited to French neoclassical tragedy than to *King Victor and King Charles*, to Polyeucte than to Polyxena. In addition, it does not make much sense. Why should Charles be blamed for keeping the crown and praised for abdicating? No sensible citizen of Savoy or Sardinia would be so inclined to blame or praise. As it turns out, all ends well so that Charles can have his crown and wear it too. For he gives the crown to his father, who thereupon promptly dies and Charles remains king. The conflict between love and duty is at an end, made possible, as it were, by a miracle. The father now dead (or dying), Charles and Polyxena are reunited not only as husband and wife but as king and queen.

In looking at the defects of the play, I do not wish to overlook some of the ironies prevalent in the previous three published works. There is not only the ironic structure but also the irony induced of self-consciousness that causes the characters to feel that they are actors in a play. As a youth Charles lives a pleasantly secluded life. If he peered out from his curtained box to look at his father and brother on the world's great stage, he was filled with pride to see them play their heroic parts before he "let the curtain drop" (1. 1. 22–28). Upon the death of his brother, he himself is forced to play a part on life's stage: "the young Prince" who serves as "the old King's foil" (1. 1. 119). To help him in his new role of crown prince, Polyxena coaches him in his part. During a rehearsal she seeks to embolden him by saying, "I fancied while you spoke / Some tones were just your father's" (1. 1. 129–30). Then she goes on to give him direction for playing a certain scene:

> you've mastered
> The fief-speech thoroughly—this other, mind,
> Is an opinion you deliver,—stay,
> Best read it slowly over once to me;
> Read—there's bare time; you read it firmly—loud
> —Rather loud—looking in his face,—don't sink
> Your eye once—ay, thus! "If Spain claims. . ."
> —Just as you look at me!
>
> (1. 1. 332–39)

Polyxena more or less directs him how to act in every situation. Charles in turn becomes so dependent upon her direction that before he can speak he must rehearse before her what he is to say: "I'll seek him," he says about a proposed interview with his father, "or, suppose / You hear first how I mean to speak my mind? / —Loudly and firmly both, this time, be sure!" (1. 1. 308–10).

Victor is also very much aware of playing a role. He sees the abdication, for example, as a theatrical exercise to be carefully acted (1. 2. 41–46). As for Charles he will suit the role Victor has chosen for him: the "earnest tone—your truth now, for effect! / It answers every purpose: with that look— / That voice," the only thing to be guarded against being Charles's possible "child's play" (1. 2. 230–33, 247). But, D'Ormea asks, if Charles is to be cast as "King Charles," "What then may you be?" Victor replies that he will be "Count Remont— / Count Tende—any little place's count" (1. 2. 252–57).

After his retirement and subsequent return, Victor sees the events about to unfold as in a play: "the masque unmasque / Of the King, crownless, grey hairs and hot blood,— / The young King, crowned, but calm before his time" (2. 1. 181–83). Or he thinks of himself in another dramatic situation, dying in battle:

> I, Victor,
> Sole to have stood up to France—bent down

> By inches, brazed to pieces finally
> By some vast unimaginable charge.
>
> (2. 1. 205–8)

His life's drama must come to the proper end: "What wants my story of completion?" (2. 2. 320). Finally, when Charles gives him back his crown, Victor struggles to enact his role correctly: "I seek for phrases / To vindicate my right"—"I am then King!" (2. 2. 310–11, 316). He is again the absolute monarch like King Louis of France: "How the world talks already of us two" (2. 2. 357). And so assured of heroic "completion," he can have his life's drama end.

Charles meanwhile has been playing the role of king, having seen through his father's design but pretending not to. At the end Polyxena tells Victor:

> Charles
> Has never ceased to be your subject, sire—
> . . . he acted you—
> Ne'er for an instant did I think it real.

Only with the death of his father can Charles be indeed King Charles.

Envisioning themselves in heroic roles and portrayed as the abstractions Power, Love, and Duty, the three major characters are almost totally wooden. Only D'Ormea has any vitality; he is a welcome but anomalous character in this "tragedy," as Browning called it in the Advertisement to the play. D'Ormea is the spirit ironic who looks with a certain detachment on himself as well as on others. Because he does not enjoy Charles's trust, D'Ormea offers his badge of office to the young king several times, only to have it returned to him: "I see / I never am to die a martyr!" (2. 1. 406–7), he says self-mockingly. Once, however, when Charles demands that he prove his charges against Victor or suffer imprisonment, D'Ormea says, presumably to himself: "And I'm at length / A martyr for the truth! No end, they say, / Of miracles. My conscious innocence!" (2. 1. 142–44). If others play roles, why can't he? Far from being the devil, he is a kind of guardian sprite whom the virtuous can never understand. "Motives, seek / You virtuous people, motives," he says to Polyxena. "Say, I serve / God at the devil's bidding—will that do?" (2. 1. 13-15). Possessed of a sense of irony, he realizes that no matter how long a matter may be considered one can never know with positive assurance that he is following the way of God or the way of Satan when he finally decides on a certain course.

King Victor and King Charles is, as DeVane noted a quarter of a century ago, probably the most neglected of all Browning's works (*Handbook*, p. 101); this is probably still true today. The poet himself regarded it as "a very indifferent substitute" for another play that he had planned to publish as the second number of *Bells and Pomegranates* and anticipated that its success would be "problematic enough" (*New Letters*, p. 25). There remains no reason to value it more highly than did the author himself. One can only be amazed that it stands, in order of publication, between *Pippa Passes* and *Dramatic Lyrics*.

CHAPTER VI
DRAMATIC LYRICS

THE VICTORIANS ARE FAMED FOR THEIR VOLUMinous writing. In the case of Browning, there is not only a huge corpus of published work but also apparently a vast amount of unpublished work as well. During the 1870s when asked why he did not write more lyrics, he replied, that he had large stacks of them at home that he had not bothered to publish because lyrics were too easy to compose.[1] This seems to have been as true of the poet during his early as well as later years. For what became the best-known volume of the *Bells and Pomegranates* series was actually put into print more or less incidentally, at the behest of Edward Moxon, his publisher, who suggested that for the sake of popularity he should publish a collection of his short poems (*Domett,* p. 36). Condescending to seek for wider appreciation, Browning presumably went to the desk or closet where he had his short poems stashed away, chose a number of them as being suitable, wrote a few more, and then gave them to Moxon to arrange on sixteen double-columned pages. *Dramatic Lyrics* appeared in November 1842.

Though slight in size, in literary and historical importance *Dramatic Lyrics* is among the most significant books of verse in English. There is an enormous range of subjects: from Euripidean Greece to medieval France, from Renaissance Italy to England of the Civil Wars to nineteenth-century France, Spain, Algeria, and England; from gods and nobles to monks, poets, soldiers, and lunatics—all reflecting Browning's zestful appetite for the multifarious variety of human personality and activity. In prosody there is likewise tremendous variation: rhyming couplets, octosyllabics, strophes of varying line-lengths, rhythm, and rhyme scheme—all somehow transformed into the language and meter of conversation: for the *Dramatic Lyrics* are designed to be heard rather than read. Here, as in

Sordello, Browning was determined to restore the old dialogic relationship between the poet and his audience.[2]

We must wonder that Browning did not rush the poems into print without the urging of his publisher. It may be that he did not regard shorter forms as important. The works published prior to *Dramatic Lyrics* were all long. Even when he had discrete shorter works such as the episodes of *Pippa Passes*—and these dramatic rather than lyric—he still managed to group them into a longer work. As for lyrics, we have noted how he seems to have identified them with the Romantics; and though he was not averse to writing songs—witness, for example, those of *Paracelsus* or *Pippa Passes*—he was concerned that they be recognized as utterances distinct and separate from the poet himself. To make sure that any short lyrics he might publish were not to be regarded as short swallow flights of song expressing the poet's own feelings, he first provided them with an obvious dramatic context and secondly linked them to other poems. Thus a poem concerned with possessivness in marriage was put into the mouth of a Renaissance Italian duke, linked to another having to do with marital fidelity and spoken by a French noblewoman of the late Middle Ages, and published under the title "Italy and France." Nearly all the shorter pieces of *Dramatic Lyrics* are thus linked to companion poems.[3] And just to make further certain that his readers fully understood that these lyrics were indeed dramatic, he prefaced the pamphlet with the famous disclaimer that the poems were "'Dramatic Pieces;' being, though for the most part Lyric in expression, always Dramatic in principle, and so many utterances of so many imaginary persons, not mine."

The best known of these pieces, such as "My Last Duchess," we today call dramatic monologues. There has been a good bit of debate as to what constitutes a dramatic monologue.[4] I shall here apply the term to those poems in which there is a speaker who is not the poet, who talks usually to someone else but occasionally to himself, and whose utterance reveals an important aspect of his character. As listeners to his monologue, we come upon the speaker in the act of talking to another person (or himself). His words and (implied) gestures capture our attention. As we focus our attention on him, we begin to deduce the speaker's purpose in speaking and we continue to follow him until we gain insight into his personality and hence his real as opposed to ostensible purpose for speaking. Browning himself did not use the term dramatic monologue; in fact, he seems never to have found a designation for such poems with which he was entirely happy, as he kept rearranging them into "Dramatic Lyrics," "Dramatic Romances," and "Men and Women" in subsequent editions.[5]

But whatever he called them, his primary interest, here as in his earlier work, lay in the revelation of character—or "soul," to employ his own word—and to this extent his monologues are logical extensions of those works that "display somewhat minutely the mood itself in its rise and progress" (preface to *Paracelsus*), that treat "Action in Character, rather than Character in Action" (preface to *Strafford*), in which the poet's "stress lay on the incidents in the development of a soul" (1863 preface to *Sordello*). The soul develops, as Browning discovered, in strange, inexplicable ways, yearning first toward this and then toward its opposite; it is torn between motives that originate in external circumstances. Hence the lyric element, the song of self that we overhear, becomes dramatic. When Browning began his career, he like his immediate predecessors and contemporaries had not learned how to represent dramatically ideas in conflict with each other or humans in conflict with ideas. The only means they had at their disposal to portray these conflicts dramatically was the confessional soliloquy—the "Intimations Ode," *Alastor, Pauline*—or, as in the case of Landor, the retrospective dialogue.[6] In the dramatic monologue Browning found a means of representing dramatic conflict within personality obliquely. What his dramatic monologues do is to internalize plot, so that instead of an open conflict of opposing forces, as on the stage or in the novel, there is an interior conflict within the character of which the speaker is often not consciously aware and, as often as not, a conflict in the reader-listener's understanding of that character. In brief—and I shall presently attempt to demonstrate by particulars what I mean—the dramatic monologue is a fragmentary, open-ended literary form that permits ironic discourse and ironic perception of that discourse.

We have already noted how Browning's irony originates partly in his desire to have a complete overview of an object or event and his simultaneous recognition that such totality is impossible; and we have seen, especially in *Sordello* and *Pippa Passes,* how any point of view is necessarily partial (in both meanings of the word) and therefore suspect and unreliable. It is not surprising then that the poet should turn increasingly toward portrayal (or examination) of various points of view. As Vladimir Jankélévitch says in his study of the ironic mode, irony practices *"l'art d'effleurer"*—the art of efflorescence, which adopts, one after another, an infinity of points of view in such a way that they correct each other, thereby allowing the ironist to escape all one-sided *centrismes* and recover the impartiality of justice and reason.[7] In his practice of the art of perspectivism, Browning manages not only to give points of view separate and distinct from his own—"so many utterances of so many imaginary persons, not mine"—but also to be present in those utterances without ever once speaking in his own voice. The dramatic monologue is thus a congenial form for one who wished to be both subjective and objective, lyric and dramatic, at the same time.

Let me illustrate what I mean by reference to "My Last Duchess" (entitled simply "Italy" in 1842), a poem much bedeviled by commentators[8] but one about which I should like to have something additional to say. Robert Langbaum argues that this monologue is a perfect example of the tension between sympathy and judgment, our initial attitude toward the duke's speech being one of sympathetic involvement, our judgment of him suspended until the dramatic moment is passed. To Langbaum the duke's speech is entirely gratuitous, an outrageous indiscretion on the part of a man who is making arrangements for his marriage to a prospective duchess: the duke breaks into song, as it were, just for the joy of singing and, being the Duke of Ferrara in the sixteenth century, is oblivious of, and perhaps even indifferent to, anyone who hears him. Langbaum sees the duke as bigger than life: his aristocratic confidence in himself and his position causes us to empathize with him, attracts and holds our sympathetic attention. Ralph Rader, on the other hand, is the most recent of those who hold that the duke's speech is not gratuitous but calculating.[9] Rader maintains that the duke uses the portrait of his last duchess as a means of indicating to the envoy that he should warn the prospective duchess to act in a way befitting the wife of the Duke of Ferrara. The duke does this obliquely because "I choose never to stoop," either to the envoy or to the woman who is to be his wife. In the end the duke turns to the statue of Neptune as a way of indicating to the envoy that he has really been talking about art all along but knowing that the envoy has well understood his message. In support of his case, Rader contends that the muffled rhymes of the couplets in which the duke speaks suggest an underlying design on the speaker's part: "If we assume that the Duke speaks purposefully, we see that the couplets have a very definite function—to give a submerged pattern running, like the Duke's hidden purpose, through the whole" (p. 139).

I myself find it very difficult to see the duke's monologue as calculating, Even though he is the Duke of Ferrara and thus in a superior position to his auditor, he would hardly designedly confess to, of all people, the envoy from the prospective duchess that he had murdered his previous wife and will likely do the same to his next if she does not act more proudly and hence worthy of a nine-hundred-years-old name. This seems to me simply not true to life, even life in Renaissance Italy. Furthermore, no matter how much the duke masks his supposed design, there is nevertheless a certain amount of "stooping" in even hinting to the envoy how he expects his new duchess to behave. It seems to me more lifelike if it happens that this cultivated autocrat simply gets carried away—into song—when talking about artifacts, of which his last duchess, "painted on the wall," is now one. I find the duke's monologue an example of what is called the feedback phenomenon: language is generative, one utterance begetting another that in turn modifies the former. Like so many of Browning's monologists, the duke speaks not in accordance with what the dramatic context requires—that is, what a future bridegroom should be saying to an agent of the father of the future bride; on the contrary, he speaks in violation of the demands of the dramatic context, speaks simply because he has spoken, because one utterance engenders another, because one musical phrase begs to be made into a song.

And this is not all: there is yet another reason why the duke speaks as he does. We noted in our examination of *Sordello* how the narrator regards speech as the means by which men justify themselves and their actions, how ultimately speech is but rationalization. In his dramatic monologues Browning shows, over and over again, how this is true. In the case of the duke, there is surely the need to justify—if not to the envoy, at least to himself—why he should have done away with his wife. Even the sixteenth-century Duke of Ferrara is not so depraved that he commits murder on a whim, for the fun of it. As the poet-narrator in *Sordello* asked concerning those the world calls "evil men past hope":

>   don't each contrive
> Despite the evil you abuse to live?
> Keeping, each losel, thro' a maze of lies,
> His own conceit of truth? to which he hies
> By obscure tortuous windings, if you will,
> But to himself not inaccessible;
> He sees it . . . ;
>   some fancied right allowed
> His vilest wrong. . . .
>   (3. 787–95)

Yes, there was a reason, a good reason why he had to get rid of his wife, the duke tells himself (and the envoy). He did the deed, justifiably, and enough said. Attempting to pass off his indiscretion as a mere bagatelle, an anecdote about a picture, he turns to another art object and makes a comment on it, as, casting aside all differences in rank, he and the envoy go down the stairs together.

The duke's speech is compelling. For the moment, the instant of speaking, we the readers are swept away by his song; we are fascinated by him—as presumably is the envoy, who makes no demur. Yet in the end, as he begins to descend the stairs, the moment of dramatic and lyric intensity passes, the spell is broken, we withdraw our sympathy and begin to see this proud and haughty man for what he is—a murderer. But even then, even in reflecting on what he has said, our later judgment of the duke does little to diminish our image of the man as bigger-than-life-size. Villain though he be, he retains, as it were, his operatic grandness. With admirable irony Browning succeeds in giving us—and causing us to hold—two conflicting views of the same individual.

Let me now turn to the prosody of the poem. I imagine that for every reader the realization that it is made up of rhyming couplets comes as a surprise, for the poet has designed the poem to be read as though it were blank verse. Why then the use of rhyme at all? Rader sees the pattern as underscoring the duke's hidden design, something like a signal on the part of the poet of his intention as to how the monologue is to be interpreted. Rader's suggestion is ingenious, and while partly agreeing with him I nevertheless come to quite a different conclusion about the function of the rhyming couplets and hence about the nature of the poem and ultimately about the dramatic monologue as Browning uses it.

Langbaum regards the dramatic monologue as an object apart from the poet and the monologist as having a life of his own. Rader, on the other hand, argues that we do not understand dramatic monologues as standing apart from their creators and the real world in semantic indeterminancy but that we understand them as "objects whose meaning and relation to the real world are fixed by the immanent intention of the indwelling poet" (p. 132). He maintains that if we assume, like Langbaum, that Browning's intention is to show the duke of "My Last Duchess" speaking inadvertently, then the muffled rhyme has no point. I agree that in his dramatic monologues Browning is often present—but not for the reason Rader states. It is my contention that the poet as Romantic Ironist manages in various ways to remind us that his monologues are not mere *tranches de vie* but art, that above the speakers there is the figure of the poet smiling at his creation and wishing to partake of it—to be both immanent and transcendent. In the instance of "My Last Duchess," the poet signals us that, after all, this is a piece of artifice by casting his monologue in rhymed couplets. It is part of his ironic playfulness that he conceals them by enjambment until almost the very close, when he end-stops the last lines and thereby calls attention to them as rhyming couplets. In addition, Browning calls attention to the poem as a poem when he has the duke refer to Neptune, "taming a sea-horse, thought a rarity, / Which Claus of Innsbruck cast in bronze for me." In that passage, whatever the speaker may or may not intend by it, we are invited by the poet to see the statue as a summarizing symbol of the duke. The poet is present in the poem, then, not to guide us in interpretation of the speaker's words but to remind us that they are, after all, but words put into the speaker's mouth by the poet. It is no wonder that the dramatic monologue, shaped from an ironic mode that was both subjective and objective, lyric and dramatic, remained for many years Browning's favorite literary form.

I have dwelt at length on "My Last Duchess" not only because it is a splendid poem but also because I wanted to demonstrate how Browning's early dramatic monologues, of which this may be taken as a paradigmatic example, operate as poems in the ironic mode. Let us now turn to the other pieces, and to consideration of the collection as a whole.

Dramatic Lyrics consisted not only of two poems previously published—the monologues now known as "Johannes Agricola in Meditation" and "Porphyria's Lover," in the *Monthly Repository* in 1836—and those that the poet had written and put aside but also of poems written in 1842 after Moxon had given him the idea of publishing a collection of small poems.[10] This suggests that Browning evidently thought of giving *Dramatic Lyrics* some kind of unity. It was not to be unity of form, because the collection contains lyrical narratives and dialogues as well as monologues. The unity that the poet had in mind was, I believe, thematic.

Let us look at the poems comprising *Dramatic Lyrics,* many with titles different from those by which they are now known. The contents of the volume were as follows:

Cavalier Tunes
    I. Marching Along
   II. Give a Rouse

III. My Wife Gertrude [later called "Boot and Saddle"]

Italy and France
　　　I. Italy [later called "My Last Duchess"]
　　　II. France [later called "Count Gismond"]

Camp and Cloister
　　　I. Camp (French) [later called "Incident of the French Camp"]
　　　II. Cloister (Spanish) [later called "Soliloquy of the Spanish Cloister"]

In a Gondola

Artemis Prologuizes

Waring

Queen-Worship
　　　I. Rudel and the Lady of Tripoli [later called "Rudel to the Lady of Tripoli"]
　　　II. Cristina

Madhouse Cells
　　　I. [later called "Johannes Agricola in Meditation"]
　　　II. [later called "Porphyria's Lover"]

Through the Metidja to Abd-el-Kadr.--1842.

The Pied Piper of Hamelin; A Child's Story.

Where "Cavalier Tunes" are concerned with loyalty to Charles I, "Italy," which we have already examined as a dramatic monologue, deals with a husand's perception of a kind of disloyalty on the part of his wife. The duke is a proud man who, alas, has married a woman who does not, in his eyes, sufficiently value his position. It is one of the beauties of the poem that though we see the duchess only through the duke's eyes, we nevertheless see her in a way different from his—as a lady of great simplicity and kindness who naturally is suited to be the duchess of Ferrara, full as she is of unaffected *noblesse oblige*. The duke, on the other hand, we see as a man who is self-consciously duke of Ferrara, constantly aware of the need to play the role of prince-ruler. It is an additional irony of the poem that the duke does not perceive that it is she far more than he who possesses the essential quality of nobility and grace; for it is to his mind just her very lack of this which causes him to have her done away with. His mistaken sense of pride will never let him play his role as duke easily.

The duke also prides himself as a collector of art, a virtuoso. Whatever he has—and he will have only the finest—must be totally his in order for him to enjoy the full pride of ownership: "none puts by / The curtain I have drawn for you, but I"; "Notice Neptune . . . / Which Claus of Innsbruck cast in bronze for *me*." Always he sees himself in the role of power, possessing utterly whatever he wants and loves and demanding constant recognition of his power from what he loves. Thus his duchess he can love only when she is dead, become a portrait that he can totally possess.

"France" is also about love, pride, and loyalty. The speaker is a woman, and what she tells is full of ambiguities. The traditional reading of the poem is that it is the story of a woman wrongly defamed and her virtue restored in the eyes of the world by a knight who comes out of nowhere to defend her name and then marry her. Yet as more recent readers have noted, there are several objections to this interpretation.[11] Why, for instance, does she lie to her husband at the end? And what is the purpose of her telling how she felt her knight's sword, bloody from the killing of her defamer, touch her side? These details seriously call into question the view that the woman is a calumniated innocent.

Like its companion poem the monologue is concerned with words. The duke of "Italy" constantly refers to speech, what people do not ask ("seemed as they would ask me, if they durst"), what Fra Pandolf said, how the duchess talked or should have talked, what the duke said, could not say, and is now saying.[12] For the duke speech is a means of control. The monologist of "France" also associates words with power, her monologue focusing on repeated use of the word "lie." Gauthier accuses her of belying her role as queen, chaste and fair, of the tournament, although why he should do this falsely we are given no motive. Gismond comes forth, pronounces

Gauthier a liar, defeats him in duel, drags him to the lady, and forces him to say he has lied to God and to her. In telling the story to her friend Adela, however, she is concerned that Gismond, now her husband, not hear her (49–50); and when he returns before her completion of the tale, she falsely tells him that she has been talking about her falcon. Evidently the countess like the duke of the preceding poem feels that if she has the right words she can exert control over the situation at hand. For the one time when she cannot speak—and at other times she speaks glibly—she is at the mercy of another person: to Gauthier's accusation, "I? What I answered? As I live / I never thought there was such thing / As answer possible to give" (61–63).

In speaking of the incident, the countess constantly refers to it as though it took place not in real life but on the stage. The "time and place and company" was a tournament where she was to play the role of queen. Her cousins dress her up "in Queen's array" (11) for "the play" (18). Before her entrance onstage she takes a moment to "adjust / The last rose in my garland, fling / A last look on the mirror" (26–28); "friends . . . kissed my cheek, / And called me Queen" (32–33); and then she takes her "state / And foolish throne amid applause" (37–38). The tournament proceeds, and just as she is about to award the prize, Gauthier stalks forth, thunders "Stay!" and recites a speech that sounds as though it had been learned from one of Dryden's plays:

> Bring torches! Wind the penance-sheet
>   About her! Let her shun the chaste
> Or lay herself before their feet!
>   Shall she, whose body I embraced
> A night long, queen it in the day?
> For Honor's sake no crowns, I say!

Whereupon, as the *deus ex machina,* appears Gismond, who strides out to slap Gauthier's mouth and call him liar. The lady is no longer at the center of the stage, willingly retiring when God "me . . . bid / Watch Gismond for my part" (83–84). Gismond defeats Gauthier, who is dragged to the lady's feet and made to confess. Gismond then kneels to ask, presumably, for her hand in marriage, and thereafter leads her away to his home in the south. So much for the play, which perhaps should be entitled "Virtue Defamed But Finally Rewarded."

But what really happened? We cannot be certain although we have some clues. As to Gauthier's accusation, we are told that "he must have schemed" (8) to make his charge just when all faces were on her, but apparently her cousins put him up to it—"'twas all their deed" (14). Why? Because they were jealous of her beauty. But this does not seem entirely plausible, for in the very next stanza we are told: "They, too, so beauteous! Each a queen / By virtue of her brow and breast; / Not needing to be crowned, I mean, / As I do" (19–22). Then follows this enigmatic utterance: "Oh, I think the cause / Of much was, they forgot no crowd / Makes up for parents in their shroud!" (40–42). Apparently the only reason for this remark is to impress upon her listener that she was a poor little orphan girl utterly defenseless against the world. But "the cause"? The cause of what? "Howe'er that be," (43) just when all eyes were upon her, her cousins cast theirs down. At this point she interrupts to say to her friend: "See! Gismond's at the gate, in talk / With his two boys: I can proceed" (49–50)

Continuing with her story she tells of Gauthier's denunciation and her inability to answer: "What says the body when they spring / Some monstrous torture-engine's whole / Strength on it?" At the very least the body says "ouch" or "stop!" But as it turns out, she need not say anything anyway, because Gismond advances to speak on her behalf. And why does Gismond, a man she had never seen before, do such a bold thing? Because "God had set / Himself to Satan" (70–71). She therefore had no doubt about the outcome of Gismond's fight with Gauthier. In fact, she enjoyed it: "This glads me most, that I enjoyed / The heart of the joy" (79–80). With exceeding pleasure she watches him don his armor:

> Did I not watch him while he let
>   His armourer just brace his greaves,
> Rivet his hauberk, on the fret

> The while! His foot..my memory leaves
> No least stamp out, nor how anon
> He pulled his ringing gauntlets on.
>
> (85–90)

The duel over and Gauthier wounded, Gismond asks, "hast thou lied?" To which he replies, "I have lied / To God and her" (101–2). This seems to me a strange, at any rate ambiguous, thing to say. Why does he not say that he has lied to the assembled crowd to whom he has made his accusation?

After it is all over, Gismond seems to have asked her to marry him. With arms around her he then leads her away; "and scarce I felt / His sword, that dripped by me and swung" (110–11). At the end, just after asking God's blessing on Gauthier's soul, she says of her two boys: "Our elder boy has got the clear / Great brow; tho' when his brother's black / Full eye shows scorn, it...," not continuing because Gismond enters. What is the meaning of this, and why does she speak of her sons immediately after mention of Gauthier? Is there not more than a slight suggestion that one of the boys may not be Gismond's?

When Gismond returns, she changes the subject and actually prevaricates about what she has been saying: "have you brought my tercel back? / I was just telling Adela / How many birds it struck since May" (124–26). There are perhaps innocent reasons why she should not want to let Gismond know what she has been talking about: for instance, she might feel it would embarrass him to hear her speak of him heroically in the presence of a third person. But in a story whose focus is on falsehood and the supposed vindication of truth, this, even if a white lie, necessarily jars on us and casts doubt as to the reliability of the truth of her tale. In addition, when we recall that this is a companion monologue to the duke's, we note how similar the ending of this poem is to that of "Italy." The predatory falcon is very much like Neptune taming a sea-horse, both literally and in function as a concluding symbol of the lady's character. In the last analysis we cannot accept the lady's story as true.[13] We may not finally be able to reconstruct, even with ardent exercise of our "co-operating fancy," the entire narrative but at least we know that, in all likelihood, things did not occur in the way the monologist says.

Does the fact that the poem is full of puzzling details even about the narrative itself mean that it is to be judged as unsuccessful?[14] If the interest in the monologue lay in the story itself, then we would be bound to say that it is not a satisfying narrative. But the emphasis here as in Browning's other monologues is on character and its revelation in speech. Many of the endings of Browning's poems are ambiguous, in part because the poet had little interest in the narrative.[15] As we saw, in *Pippa Passes* we do not know, for instance, whether the bishop restores to Pippa her rightful inheritance or keeps it for the Church. And it does not matter because it is not the story we are invited to be interested in; it is, rather, on character that the poet wishes to concentrate. Those commentators who most misrepresent Browning's poetry do so because they study the monologues for stories or themes or morals instead of witnessing the drama of character unfold.

In "France" as in most of the early Browning, there is a tension between form and meaning as well as between content and meaning. Cast in the form of a metrical romance—stanzaic tetrameters—the monologue appears as a version of medieval romance: trial by combat, vindication of the just, love winning through. Yet as we have just seen, the poem is about the pathology of love, if indeed love it can be called. The speaker gives more than a hint about the implication of love with respect to power, of how love can be realized only when it is somehow connected with power, the power to conquer and even to kill. Like nearly all the other poems in *Dramatic Lyrics*, "France" deals with death.

The next pair of poems, "Camp and Cloister," which are fairly artificially connected, focus on their speakers' belief in forms of behavior inculcated by the organization to which they belong. "Camp" is a third-person narrative of a youth who follows a military code of heroism in battle even though it means his death, his only reward being that he has served his emperor—who is preoccupied with matters other than the young soldier's mortal wounds. In "Cloister," a dramatic monologue, the speaker adheres to the rules of monastic life but is devoid of belief in the informing spiritual principle behind them, unwittingly damning himself in our eyes as a type of Satan while commending the saintly Brother Lawrence, whom he hates, as a true follower of Christ. Like Napoleon in the companion poem, the speaker is concerned only with mind and power whereas Brother Lawrence, like the boy soldier, is shown to be governed by emotion and love.

"In a Gondola" is a study of the psychology of romantic love reminiscent of the Ottima and Sebald episode of *Pippa Passes*. A clue to interpretation may be found in the first mention Browning made of it. The poem began, says Browning, as an illustration of a picture by Daniel Maclise entitled "The Serenade"; "All the 'properties,' as we say, were given—and the problem was how to cataloguize them in rhyme and unreason." The picture contained, in other words, all the stuff of storybook love: "I send my heart up to thee—all my heart. . . . Singing and stars and night and Venice streets in depths of shade and space are 'properties,' do you please to see" (Hood, *Letters*, p. 7).

The varying line-lengths, rhythms, and rhyme schemes of the dialogue between a young man and his inamorata carry the two lovers through a variety of moods. She apparently a married woman, they must meet in secret. It is the danger associated with their trysts that makes their furtive meetings so rapturous. Discovery and death are never far away. What if they are caught? Paul throws a cloak over the lover's head, Gian pinions his arms, "Himself" (presumably the husband) thrusts a stiletto through his back: "I reel; / And...is it Thee I feel?" (108–9). Or they force him to the graveyard of the Lido and to the grave in which they propose to shove him, "roll me to its brink, / And...on Thy breast I sink" (114–15). She replies that indeed death is nothing to fear: "were Death so unlike Sleep / Caught this way?" (117–18). Death is not to be avoided but sought actively: dying into love, they would be free of the world's falseness and annoy, of a Venice where marriages are arranged for money between old men and young girls and where everyone is indifferent to feelings of any kind (37–48). There in the darkness of death, removed from "the daylight world" (27), they could find the refuge that would permit them to love forever.

In the meantime, what to do? Real life being hideous, they must live in fancy. She says,

> Kiss me as you made believe
> You were not sure this eve,
> How my face, your flower, had pursed
> Its petals up.
>
> (50–53)

He thereupon engages in some instances of make-believe, at the end of each "shattering" the fancy so that "as of old, I am I, Thou art Thou" (70, 78). Yet remaining "as of old" is not for long because he is then led into a bigger fancy, from which he retreats:

> Rescue me thou, the only real!
> And scare away this mad Ideal
> That came, nor motions to depart!
> Thanks! Now, stay ever as thou art!
>
> (99–102)

But having this uttered, he then proceeds with even more fantastic visions.

The lovers in the poem constantly engage in little dramas to sustain the rapture of love, occasionally even telling the other the lines of the script that he or she is to speak. Thus,

> Say after me, and try to say
> My words as if each word
> Came from you of your own accord,
> In your own voice, in your own way.
>
> (8–11)

But why deal at all with the phenomenal world, of which language is but part? "And yet once more say...no word more! /

Since words are only words" (18–19). Death alone will sustain the fervor that each desires, so speak no word unless it be a means to that land of bliss:

> no word more!
> . . . Give o'er!
> Unless you call me, as the same,
> Familiarly by my pet-name
> Which if the Three should hear you call
> And me reply to, would proclaim
> At once our secret to them all:
> Ask of me, too, command me, blame—
> Do break down the partition-wall
> 'Twixt us the daylight world beholds
> Curtained in dusk and splendid folds.
>
> (20–28)

Finally, the gondola ride over, they are surprised by "the Three" and he is stabbed, almost as he had foretold. Yes, they say, it was ordained to be, although in fact the lovers took fate into their own hands and made their play of love end as they wanted. Echoing Sebald's sentiment, the serenader asks what matters their recklessness. The world, of which the Three are but all too real a part, is not alive, its inhabitants have never lived: "but I," says the dying lover, "have lived indeed, and so—(yet one more kiss)—can die" (230–31).[16]

It has been customary to regard "In a Gondola" as reflecting Browning's belief that love conquers all.[17] Such a view seems to me to stem from a serious misreading of this poem of "rhyme and unreason." Even at its inception Browning appears to have had in mind a study of the pathology of romantic love, and when we place it in the context of a volume of poems many of which, such as "Count Gismond," deal with the relationship between love and death, I think it behooves us to investigate the psychology that results in this death in Venice.

Like "Artemis Prologuizes," which precedes it, "Waring" is also a narrative that deals with loyalty and pride. It is in two parts—a monologue and a dialogue. The setting is not given, but a London club would seem just right.[18] Disaffected by a lack of recognition in London, Waring suddenly disappeared without even so much as a good-bye to his friends. The speaker tells how he misses Waring, guesses where the lost man might be, and predicts a brilliant future for him no matter where he eventually turns up. On the surface that is all there is to the poem. But when we look into it more closely, we learn that the speaker's attitude toward his friend is more complex and less admiring than initially it seems.

If on the eve of Waring's departure the speaker did leave his friend's arm for the new prose-poet, how was he to know that Waring meant to slip away that very next morning? Waring was proud, and he was disappointed that no one made enough of him. True, he had not done anything, although he had achieved "certain first steps"; but who goes gleaning along the hedges when full-sheaved cornfields are by? But oh, if one could only bring him back once more! Faced with him, "so hungry for acknowledgement / Like mine," one would "fool him to his bent" and say that great works conceived and planned surpass little works achieved—just the sort of nonsense he would like to hear. One would lie and make havoc of the claims of the "distinguished names." Changing tone from condescending banter, the speaker asks Waring truly to come back and rouse the country from its torpor:

> Our men scarce seem in earnest now;
> Distinguished names, but 'tis, somehow,
> As if they played at being names
> Still more distinguished. . . .
>
> (201–4)

In the second part of the poem, another person reports seeing Waring on the Illyrian coast. The first speaker, heartened by the news but apparently having paid little attention to what was actually said, observes, "Oh, never star / Was lost here, but it rose afar." And as if asking whether his earlier prophecy concerning Waring might not be true, he says: "In Vishnu-land what Avatar?" (259–62).

The picture of the speaker that emerges is of a loquacious

bore, a clubman who makes it a point to know the "distinguished names." He speaks of Waring as one who wishes to be recognized as a "distinguished name" without ever having accomplished that which would make his name famous. But the more he talks, the more he realizes that he really does miss his friend, feels guilty for having been so condescending and patronizing in his attitude toward Waring, and comes to suspect that the "distinguished names" are perhaps less worthy of distinction than he had made them out to be. And we as listeners become increasingly aware of the real reason why Waring left: because he was bored with the empty life such as the monologist represents. But whatever the speaker says or does not say, he still values Waring more as a topic of conversation—a distinguished name *manqué* whom he has known well—than as a friend. In part two of the poem when someone, presumably another member of the club, relates "when I last saw Waring," the first speaker asks increduously, "You saw Waring?" (211). And then at the end of the tale when the other clubman concludes, "so I saw the last of Waring," the first speaker is again moved to ask, "You?" as though no one had any right to speak of Waring but him.

In the two poems under the joint title "Queen-Worship," we find the old fondness on the part of Browning's lovers for strong women who assume the position of power in the sexual relationship. Both lyrics have as their speakers men who would willingly sacrifice the world for love. In "Rudel and the Lady of Tripoli," the French troubadour figures himself as a sunflower ever bending toward the sun, which represents both love and his lady. In "Cristina" the speaker claims that when he and the lady met, she flirtingly fixed him with her eyes: all of a sudden their souls rushed together. She recognized it as well as he, but she withdrew for the sake of "the world's honours," which "trampled out the light for ever." He, on the other hand, has remained faithful to this ecstatic moment of their soul's union and consequently has grown greater than she: "She has lost me—I have gained her." All that now remains to him is the proving of their separate powers: which is greater, she without him, he with her?

Traditionally the monologue is regarded as a lyric representing Browning's most cherished beliefs.[19] But upon investigation we discover here as in "Count Gismond" certain puzzling statements that give us pause and make us wonder how much of the speaker's story is accurate. In the very first stanza, we learn that, although the lovers had apparently never met before, she was aware of the kind of man he was, "knew it / When she fixed me." And then though she was as transfixed as he by their encounter, he is not sure that she was aware of it: "To fix me thus meant nothing? / But I can't tell...there's my weakness.. / What her look said." This was one of those times when time has a stop and the world becomes nothing. "Doubt you," he twice asks (33, 46), that she was aware of this? Finally, his claim to have "grown perfect" strikes us as a bit excessive. We are left with the strong suspicion that the speaker is trying to convince his listener that once upon a time a queen fell in love with him but, refusing to act on soul's truth, departed from the relationship because of worldly inducements.

In the end we come to the conclusion that "Cristina" is a dramatic monologue uttered by one whose mental balance may be doubted, not only because of what he ways but also because of the way he says it. The opening lines are spoken in a halting, nervous rhythm:

> She should not have looked at me,
>   If she meant I should not love her:
> There's plenty..men, you call such,
>   I suppose..she may discover
> All her soul to, if she pleases,
>   And yet leave much as she found them.
> But I'm not so, and she knew it
>   When she fixed me, glancing round them.

And the repetition of the word "fix" in the first line of the very next stanza goes further to impress upon us the notion of fixation, of the speaker's feeling that time stopped, was fixed at the romantic moment of souls' meeting, and of his need to refer to it constantly.[20]

As to the madness of the speakers in the next pair of poems

there is no doubt, since Browning entitled them "Madhouse Cells." Both are identical in meter, rhyme scheme, and length. The first, "Johannes Agricola in Meditation" as it came eventually to be called, is the monologue of one who feels himself predestined by God for salvation, thus being unable to do wrong and also being exempt from the necessity of good works. Johannes shows himself to be, somewhat like the soliloquizer of the Spanish cloister, one who though versed in Christian theology is not a Christian. It is Browning's point that those who believe themselves relieved by fate or ordination of the trials and tests of life are mad. Like Pauline's lover and Paracelsus, Johannes aims "to get to God," to "God's breast, my own abode." His pride as one of the elect leads him to declare that God created him before the heavens and ordained that he should grow, "guiltless for ever." The Creator did this because he needed the creature as the vessel for his love. Thus whatever Johannes does, no matter how sinful its nature, is turned to "blossoming gladness," while the good works of the unelect can never win God's love, "all their striving turned to sin."

"Porphyria's Lover" is the monologue of one who has strangled his beloved in order to preserve the good moment and make her his forever: "That moment she was mine, mine, fair, / Perfectly pure and good." His justification of the act is that Porphyria herself wished it too: her head now propped on his shoulder "glad it has its utmost will, / That all it scorned at once is fled, / And I, its love, am gained instead." Furthermore, all night long his and her bodies have been together side by side, "And yet God has not said a word!" The lover may be mad, but he has still enough sanity to be dimly aware that murder is wrong, forbidden by God. Yet if God does not speak in condemnation of him and his deed, then surely the act is to be condoned. Like the duke of Ferrara, Porphyria's lover demands the total possession of another person, which cannot be achieved in life.

There is more plot in "Porphyria's Lover" than in the other monologues of *Dramatic Lyrics*. The story material could easily have been the basis for an early Victorian play, novel, or verse narrative. The girl forced by concern (probably on the part of her family) for financial reward and social status to marry a man she does not love, the boy of inferior social status whom she does love, his dejection, her feelings of guilt, her slipping away from a fancy dinner held to announce her engagement to be married, her visit to the boy's cottage during a storm, her giving herself to him sexually—all this is the kind of stuff, the conventions and clichés, out of which so much early nineteenth-century literature was made. It is, for example, something like the story of Keats's *The Eve of St. Agnes,* and it may be that the name Porphyria was suggested by the name Porphyro in Keats's poem.[21] It is also reminiscent of the stories of Tennyson's "Locksley Hall" and "Maud," both of which were published after "Porphyria's Lover" but which nevertheless contain stock Victorian narrative details. Browning, however, adds his own twist (and in doing so may be satirizing early nineteenth-century narratives): first, by having the lover kill the girl to prevent the loveless marriage, and second, by having him narrate the story so as to justify his part in it. Casting it as a monologue, Browning lets us see the story from the inside, as it were, as the lover seeks for ways to show that the deed, though done in a moment of passion, was the right thing to do. Porphyria having come through wind and rain from the "gay feast" for the sake of one so pale from love of her, he—"proud, very proud"—at last knew that she worshiped him. How could he prevent the arranged marriage and keep her true to the one she really adored? "I debated what to do." Then "I found / A thing to do":

> all her hair
> In one long yellow string I wound
> Three times her little throat around,
> And strangled her.

It was all so natural: no rope or cord but her own hair used for the deed; and three times around, almost as if it were illustrative of Trinitarian doctrine. "No pain felt she: / I am quite sure she felt no pain." Furthermore, she seems in death as if she approved: her blue eyes (when pried open) laugh, her cheek blushes bright, her rosy little head smiles—no sign of disapproval at all. Yes, surely, it was the "thing to do."[22] A thing to do: he makes murder sound so innocent. It is this insane narrative of self-justification stated with such matter-of-fact simplicity and in a verse form—highly regular tetrameter lines that, mostly end-stopped, call attention to the highly patterned male rhyme—suggestive of perfect rational control—it is this that gives the poem its ironic power. When we recall that "Porphyria's Lover" was first published in 1836—and perhaps composed two years earlier, when Browning was but twenty-two years old—we see how from the beginning of his career the poet was a master ironist.

The last two poems in the collection are linked by the themes of loyalty and pride. "Through the Metidja to Abd-El-Kadr.—1842" is the lyrical soliloquy of an Arab proudly riding on horseback through the Algerian desert plain to join his chief in the fight against the French for an independent Algeria. "The Pied Piper of Hamelin" is a third-person narrative that tells of a fabulous piper who by his piping freed the town of Hamelin from rats. When he has completed his job of pest control and is not paid for the deed according to contract, he entices the children of the town away into an opening in a mountain and disappears with them forever.

As we glance back over the poems of this small volume, we see that all touch on loyalty and pride. The first line in the collection, spoken by a southern Loyalist, is "Kentish Sir Byng stood for his King." The last line, spoken by the narrator of "The Pied Piper," is "If we've promised them aught, let us keep our promise." With their varying ideas as to what constitutes loyalty (or disloyalty) the actors in the monologues die in battle, kill their wives and lovers or bring them back from the dead, make pacts with the Devil or act as the elect of God. Whatever misdeed or good work is performed, it is done in accordance with the individual's notion of loyalty, of which he is extremely (and sometimes madly) proud. Each acts, in other words, the way he believes the loyal man or woman should act; which is to say, each plays a role, speaks the words proper to that role, and feels that the role has been ordained. The actors are intensely self-conscious and long to explain why, in fulfillment of their roles, they have acted in a certain fashion, more or less according to a script written by a master dramatist. They are thus characterized by the irony that causes them to view themselves both as free agents and as puppets. We as listeners observe their sense of power that conflicts with their striving to unbend and submerge themselves in love—to manifest pride as loyalty, to submit ego to some form of "out-soul." The dialectic of self and other thus remains a chief topic in Browning's study of soul-making and the ironies it involves.

CHAPTER VII
THE RETURN OF THE DRUSES
A BLOT IN THE 'SCUTCHEON
AND
COLOMBE'S BIRTHDAY

IN WRITING TO FANNY HAWORTH IN 1837 THAT HE was soon "to begin the finishing *Sordello*" and "to begin thinking a Tragedy" (presumably *King Victor and King Charles*), Browning said that he wished also "to have *another* tragedy in prospect." "I want a subject of the most wild and passionate love, to contrast with the one [*King Victor*] I mean to have ready in a short time. I have many half-conceptions, floating fancies: give me your notion of a thorough self-devotement, self-forgetting; should it be a woman who loves thus, or a man?" (Orr, *Life*, pp. 103–4). The subject that he came up with was made into the play entitled *The Return of the Druses*.

Originally in three acts, the play was expanded to five at the suggestion of Macready. Macready however was not pleased: "Read Browning's play," he recorded in his diary on 3 August 1840, "and with deepest concern, I yield to the belief that he will *never write again*—to any purpose. I fear his intellect is not quite clear" (*Diaries*, 2:73). Browning nevertheless continued to argue his case for the play's suitability for the stage. Macready reread what he could but found it "mystical, strange and heavy" (*Diaries*, 2:80). Finally Browning retrieved the manuscript from the obdurate Macready, put it away, and did not publish it till January 1843, when it appeared, with some revision, as the fourth pamphlet of *Bells and Pomegranates*.

It seems that the more he revised the play, the more "mystical" and "strange" it became; which is to say, it grew increasingly ironic. One is not surprised that Macready did not know what to make of it, for the play permits, and indeed encourages, the audience to take two opposite views of the motives of the chief characters, whose actions in turn are presented in a series of ironic reversals. In *The Return of the Druses*, somewhat as in *Strafford*, Browning constantly undercuts his protagonists—in consequence demolishing sympathy for them—only in the end to represent them in such fashion as to elicit the audience's compassion for their plight. The effect is indeed "mystical, strange," and perhaps even "heavy."

The basic theme of the play is deception. "We live and breathe deceiving and deceived," said Paracelsus (4. 625). Working with this early insight, Browning has the hero of *The Return of the Druses* say upon first appearance, "I am found deceiving and deceived" (2. 35). The question is enlarged to encompass a consideration of the degree to which deception is necessary and justifiable in human affairs and of the extent to which deception takes on a reality that is the thing itself. In other words, is not the robe (or veil) of the thing ultimately, in the phenomenal world, the *ding an sich*?

Djabal has plotted the death of the hated governor of the island and secured the protection of Venice, whose ships are to take the Druses to Lebanon. Now that deliverance is at hand, he questions why he should declare himself the reincarnate Hakeem, as his people expect their deliverer to be. Is it not enough to be Djabal? Has he not deceived himself and others as to his nature? Surely he is but a man, not God: "And I feel this first to-day!" (2. 14). But having pursued his goal with concentrated fervor and having accomplished all that Hakeem promised, "Would it be wondrous that delusions grew?" he asks himself. "Could I call / My mission aught but Hakeem's?" (2. 47, 53–54). Is the man who accomplishes the work of deity not an incarnation of deity? In answering the question, the play is worked out in terms of a dialectic of power and love involving Djabel and Anael, his bride-to-be.

As the child of murdered parents, Djabal has a personal as well as tribal motive for his actions. In pursuit of his end—the death of the prefect and the subsequent return of his people to Lebanon—he has resorted to any means: the chill policy and lore of Europe as well as the hot-headed pride and deviousness of Syria. Through power he has become the leader of the Druses, and through power he will deliver them. As the play opens, it is Hakeem the God of power that he represents himself to be. But the nature of this manifestation of Hakeem—if indeed he is Hakeem—troubles him. Surely, he asks at the beginning of act two, he could have attained the power simply as Djabal: what he has done "took / No less than Hakeem?" "What of Hakeem?" he ponders. His has been thus far a strangely deficient notion of what God is, who certainly is more than power. But what else? At this point Djabal does not know, and consequently, convinced that his "delusion mixed itself / Insensibly with this career," he determines to renounce all claims to be the incarnate God.

But just at this moment, Khalil enters, greets him as Hakeem, and announces that the people are instituting choirs and dances to the returned caliph "as of old / 'Tis chronicled you bade them" (2. 71–72). Determined to abjure what he now fears to have been imposture, Djabal asks his faithful lieutenant why he, Khalil, never essayed to save the Druses. Khalil replies that only belief in the power of Hakeem has united his people and goaded them on from seeking some selfish prize. Djabal begins to rethink his position, and his interview soon thereafter with Anael, his betrothed, further convinces him that he cannot confess to being a mere pretender.

For her part Anael feels unworthy because she can feel no awe for the godlike, only love for the human in Djabal. To prove her faith in his divinity, she undertakes to kill the prefect. Having done the deed, she calls upon Djabal to exalt himself and her with him. Djabal, however, overcome with the result of his duplicity, tells her the truth. Momentarily her revulsion is extreme, but then aware that he is merely human after all, she loves him more than ever. She insists that he confess to the Druses that he was an impostor and that in his abasement their true love will be realized: "Oh, best of all I love thee! / Shame with the man, no triumph with the God" (4. 113–14).

But Djabal draws back. His pride will not allow him to perform this act of degradation. Once more possessed of a sense of power, he insists that he is indeed a god: "for I know myself, / And what I am to personate" (4. 137–38). And so as Hakeem, the God of power, he exclaims: "Thus I grasp thee, sword! / Druses, 'tis Hakeem saves you!" (4. 149–50).

In the last act Anael comes to denounce him before all the Druses. To her he turns to repent the course of action that grew out of the conflict between his Arab instinct and his Frank brain. From the clash there now arises "my mere Man's nature" that allows him to love her as he never loved before (4. 270–80). He submits to her and awaits his doom from her lips. Anael, however, become aware that through love the divine is incarnated in the human, utters "Hakeem!" and then dies. As if inspired, Djabal turns to the crowd to remind them of what has been done for them and to ask, "Am I *not* Hakeem?" Through love power has grown to godhead.

Browning had been intrigued with the notion of growth toward godhead ever since *Paracelsus*, in which his protagonist describes "a tendency to God" (5 .722) arising from the interplay of love with power in human life. In *Sordello* the poet-narrator had spoken of Sordello's need for a revelation of power through love, presumably in an incarnation of deity (6. 590–602). And now in *The Return of the Druses*, Browning turned to consideration of incarnation not so much as a revelation but as development of human character, of "soul." This is very much akin to the theory of progress enunciated in *Paracelsus* but with this difference: the fulfillment of the "tendency to God" is not an eschatological expectation but a possibility of present realization. The Incarnation of Christ, by implication, was thus not a historical event that happened once for all but is ever being repeated in acts of sacrificial love.

This is the "mystical" view of the tragedy. Regarded in this way, *The Return of the Druses* is hardly a play "of the most wild and passionate love" that Browning referred to in his letter to Miss Haworth. But seen from a different angle, the drama does focus on human passion, is in fact a study in the psychopathology of romantic love.

Not until he saw Anael did Djabal announce that his was the promised mission of Hakeem (2. 224–27). When he first speaks of her, he seems to regard her as a distraction from what he thought he ought to be about (2. 93–94). Yet later, in talking to Anael, he says that the people needed a miracle if they were to be freed, and so "I said / 'Be there a miracle!'—for I saw you!" (4. 66–67). He was to exalt her as the beloved of Hakeem. But, he erroneously believes, he receives from Anael not love but worship: she adores the god, not the man. Djabal, however, in common with Browning's lovers whom we have met previously, can only love the woman whom he can worship. Not until the end does she achieve the requisite superior position when he can tell her, "I love thee—I—who did not love before!" (5. 280). "How," he asks, "could I love while thou adoredst me?" (5. 282). But now that she despises him and is above him so immeasurably, he can love her fully. What elevates her in his mind is her present power to doom him to death: "Oh, luxury to worship, to submit, / To be transcended, doomed to death by thee!" (5. 287–88). And so he stabs himself to join Anael in the exaltation of death. Djabal manifests the same pathology as the lovers in earlier works who have need of "queens" as objects of their love.

Though Browning's lovers studied previously yearn for the full realization of their love that can come about only in a world beyond that of quotidian reality—in death, in other words—none had specifically envisioned their "dying into love" as exaltation. In *The Return of the Druses*, on the other hand, the two lovers almost explicitly see death as means of translation to a higher sphere of pure love where they are deified as love's lovers. "What remains," asks Djabal of Anael's dead body, "But to press to thee, exalt myself to thee?" And then just as he stabs himself: "Thus I exalt myself, set free my soul!" (5. 389–91).

Anael tells that she can only love one who can redeem her people (3. 17–20). But as it happened, she fell in love with Djabal at first sight. Although she says that she realized he was not fully human, it was Djabal the man, not Djabal the god, she loved (3. 92–106). And then, lest she lose sight of her people entirely under this spell of passion, "I vowed at once a certain vow— . . . / Not to embrace you till my tribe was saved" (3. 107–8). Thereafter she has consciously repressed her passion for the man so as to achieve a higher love for the god. But she has not been at ease in her "man's preference" (3. 74)—"Never a God to me! 'Tis the Man's hand, / Eye, voice!" (2. 260–61)—and feels constantly reproached by Djabal for her inability to love on a more elevated, less passionate plane.

To prove her faith in him as Hakeem, she will kill the prefect. Although appearing fearful of the deed, she nevertheless seems more than half in love with death:

> Death!—a fire curls within us
> From the foot's palm, and fills up to the brain,
> Up, out, then shatters the whole bubble-shell
> Of flesh perchance!
>   Death!—witness I would die, . . .
> Be worthy you!
>
>   (3. 115–24)

Afterward she speaks of the assassination as if it had been performed at the behest of Djabal, as if indeed Djabal himself had committed it (4. 29–42, 91–93). Finally, when Djabal confesses that he has spoken falsely and is but a man, Anael exclaims: "I . . . better love thee / Perchance than ever. . . . / Shame with the man, no triumph with the God" (4. 110–14). No longer need she pretend to anything other than romantic passion.

Her passion is not, however, to be realized, for Djabal insists that he will continue to be Hakeem with Anael as his exalted bride. At the end, when she is to expose him, Djabal says that he repents, that his is now a "mere Man's nature" that loves her more than ever and is "doomed to death" by her (5. 279–88). Whereupon she does not betray him as intended but screams "Hakeem" (5.293) and dies into what she doubtless envisions as a paradise of love.

Understanding of the play depends upon interpretation of that one word "Hakeem" that Anael utters. Does it mean that she recognizes Djabal as the incarnation of deity or that she lies to the crowd to save him? We can never know. The arguments to be made are fully as good on one side as the other. And Browning has, I believe, designed it to be so. The indeterminacy of meaning is the meaning. Or to put it another way, *The Return of the Druses* is an ironic play.

Some of the ambiguities and ironies of love are manifest in the character of Loÿs. Soon to become a Knight Hospitaller and take the vow of chastity, he has returned from Rhodes to replace the old prefect and rule the Druses on the island as though he were one of them. His heart leaps up to be back among the tribe, but clearly he is most thrilled to be again near Anael—Anael with "the great black eyes I must forget" (1. 364). Unable to control his feelings, he declares his love in language that is strongly sacramental, as though in loving her he were supplanting one passion with another: "your breathing passes thro' me, changes / My blood to spirit, and my spirit to you, / As Heaven the sacrificer's wine to it" (3. 12–14). Anael tells him that she does not love in return but in such a way that Loÿs is misled into believing that she does. He thereupon admits that his espousal of the cause of the Druses was not altruistic but was for the sake of Anael, whom he now proposes to marry. Renouncing his knighthood in the Christian order, Loÿs goes to inform Djabal what he proposes to do, only to discover that Anael is the Druse's intended bride. Loÿs refuses to believe what Djabal tells him, and when in the last act Anael comes to denounce Djabal as an impostor, he exults that of all these Druses she alone was true and makes an impassioned plea for her love. Anael, however, chooses Djabal and then dies, leaving Loÿs without love and, from his witness of the Church's impurity, with a shaken religious faith. For Loÿs as for some of Browning's other lovers, love is a kind of religion.

Also like the characters in previous works, those in *The Return of the Druses* see themselves as playing roles assigned by fate. Thus Djabal must stay to kill the prefect: "'tis forced on me!"; "all things conspire to hound me on!" (3. 148, 158). When Anael insists that he must confess his fraudulence, he momentarily acquiesces: "How can I longer strive with Fate?" (4. 118). In the end—"See fate!" (5. 268)—when he asks Anael to speak his judgment, he gathers the Druses close to hear: "I am out of reach of fate" (5. 290).

In playing their parts the characters assume various costumes, mainly robes and veils, which they are ever putting on and taking off. "I dare / Assume my Nation's Robe," says

Djabal, when he comes to a new conception of "what I am to personate" (4. 149–50). Finally, when the Nuncio demands that he "cast off that husk, thy form," Djabal asks, in full assurance that his is the right role and that he is decked in the right clothes, "Am I *not* Hakeem?" (5. 332, 339). Loÿs, the only one able to "unmask" Djabal (2. 321) and "unveil" the prefect (3. 280), finds that Anael's eye breaks his own "faint disguise away" (3. 40). The Druses impatiently await the time when they can "off—with disguise at last" and "from our forms this hateful garb . . . strip" (1. 16–17).

Just as clothes disguise or reveal, so do words enrobe personality and thereby permit it to work its will. Djabal is a master of speech, "his voice a spell / From first to last" (3. 48–49). But for him, as for the Duke of Ferrara, language is only an instrument of power: "Babels men block out, Babylons they build" (4. 130). When, however, it is necessary to communicate on the level of intimacy and love, he cannot find the proper words: "To yearn to tell her, and yet have no one / Great heart's word that will tell her" (2 .102–3). "In what words / Avow that all she loves in me is false?" (2. 287–88). It is this linguistic inability on the part of Djabal and the other characters as well that makes for the misunderstandings that trigger so much of the action of the drama. Only when he finds the language proper to to his "mere Man's nature" does Anael speak the one word—"Hakeem"—on which the whole plot turns. Toward that utterance point all the "glozing accents" (1. 18), "mad words" (3. 5), vows (3. 66, 107), euphemisms (3. 131–33), babblings in foreign languages (5. 50–58). Up to this moment faith in the incarnation is but faith in the report: "After all," say the Druses, "I know nothing of Djabal beyond what Karshook says, he knows but what Khalil says, who knows just what Djabal says himself" (5. 83–85). After the pentecostal moment the Druses address Djabal as Hakeem, and Djabal gives his blessing to his apostle Khalil by laying on of hands and saying: "Thou art full of me—I fill / Thee full—my hands thus fill thee!" (5. 356–57). With this gift of the spirit, language is no longer problematic, is indeed unnecessary: no longer "requiring words of mine," "now, thou hast all gifts in one," Djabal tells Khalil: "With truth and purity go other gifts! / All gifts come clustering to that" (5. 359–62). The messianic expectation realized, Djabal "his last word to the living speaks" (5. 382).

The Return of the Druses is one of Browning's most complex and beautiful plays. This is not however the general view of this work. Few agree with Chesterton that it "contains more of Browning's typical qualities exhibited in an exquisite literary shape, than can easily be counted."[1] At the beginning we discover a sheer gorgeousness of language not previously encountered in the two dramas intended for the stage:

> The moon is carried off in purple fire:
> Day breaks at last! Break glory, with the day
> On Djabal, ready to resume his shape
> Of Hakeem, as the Khalif vanished erst
> On red Mokattam's brow—our Founder's flesh,
> As he resumes our Founder's function!
>
> (1. 1–6)

In Anael's denunciation of Djabal as an impostor, there is a wealth of suggestion and strength of imagery that displays Browning at his best:

> Hakeem would save me! Thou art Djabal! Crouch!
> Bow to the dust, thou basest of our kind!
> The pile of thee I reared up to the cloud—
> Full, midway, of our Fathers' trophied tombs,
> Based on the living rock, devoured not by
> The unstable desert's jaws of sand,—falls prone!
> Fire, music, quenched: and now thou liest there
> A ruin obscene creatures will moan thro'!
>
> (4. 95–102)

Anael had built up her idol into the sky and girded it round with the symbols of her tribe's inherited belief only to discover that like a statue in the desert it collapses to lie there and be degraded by beasts. This imagery of the bestial and the godlike, the sands and the empyrean, throws a dramatic flash of light on the nature of the love of Anael and Djabal and on the conception of the incarnation worked out in the next act.

As for the characters, Djabal is splendidly conceived.[2] One is surprised like Browning that, whatever the defects of the piece as a play, Macready was not smitten with the part (*New Letters*, p. 21). There is not only a good bit of swashbuckling dash about him but also an appealing self-consciousness that makes even his imposture (if such it is) attractive. For he is, as he says, both deceived and deceiving—and he may or may not be so till the end. It is the enigmatic quality of his character that invites comparison with such a role as Hamlet. Anael, on the other hand, is a bit too hysterical from beginning to end. She is interesting not so much as a character as a medium for working out an idea. Loÿs is mainly an instrument for the complication of the plot and for the underscoring of the ironic nature of the play; as a character, the boy-knight is a bore.

The structure of the play is ironic. Djabal is that day to be proclaimed Hakeem (act one); Djabal, disavowing deception, plans to excape from the island without claiming to be Hakeem and without marrying Anael but is prevented from doing so by the return of Loÿs (act two); Loÿs misunderstands Anael and believes she is to marry him while Anael misunderstands Djabal and believes he will not marry her until she has proven her faith in him (act three); Anael murders the prefect, discovers Djabal's fraudulence, and goes to denounce him (act four); Anael appears before the assembled Druses, proclaims Djabal Hakeem, and dies, and Djabal accepts the role of Hakeem and kills himself so as to be exalted to Anael (act five). These ironies are intensified by the story of Loÿs—his idealization of Djabal, his discovery of the veniality of his order, the superfluousness of his replacing the prefect and the complications resulting from his return, so that in the end he is left with neither love nor unblemished religious faith: he is a man whose life and work have, despite the best intentions, come to naught. Browning called the play a tragedy, but it more nearly resembles ironic domestic drama, differing in genre and mode from a play by Ibsen, say, mainly in its affinity with heroic drama.

It is this unstable combination of the heroic and ironic that probably caused Macready such uneasiness. In outward form Browning borrows heavily from the heroic play.[3] In fact, on the surface it is not dissimilar to a French neoclassical tragedy. As in Corneille, for example, there is unity of time and place—the day of the revelation of Hakeem on the island in the Sporades; concentration of the action on one inevitable crisis—the proving true or false of Djabal's claim to be Hakeem; the characters' constant analyses of the motives that cause them to act—the many asides in which Djabal, for instance, examines his reasons for advancing his claim; new action resulting from, and explained by, each self-analysis—Anael will assassinate the prefect to prove her faith in Djabal, whom she has ever regarded more as man than god. On the stage these frequent asides make for a static play. Djabal's soliloquy at the beginning of act two takes sixty-two lines. In Djabal's first interview with Anael, their colloquy is interrupted by eight asides, one by Anael taking seventeen lines immediately followed by one by Djabal lasting for thirty-seven lines (2. 269–85, 286–322). Both of these are highly interesting monologues of a metaphysical nature in which the actors reflect on love, truth, faith, and doubt, and the degree to which they are intertwined; but whatever their intellectual interest, they effectively halt the action of the play for a considerable length of time. When to this static quality is added ironic action that undercuts or in some way calls into question the essential truth or even necessity of the monologue, the effect upon the audience must be that of pure mystification. Browning always set great store by *The Return of the Druses*, but it is understandable that from the time of Macready on no one has ever wished to produce it on the commercial stage.

After Macready refused *The Return of the Druses*, Browning composed still another play in hopes that it would be acceptable to the actor-manager. " 'The luck of the third adventure' is proverbial," he wrote Macready. "I have written a spick and span new Tragedy (a sort of compromise between my own notion and yours—as I understand it, at least). . . . There is *action* in it, drabbing, stabbing, *et autres gentillesses*—who knows but the Gods may make me good even yet?" (Hood,

Letters, p.5). Macready, who was already half-convinced that "he [Browning] is for ever gone" (*Diaries*, 2:76), did not even bother to read the play till September 1841, and then took another sixteen months to begin preparations for production. After several weeks of bitterness and recriminations between Browning and Macready,[4] *A Blot in the 'Scutcheon* was performed on 11 February 1843. On the same day it was published as the fifth pamphlet of *Bells and Pomegranates* to prevent Macready from further alteration of the text.[5] The play vanished from the boards after three performances, from which point Browning's break with Macready was complete.

A Blot in the 'Scutcheon is Browning's worst play and may well be the worst piece he ever published under his name.[6] Wanting desperately to be a successful dramatist—"who knows but the Gods may make me good even yet?"—he was willing to go to any lengths to receive applause from a theatrical audience. For titillation he offered "drabbing"—that is, whoring—and "stabbing" treated in a melodramatic mode in a three-act structure approximating the French *pièce bien faite*.[7] For sentiment he offered the pathos of young love and life cruelly cut off by an uncomprehending elder whose only concern is for the ways of the world. For sophisticated amusement he presented a smart young woman who comments wittily on the events unfolding. In addition, he borrowed heavily from Aeschylus, Shakespeare, Milton, and Keats, obvious imitations and echoes of whom were probably designed to impress the audience with the "literary" quality of this drama that also had "*action* in it." In brief, the play is a farrago of literary and theatrical clichés.[8]

The plot is largely based on *Romeo and Juliet*: two lovers from neighboring households meet at night in secret after the lover scales the balcony into her bedroom from a grove of trees, their trysts are discovered, the lover is killed in a duel by her brother, the beloved dies (presumably of a broken heart), the brother of the girl commits suicide by poison. So that no one would overlook the resemblance to Shakespeare's tragedy, Browning made the girl to be fourteen years old, the same age as Juliet, and employed the light-dark dramatic imagery of that play. The medieval setting, the lights showing through stained glass with heraldic devices, the gules of the escutcheon—these seem to come from *The Eve of St. Agnes*, which of course also bears marked similarities to the Shakespearean play. Tresham seeking vengeance and lamenting the pity of the situation appears to be modeled on Othello, and Tresham believing himself to have let loose the Furies that must inflict punishment on himself and others of his family seems to come from the *Oresteia*. Guendolyn and Austin, who have little relation to the plot, are borrowed from *Much Ado About Nothing*: her witty, slightly acerb remarks and her loyalty to Mildred recall Beatrice, and Austin, won over by his fiancée to Mildred's cause, seems to be based on Benedick. The frequent references to pride, Paradise, sin, the snake in the garden—these obviously echo *Paradise Lost*.

With so much borrowed from other authors, is there then anything that is distinctively Browning's? More than anything else, the characters' sense of playing roles in a drama written and controlled by a master playwright-director, called God or Fate, is what gives them the ironic dimension characteristically Browningesque. Like the duke of Ferrara, Thorold is preoccupied with his ancient lineage and therefore highly conscious of himself and his position as the present earl of Tresham. He is "all accomplished—courted everywhere— / The scholar and the gentleman" (3. 1. 135–36), at home equally in the library poring over genealogical records or in the world displaying his courtly manners; in short, he is the eighteenth-century *honnête homme*, the embodiment of "the perfect spirit of honor" (1. 3. 38). It is his sense of family pride and, closely allied to it, his sense of honor that lead him to assume various roles in the play and that result in tragedy.

In the beginning Tresham is the *grand seigneur* and loving brother—"what a nobleman should be! / . . . like / A House's Head!" (1. 1. 64–66)—who wishes more than anything else to marry his sister off to someone of impeccable pedigree. He finds his highest hopes fulfilled in Henry Mertoun; but his plan is frustrated by Mildred, whom he discovers to have a lover and who ceases in his eyes to be his sister but is "the woman there"—"Mildred once!"—who would betray Mertoun, "honor's self" (2. 265–69, 306). Tresham thereupon becomes the stern judge: "I curse her to her face before you all! / Shame hunt her from the earth!" (2. 325–26).

For the most part thereafter, Tresham envisions himself as the Archangel Michael in battle with Satan. When he apprehends Mertoun in the grove beneath Mildred's window, he asks how one deals with such a culprit and then answers that one "sets the foot upon his mouth" (3. 1. 89). "What right," asks Mertoun of him later, "have you to set / . . . foot upon her life and mine?" (3. 1. 152–53). With his misguided sense of honor and trapped in the role he has assumed, Tresham mortally wounds Mertoun in a duel that there is no need to fight, either pragmatically or for principle. As the tragedy reaches its end and Tresham learns he has acted precipitately and wrongly, he renounces his assumed role of judge and avenger.

But Tresham does not yield up one role without assuming another. For without his role—his dramatic mask, as it were—he is nothing.[9] When he ceases to be God or God's avenging angel, he reverses roles and becomes the accursed whose evil deed, as in the *Oresteia*, "lets loose a fury—free to lead / Her miserable dance amidst you all" (3. 1. 220–21). Only at the end, when it is no longer necessary to present a face to the world, does he forgo all roles on life's stage, where other players continue the drama without him:

> There are blind ways provided, the foredone
> Heart-weary player in this pageant-world
> Drops out by, letting the main Masque defile
> By the conspicuous Portal:—I am thro'—
> Just through!—
>
> (3. 2. 137–41)

To Mildred role-playing is nothing less than dissimulation and hence "deliberate wickedness": "I / Shall murmur no smooth speeches got by heart" (1.3. 144, 146–47). But she does not remain true to her resolve, for when adversity is experienced rather than anticipated, she too envisions herself in a role: the role of Mildred the suffering penitent: "I must have crept / Out of myself. . . . 'Tis she, / Mildred, will break her heart, not I" (3. 2. 20–24). It is this Mildred who three times pictures herself as the young, loving orphan who fell into sin (1. 3. 238–40; 2. 371–73, 411–13).

As for Mertoun, he is so little given to role-playing that the one time he does assume a role he plays it badly enough that the other characters comment on his inadequacy in the part. Of Mertoun's asking for permission to press his suit to Mildred, Austin says that he would have played the scene differently and Guendolyn agrees that she would have too. Tresham concurs in their appraisal of Mertoun's performance and then proceeds to play the part for him: "He should have said what now I say for him" (1. 2. 151).

Consideration of the appropriateness and adequacy of words is never far from the characters' thoughts and is, in fact, related to the basic theme of the drama—deception. What's in a name?—this is the question that the play tacitly poses.[10] One answer is that kind hearts are more than coronets and simple faith more than Norman blood. Another answer is that names—words—conceal as much as they reveal. Extending greetings to Mertoun, Tresham says: "your name / Would win you welcome"; for the young earl is "a name! a blazon!" (1. 2. 8–9, 130). Tresham is, Guendolyn remarks, totally absorbed in Mertoun's "old name and fame" (1. 2. 144). When he learns that Mildred has been receiving a lover nightly, Tresham demands to know his name (2. 229–31). When he apprehends the disguised Mertoun, Tresham again demands to know the man's name. Learning that it is Mertoun, he discovers to his great dismay that word and thing are not identical, at least do not seem to be so.

Yet it is Tresham's adamant refusal to listen to the words that Mertoun does wish to speak that results in tragedy. Disturbed that things are not always what they seem, Tresham comes to fear language as the chief instrument for deception. "Not one least word on your life!" he tells Mertoun. "Be sure that I will strangle in your throat / The least word that informs me how you live / And yet are what you are!" (3. 1. 74–76). He fears this for the very reason that Mertoun might somehow be capable of a verbal magic that would teach the unteachable and so explain "how you can live so, and so lie!" (3. 1. 80). It is better not to know how things can be other than they appear and yet be true.[11]

It is the Romantic Ironist's view of life—the ability to hold contradictions in mind and accept them—that Tresham cannot tolerate. When old Gerard tells him the story of having seen for the past month someone climb into Mildred's bedroom at night, Tresham momentarily is faced with the possibility that Gerard is not to be doubted and also that Mildred is not guilty of lust: "oh, no, no!" he exclaims, "both tales are true" (2. 96). But he cannot live with this possibility, and so he yields to belief in his sister's near-total depravity. When he discovers that Mertoun also is untrue, no escutcheon is left unblotted to shield him from the perception that things are not what they seem. No, indeed, he will not listen to Mertoun's glozings—and thereupon runs his sword into the young earl's body.

In his dying breath Mertoun insists, "You'll hear me now!" (3. 1. 94). For the man has the right to speak in his own defense who "presently . . . may have . . . to speak before his God / His whole defence" (3. 1. 97–99). Mertoun then tells why he had not asked earlier for Mildred's hand and, for purposes of the play, this explains all: "Tresham—oh, had you but heard! / Had you but heard!" (3. 1. 150–51). And Tresham himself regrets, "Had I but heard him—had I let him speak / Half the truth . . . / I had desisted!" (3. 2. 94–96). Had he but listened, he would have seen "thro / The troubled surface of his crime and yours / A depth of purity immovable!" (3. 2. 98–100). Only in his last moments does Tresham arrive at the ironist's understanding that two different tales can be alike true. Like other of Browning's protagonists, Tresham comes to knowledge when it is too late to act on it.

Mildred also turns during her last few moments of life to the necessity and yet inadequacy of language. Tresham had agreed to bear Mertoun's last words to her, but when he comes to repeat them, Mildred prevents him: "*You* / Tell me his last words? *He* shall tell me them, / And take my answer—not in words, but reading / Himself the heart I had to read him late" (3. 2. 72–75). Only in death are words unnecessary.

Although Mildred and Mertoun do not aim their lives so

explicitly toward a *Liebestod* as do some of Browning's other lovers, they nevertheless view their love as something apart from ordinary life. Early on, Mertoun says that they will soon find "happiness / Such as the world contains not" (1. 2. 96–97), but Mildred has a dim intuition that this cannot be: for how can they have happiness that is not of this world if they are alive? "Our happiness," she insists, "would exceed / The whole world's best of blisses." No, she says, tell your soul what mine has grown used to hear "like a death-knell": "this will not be!" (1. 3. 98–103). The world simply cannot admit such ecstasy. When confronted by her brother, she asks him to kill her, "so should I glide / Like an arch-cheat into extremest bliss!" (2. 241–42). As Mertoun is about to expire, he apostrophizes his beloved: 'Die, Mildred! leave / Their honorable world to them—for God / We're good enough, tho' the world casts us out!" (3. 1. 174–76). And Mildred, needing not "to hide love from the loveless, any more," feels that her soul has been "loosed . . . of all its cares at once— / Death makes me sure of him for ever!" (3. 2. 14, 71–72).

The uneasiness and fear that Mildred feels concerning their earthly happiness, even long before their liaison is discovered, seem to stem from a belief that their lives are somehow beyond their own control. How did "sin the snake" glide "into the Paradise Heaven meant us both?" The answer: "Sin has surprised us" (1. 3. 79–80, 120). But how was this possible? Not because she has not been on her guard, as Milton's Raphael warned Adam and Eve to be, but because "I was so young—I loved him so—I had / No mother—God forgot me—and I fell" (1. 3. 238–40). This is her plea, which becomes a refrain throughout the play; yet God does not seem entirely to have forgot her because, according to her, he seems indulgent (2. 413) and to hear her (3. 2. 30).

Tresham also wonders how in his Paradise, the ancestral home of the Treshams, there has sprung up this "poison-tree, to thrust from Hell its roots" and stretch "its strange snaky arms" (3. 1.24–26). For him the answer is that it was Fate (3. 1. 219–21). No longer a free agent, he is brought by the trees and river to the yew beneath Mildred's window: "I'll shun / Their will no longer—do your will with me!" (3. 1. 11–

12). Acting in concord with their will, he then determines "Mertoun's fate" (3. 1. 203). Yes, it is fated that only blood can wash away a blot on the escutcheon (3. 2. 147–149).

In his as in Mildred's case, there are ironies in Tresham's attitude toward God or Fate. For his "fate" is his "perfect spirit of honor," which means living in the past, among his glorious ancestors. He must act in such and such a way because his honor demands it.[12] He is, furthermore, the preserver of that chivalric code of honor which in the eighteenth century is being threatened from all sides: "With God's help I will keep . . . / The old belief," whereas those like Mertoun are "unable to recall the Past" (3. 1. 81–82, 128). Yet in the end he acts in a way contrary to what his code requires. Mildred observes that surely Tresham has let Mertoun plead his case before the duel "because your code / Of honor bids you hear before you strike" (3. 2. 90–91). As we have already noted, Tresham refused to hear a word from Mertoun, and this he admits to his sister, who comments simply that heaven "needs no code to keep its grace from stain" (3. 2. 107). An additional irony is that, despite all that has gone before, Tresham dies with the admonition to "hold our 'Scutcheon up" with "no Blot on it." For it is required by "fate" or "honor" that "blood / Must wash one blot away" (3. 2. 146–48). In this tragedy the protagonist dies unenlightened.[13]

Guendolyn and Austin are so much on the periphery of the action that it is difficult even to speak of their roles, much less of their role-playing. Yet on Guendolyn's part there is sufficient awareness of, and detachment from, the events to earn her the right to be the voice ironic in the play. Like D'Ormea in *King Victor and King Charles*, she hovers near the chief figures, seeing more than they see and urging them to act in certain ways. Also like D'Ormea she possesses the self-awareness that permits her to recognize her role-playing for what it is. She speaks, for example, of her "attempted smartnesses" and can refer to herself as "foolish" (1. 3. 20, 56). Furthermore, she possesses exactly that quality of which Tresham speaks and most lacks—the ability to "join hands in frantic sympathy" (3. 1. 78). She has this by virtue of her detachment, self-awareness, openness to experience, and power of empathetic insight. "I divined— / Felt by instinct how it was," she says to Mildred upon realizing that Mertoun is the clandestine lover (2. 425–26). Not only is she aware of her own role-playing but also she can penetrate the roles and disguises of others, what she calls "the world's seemings and realities" (2. 398). Guendolyn is, however, but forced on the play. She has no more integral part in it than her betrothed, Austin, who is only a stick figure. We welcome her presence, nevertheless, just as we welcome D'Ormea's in *King Victor and King Charles*, because she at least has some vitality, which is more than can be said for Tresham, Mildred, and—albeit he sings and climbs trees[14]—Mertoun.

If the characters do not elicit our interest, even less does the action capture our attention. Most of it is incredible. Why should Mertoun not have wooed and won Mildred in the accepted way? Why does Mildred yield her virtue so readily? Why, after having spoken for Mildred's hand and expecting a positive answer the next day, does he jeopardize their future by stealing into her bedroom on the night of his first visit to Tresham? Why does Mildred display the light that allows him to enter? Why in his clandestine approach does he sing a song? Or even more basically, why being close neighbors have Mertoun and the Treshams not met?[15] *A Blot in the 'Scutcheon* is incredible in its every aspect, including the fact that Browning wrote it. The anonymous reviewer of it in the *Times* for 13 February 1843 gets to the root of the play's failure when he remarks of the dramatist: "His whole thoughts seem to have been directed to the production of striking effects, and these, in some instances, he certainly has obtained, but it has been at the expense of nature and probability." In sum, Browning violated his own dramatic principle: instead of focusing on action in character, he tried to put character in action—and he failed.

Having quarreled with Macready, Browning was forced to look to other theatrical managers as prospective producers of his play. Charles Kean—the son of the great Edmund Kean, whose brilliance as an actor first turned Browning toward dramatic writing—offered the young poet-playwright a goodly sum for a new play. In March 1844 he read his play to Kean, who seems to have liked it but could not promise to produce it before Easter of the following year. Greatly surprised, Browning decided to forgo the money Kean promised and publish the piece. As he wrote a friend, "something I *must* print, or risk the hold, such as it is, I have at present on *my* public: . . . and two or three hundred pounds [from Kean] will pay me but indifferently for hasarding the good fortune which appears slowly but not mistakeably setting in upon me, just now" (Hood, *Letters*, pp. 9–10). Unless he was seriously deluded, Browning was apparently winning a select but growing audience, however badly his plays might fare on or off the stage. *Colombe's Birthday* appeared as the sixth number of *Bells and Pomegranates* in April 1844.

Despite its later date of composition, the play is thematically more closely akin to *Sordello* than any of the other subsequent works we have examined. In the first place, it has a political theme. Although the other plays, with the exception of *A Blot in the 'Scutcheon*, have political subjects, none of them is truly political in focus, the relationships between rulers and ruled being examined more in terms of the individual than of governed society. As we saw, this is not the case in *Sordello*, which has as one of its major concerns the question as to which means of government will best serve the society at large and, further, how the individual can effectively work for the establishment of such government. In *Colombe's Birthday* Browning again presents a society in the process of transition—from autocratic rule to representative government. Valence appears as the new type of political leader, the "advocate" chosen by the people to speak for them, enjoying their confidence, and embracing their causes and sufferings as his own.[16] Prince Berthold represents the old autocratic ruler whose main concern is possession and power. He is the more modern type of Charlemagne, and Valence is the more modern type of Hildebrand—the types of strength and feeling adduced in book five of *Sordello*. Both know that in the seventeenth century—the play is dated "16__"—the days of empire are numbered. Valence speaks of "the old shapes" that are worn out and of the new ones now appearing that are to supplant "Marshall, Chamberlain, and Chancellor" and that are to be cates of the people (3. 247–50). The prince, realizing the old European order is near an end, speaks of the favored few who may perhaps be allowed to finish out their days in the "masque" of Europe and of the "dim grim kind of tipstaves at the doorway" who stands there to bar entry to newcomers (5. 23–45).

It is apparent that Valence and Berthold contesting for Colombe represent the Browningesque dialectic struggle of love and power that we have so frequently noted, the difference here being that the conflict is translated into more overtly political terms than was the case in the other plays. Love wins out, and power is left to pursue its course wearily; but it is not the least of the ironies of the play that, as we shall see, power is more attractive than love. *Colombe's Birthday* perfectly displays that ambivalence which Browning admitted to in correspondence with his future wife: " . . . I have been all my life asking what connection there is between the satisfaction at the display of power, and the sympathy with—ever-increasing sympathy with—all imaginable weakness" (Kintner, 1:270).

On the personal level love is shown to be superior. As Valence says, the prince may conquer the people by force but never rule effectively without the people's love: he can be their despot but not their duke (3. 260–68). In addition, power without love is shown to be devoid of vivacity, as the prince prepares to go his old way "somewhat wearily" (5. 387). Finally, Colombe chooses love, in the person of Valence, after having been required to judge the two almost allegorical figures on the "stage . . . for the world's sake" and "vindicate / Our earth and be its angel" (4. 402–7). But the choice that she makes in the end is by no means clear-cut—she wishes to wed Valence and keep her duchy too, which is to say that she wants both love *and* power. But it is a matter of one or the other and so perforce she gives up "Juliers and the world" (5. 354). In its conclusion the play shows that love and power cannot coexist, which in political terms means that enlightened, effective government is not possible. The prince goes forth to accumulate more power, and as his deputy in Juliers he leaves behind Dietrich the black Barnabite "to ply his trade" (5. 380–82) while Valence and Colombe retire to the floral seculsion of Ravestein. Unlike Sordello, Colombe arrives at a decision, one that is in effect forced on her; but her choice means turning her back on the world—on Cleves, whom she has promised to help—and seeking personal fulfillment at the expense of society. One is left wondering, if but ever so slightly, whether she might not better have chosen the prince.

Browning also seems to have had mixed feelings about her decision. For he built his play around the irony that makes Berthold, the loser, a more attractive character than Valence, the winner, just as in *Strafford* he made the more appealing character represent the worse cause. Valence is first in love with Cleves and then with the duchess, for whom he gives up his fellow townsmen and their troubles, although he is, at least in the penultimate act, uncomfortable about doing so. He is entirely selfless as far as Colombe is concerned and is willing to sacrifice all for her, and comforts himself that his love for her, which resulted from his first sight of her, is "Heaven's gift" (2. 88, 3. 364, 4. 118). Humorless and physically unattractive, "ungainly, old before his time" (2. 87), he is also poor, being able to offer Colombe nothing but himself. The prince, on the other hand, is a splendid man of the world. He can offer Colombe everything but "love." Unlike Valence he does not fall in love at first sight, having already had some unhappy experience along the lines of passion: "I am past illusion on that score" (5. 79). But he can offer respect and admiration, which may grow into affection.

Colombe's Birthday is, in the second place, like *Sordello* in that Colombe herself resembles Palma. A duchess in name only during the year's time that she has occupied the throne, she has been awaiting what Palma called an out-soul—but what Colombe calls a power above her power, someone of "greater potencies," a man who though constantly by her side she could "still keep distant from, / And so adore" (4. 253–58). She recognizes this man in Valence whose "renovating" force on her nature she discovers on first meeting (3. 347). Yet she does not give herself entirely to her protector until she learns what another contending power might have to offer:

> Devotion, zeal, faith, loyalty—mere love!
> And, love in question, what may Berthold's be?
> I did ill to mistrust the world so soon—
> Already was this Berthold at my side!
> The valley-level has its hawks, no doubt:
> May not the rock-top have its eagles, too?
> Yet Valence...let me see his Rival then!
>
> (4.413–19)

The eagle turns out to fly too loftily for such as she, and so she contents herself with the home bird: "I take him—give up Juliers and the world! / This is my Birth-day" (5 354–55).

As I propose to show to greater extent presently, Colombe is only a play duchess, being by nature more like a violet by a mossy bank half-hidden from the eye. As the motto asks: "Ivy and violet, what do you here / With blossom and shoot in the warm springweather, / Hiding the arms of Monchenci and Vere?" Before becoming duchess Colombe lived as "queen / Over the water-buds" (1. 16–17). Like a flower she was plucked and put on display. She did not crown herself—in fact, claimed a right to the throne no more than church flowers claim to have written the words in the saint's book near which they are placed (2. 164–66). Better far that she return to her old life "among the flowers" (2. 186). After many associations of Colombe with flowers, mainly by Valence (for example, 3. 266–67, 4. 288, 5. 348), the prince sums up by saying to her: "Too costly a flower were you . . . / To pluck and put upon my barren helm / To wither" (5. 362–64). "Any garish plume will do" (5. 364) for the eagle. The violet is better returned to its mossy banks, not "hiding the arms of Monchenci and Vere."

Superficially *Colombe's Birthday* is domestic drama with strong overtones of Shakespearean romance. But here the heroine does not win a handsome lover who also turns out to be a prince; instead she chooses the poor, plain suitor who is no other than he appears. Not the eagle of the heights but the hawk of the valley captures this dove (*colombe*). The "hero," as Melchior calls him (5. 355), does not get the girl and, in not getting her, is certain she has made the proper choice. To

Colombe and Valence he says: "I could not imitate—I hardly envy— / I do admire you. All is for the best" (5. 360–61). What we have then is neither domestic drama nor ordinary romance but ironic romance, which in this instance does not lead to tragedy, as in the earlier plays, but to a conclusion satisfactory to all, although the audience is left with some doubts. All the other theatrical pieces, both before and after, are called tragedies; this one alone is simply called "a play."[17]

The ironic nature of this play is underlined, as in the case of the other dramas, by the constant reminder that the action and the characters are only fictions. So numerous are the documents that are passed around, studied, and quoted that they are elevated from the position of subtext—as in *Strafford*, say—to become part of the actual text from which the characters read and speak as though it were a script for a dramatic performance. This means that the characters see themselves as playing parts in a drama whose text thus becomes what Colombe calls a "rescript" (2. 182).

The play opens with Guibert, one of the duchess's courtiers, "*reading a paper*," which turns out to be a demand from Prince Berthold that Colombe yield the duchy according to Salic law. She has for the past year, therefore, been but playing the role of duchess, and on this first anniversary of her "investiture," which is also her birthday, while she has been "wreathing her hair" (1. 98) to receive the good wishes of her subjects, someone must present her with the prince's letter telling that she has been incorrectly cast in the part that she must now yield. When she learns that she has been but a "play-queen" (3. 265), she is much shaken and insists that she will keep the ducal crown. She did not ask for the role, she tells her courtiers; she did not write the words for her part (2. 165–66). Yet now they want to revise the play just when she is settling into the role. But she has no recourse; she must do as the prince demands and as they say: she will return to her life "among the flowers" in her old role, "Colombe of Ravestein . . . no longer Duchess here" (2. 186–87). Speak then no further of "rescripts," she says, as she takes off her coronet (2. 181–88), although as it happens the rescript is rescripted.

Up to this point Colombe has been like a May queen,

decked out for display but having no real authority. Her life for this past year has been one of "pure pleasure," during which she could not find out the loves of her people and would not look for their fears (2. 100, 184–86). Colombe has in fact been cast pretty much in the same role as Countess Gismond (as she later became) at the tournament. And then, as in the case of the Countess, there steps forth an "advocate," Valence of Cleves, who brings with him a petition from his townsmen for the redress of their wrongs. Colombe receives the paper, looks it over, accepts it, and returns the prince's paper to her courtiers with contempt. She will remain in the role of duchess, with a new supporting cast consisting of Valence and the people of Cleves, and with every intention of revising "established form," which is in need of "new consecration" (2. 292, 296).

Valence has come to the court at Juliers as the representative of the people of Cleves. So much engrossed is he in his role as their advocate that he comes to think of himself as Cleves (2. 92–94). He has arrived to utter no "grand harangue," the language of courtiers, but unheroic speech on behalf of Cleves. But he has difficulty in speaking at all, and he keeps glancing at the paper he holds for the proper words. "Cleves, speak for me!" he says (1. 229). Having gained admission to Colombe's chamber by agreeing to carry to her the prince's letter, he is tongue-tied and *"suddenly occupying himself with his paper,"* as the stage directions indicate, he can speak only when he reads from the script in which the people of Cleves have told him to "take from our mouths / Our wrongs and show them" (2. 148–49). Having unwittingly become the "instrument" of Colombe's disgrace, he speaks in defense of the duchess, who names him her "Marshall, Chancellor, and Chamberlain"[18] as well as her "only subject" (2. 190, 288–93, 348). He becomes, in short, "the leading man" (3. 280).

Prince Berthold then appears in act three, and it becomes only too apparent that Colombe and Valence are but engaging in make-believe. Colombe is but a "shadow" duchess after all (3. 190), and she will have to yield her throne. Yet she cannot bring herself to give up the part all of a sudden, for it will ruin her reputation. "How will it be read, sir? How be sung about?" she asks Valence, commissioning him to appear before the prince and speak "what I shall call to mind I should have urged / When time's gone by" (3. 209, 203–5).

The prince himself has been playing the role of conqueror and, finding no apparent opposition to his claim to the duchy, is concerned for what nowadays is called his "image." If he gain conquests so easily, he will have to forgo the role of "victor" (3. 12–13, 52). Then appear the courtiers, who have been acting out their roles in the "masque" and "mummery" till the claimant arrived (1. 94, 95). It is expected that they will speak and act exactly like the courtiers at the other cities the prince has claimed (3. 65–68), but to Berthold's surprise they return his letter to the duchess by crumpling it in a gesture of contempt in the same way that she had done. Somewhat amused and not entirely displeased, the prince finds them "better actors" than he had anticipated and himself looking "much bolder" than he knew (3. 143, 142).

In the interview with the prince, Valence, refusing to employ the "faded language" of courtiers (3. 331), impresses Berthold with his playing of his role: Valence's "method" of acting is by "feeling's play" (4. 174). Berthold in turn impresses Valence as the perfect actor of the role of the gracious and courteous prince. Berthold is, says Valence, "a noble spirit in noble form," although he could wish that the prince "less had bent that brow to smile / As with the fancy how he could subject / Himself upon occasion to—himself" (3. 324–27).

Valence comes away from the interview with the papers, "cold hard words" (3. 319), that the prince has originally sent to Colombe and that the courtiers had returned to him. Reading them, Valence concludes that Berthold is the true duke and that Colombe has been allowed to play her "shadow" role only by the connivance of kings and popes, whose pleasure it temporarily served. The courtiers meanwhile fear that the duchess has so captivated the prince that he has become "her puppet" (4. 33) and that Valence will end up as "the very thing he plays, / The actual Duke of Juliers" and the prince dismissed "with thanks for playing his mock part so well" (4. 46–47, 60, added in 1849 edition). Only later does it occur to them that another part of the script by which roles are enacted lies in the archives—the old duke's will that forbids Colombe to marry one of her subjects and retain the ducal crown.

Valence himself is concerned that he has become Colombe's advocate more than Cleve's. He rationalizes that his life continues Cleves's and Cleves's his, but if he were "to take God's gift . . . swerve no step," might he not then be the advocate of both (4. 114–16)? Considering further this possibility, he sees a new role for himself: "I that spoke for Cleves, can speak / For Man" (4. 384–85), but to convey his love directly to Colombe he finds "there's no language helps here" (4. 399). She, however, discovers how to communicate her love for him by telling him what he should say to his supposed inamorata (4. 357–64), all the while finding it "mournful—that nothing's what it calls itself" (4. 412).

Berthold is surer of his language, doubtless because he is more authentic in his role. He is a real prince, whereas Valence is a make-believe marshall, chancellor, and chamberlain and Colombe a fairy princess. He believes it good policy to marry Colombe. At the moment he is sure of his claim to the duchy, but he recognizes that scripts can be rewritten—"a new gloss on the ancient law, / O'er-looked provisoes, past o'er premises" (5. 16–17). Appointing Valence to carry to Colombe his suit for marriage, he rehearses Valence in the language to use, fully aware of his own clichés (4. 182–85) and those of others (4. 131–32.)[19]

In the last act—which Valence sees as a kind of morality play, "a stage / For trial" (4. 402–3)—Berthold speaks for himself. He woos Colombe not by expressions of love but by considerations of policy. In the "great masque" of politics in which his part is to "career on all the world for stage," like a new Alexander of Macedonia, he needs someone to play the part of his "representative" at home (5. 29, 93, 94). He himself is "nothing" as a human being—he is only the role he plays—and he does not therefore urge her to marry himself, Berthold, but "the Empire" (5. 221–22). Having been ready to be swept off her feet by the prince's protestations of passion, she concludes that she can win his respect only "by putting on a calculating mood" (1. 122). She writes her reply to his proposal on his requisition. "Read it and have done!" she says, ready for a new script and a new role (5. 353). The prince then accepts her refusal, congratulates the pair in a "few words," assumes the dukedom, and commands the courtiers to go copy "the precedents / Of every installation, proper styles, / And pedigrees of all your Juliers' Dukes" (5. 383–85). He is ready to depart for the next act in the masque of European politics.

In general, the characters in *Colombe's Birthday* play their roles with perhaps a greater degree of self-consciousness yet also with a greater sense of freedom of will than those we have met previously. To be sure, they feel themselves partially bounded by various fateful documents, but at the same time they realize that it is possible to revise them in some degree—with new glosses, for example—so as to render them as "rescripts." Only Colombe feels her life, to any great extent, determined by fate. Next year will not be like the last, she says in echo of Mildred in *A Blot in the 'Scutcheon*: "It cannot be! It is too late to be! " "What part had I," she asks, "or choice in all of it?" (2. 52–53). She has been, she feels, a mere puppet; and of all the characters in the play, she alone refers to "my fate" (4. 198). It takes Berthold, who feels constrained by neither fate nor anything else, to remind her that her "will and choice are still as ever, free" (5. 215).

The degree of free will permitted the characters is perhaps best exemplified in Guibert, who wavers between selfishness and altruism. His susceptibility to "conversion" is suggested by the fact that he swears by Saint Paul (1. 286, 3. 113), although his crest ironically has the motto "Scorning to waver" (2. 208). "Whoever's my kind saint," he says, "do let alone / These pushings to and fro, and pullings back" (1. 343–44). For him it is constantly a matter of scripts and visions succeeded by rescripts and revisions.[20] Where in act three he follows on the heels of Valence and would stand with him (139–40, 305–6), in act four he decides that "selfishness is best again. / I thought of turning honest—what a dream!" (51–52). In the end, however, he submits to conversion, not without some ironic detachment: " 'Tis my Birth-day, too" (5. 378). Guibert is very much of the same mold as Guendolyn of *A Blot in the 'Scutcheon*.[21]

There are some spendid scenes in *Colombe's Birthday*. The romantic colloquy between Colombe and Valence in act four recalls the wooing scenes between Rosalind and Orlando in *As You Like It*. There is also some excellent poetry—for example, Valence's defense of Colombe in act three or, even better, Valence's prophecy of Berthold's career:

> He stands, a man, now; stately, strong and wise—
> One great aim, like a guiding-star, before—
> Which tasks strength, wisdom, stateliness to follow,
> As, not its substance, but its shine he tracks,
> Nor dreams of more than, just evolving these
> To fulness, will suffice him to life's end.
> After this star, out of a night he springs;
> A beggar's cradle for the throne of thrones
> He quits, so, mounting, feels each step he mounts,
> Nor, as from each to each exultingly
> He passes, overleaps one grade of joy.
> This, for his own good:—with the world, each gift
> of God and man,—Reality, Tradition,
> Fancy and Fact—so well environ him,
> That as a mystic panoply they serve—
> Of force, untenanted, to awe mankind,
> And work his purpose out with half the world,
> While he, their master, dexterously slipt
> From such encumbrance, is meantime employed
> In his own prowess with the other half.
> So shall he go on, every day's success
> Adding, to what is He, a solid strength—
> An airy might to what encircles him,
> Till at the last, so life's routine shall grow,
> That as the Emperor only breathes and moves,
> His shadow shall be watched, his step or stalk
> Become a comfort or a portent; how
> He trails his ermine take significance,—
> Till even his power shall cease his power to be,
> And most his weakness men shall fear, nor vanquish
> Their typified invincibility.
> So shall he go on, so at last shall end,

> The man of men, the spiritit of all flesh,
> The fiery centre of an earthy world!
>
> (4. 209–51)

One looks to Shakespeare—to Cranmer's compliment to the future Queen Elizabeth in *Henry VIII*, for example—for comparable splendor. In general, the language of *Colombe's Birthday* is simpler, less convoluted than in the other dramatic pieces.

The play is demonstrably better in the last three acts than in the first two. Browning himself seemed to be aware of having got stronger as the play progressed (*Domett*, p. 106). Something had happened to give him—in the writing of this play, at any rate—a new attitude toward love. In the last two acts, there is little evidence of the pathology of romantic love that we have earlier witnessed so frequently, no talk of "queens" but of "play-queens" bringing the happy fulfillment of Valence's love for Colombe. The author does, of course, allow Colombe to dally with her advocate in act four. As the anonymous reviewer in the *Athenaeum* for 19 October 1844 notes, she "flatters him with brilliant hopes, and then, like a true daughter of Eve, turns him over to the rack of suspense, unable herself to decide betwixt power and love"; but the resolution in act five is a happy one in which the duchess, according to the stage directions, "*with a light joyous laugh*" turns to her lover and says: "Come, Valence to our friends—God's earth—" which "*as she falls into his arms*" he completes by saying "—And Thee!" Colombe accepts her unromantic lover, part of "God's earth," and does so happily, in spite of the fact that she must give up the duchy. The dialectic of love and power is left unresolved but for the first time definitely concluded, not by a joining of the two but by a rejection of one in favor of the other.[22]

On her birthday Colombe is reborn, and the play that tells the story of her soul's achievement is thus a comedy. This new kind of dramatic mode does not, as it might seem, preclude an irony of form. On the contrary, comedy—particularly realistic comedy, as this approaches being—opens up an irony of possibilities: it does not assert that the lovers lived happily ever after, as the ordinary romance asks us to believe, but leaves us with questions like these: Will not Valence in his flowery retreat at Ravestein regret turning his back on the poverty of Cleves? Will Colombe find "devotion, zeal, faith, loyalty—mere love" (4.413) sufficient? In other words, what seems like a perfectly enclosed play, proceeding through five acts from morning to night of one day, is in fact more open-ended than the tragedies of earlier date. For all its external qualities seemingly pointing toward finality, *Colombe's Birthday* is an ironic drama that defers closure to a point beyond the play itself.

CHAPTER VIII
DRAMATIC ROMANCES AND LYRICS

SEVERAL MONTHS AFTER THE PUBLICATION OF *Colombe's Birthday*, Browning wrote to his friend Domett enclosing a copy of his play: " . . . I feel myself so much stronger, if flattery not deceive, that I shall stop some things that were meant to follow, and begin again" (*Domett*, p. 106). The things meant to follow seem to have been plays, for although two more were soon to be published, neither was intended for stage production. Beginning again apparently meant returning to shorter pieces of the kind that had appeared in *Dramatic Lyrics* three years earlier. Yet before he could begin—"I really seem to have something fresh to say"—Browning felt himself in need of a change, a trip to southern Italy to complement his visit in 1838 to northern Italy, where he had found artistic renewal. After which, "I never took so earnestly to the craft as I think I shall—or may, for these things are with God" (*Domett*, p.106).

The second journey to Italy made between August and December 1844, proved remarkably fruitful. He not only wrote verse on the way there and back but also was inspired by Italian scenes to compose a number of poems upon his return. Again in England, he began correspondence with Elizabeth Barrett in January 1845 and finally met her in person some four months later. She too may have inspired some of the short poems that Browning now wrote. She did, at any rate, see a number of them in manuscript and in page proof and made suggestions for changes in them.[1] The verses were published as *Dramatic Romances and Lyrics*, the seventh number of *Bells and Pomegranates*, in November 1845.

As he was completing *Colombe's Birthday*, Browning seems to have discovered that ironic romance was a more salutary mode for him than tragedy, certainly as far as playwriting was concerned. *Dramatic Lyrics* of 1842 had proved, in the words of John Forster in the *Examiner* for 26 November 1842, a "continued advance in the right direction"—lyrics for the most part dramatic that are "full of the quick turns of feelings, the local truth, and the picturesque force of expression, which the stage so much delights in" and that redeem his genius from "mere metaphysical abstraction." Where Browning excelled, said Richard Hengist Horne, was in "dramatic portraiture."[2] By 1844 Browning could have had no doubt that his genius was essentially ironic. For some years now he had been forcing his native gift into literary forms alien to it—namely, the dramatic tragedy, basically a closed-end form that gravitates toward judgment in favor of one particular side of a dilemma. Browning had struggled mightily with the form, attempting to provide it with the multiple perspectives, even in its closure, that his genius dictated. But it was all wrong, for only with the greatest wrenching of the plot could he force it to yield the ironic possibilities of character portrayal—"dramatic portraiture"—that he found most congenial. Writing for the stage would simply no longer do. As he told Elizabeth Barrett, he would compose no more plays after the one he was currently working on (Kintner, 1:26).

We have already noted how the dramatic monologue—what Browning called the dramatic lyric—is a salutary form for an author who hangs between immanence and transcendence, involvement and detachment, the lyric and the dramatic. We have also noted how those dramatic lyrics in which an ironic conflict is most strongly felt are those that realize most fully the potentialities of the form. But what of poems in which ironic tensions are significantly diminished, as for example in those works where the conflict between love and power is concluded by the choosing of one and the suppression (or forgetting) of the other? We have seen in *Colombe's Birthday* how Valence and Colombe choose love and Berthold chooses power and how their decisions force the play into the mold of ironic romance. Shorter forms dealing with such subject matter would then also be romances. Irony would not cease to inform poems of this nature, but ironic tensions would be reduced. As a result the emphasis would lie more heavily on narrative than on revelation of character. Browning decided therefore to call such poems dramatic romances. One cannot be sure exactly which of the *Dramatic Romances and Lyrics* the poet had in mind as romances. In the edition of 1863, at any rate, six of the poems of this volume come under the head of "Dramatic Romances."³

Like *Dramatic Lyrics* this collection covers a wide range of subjects treated from many different points of view and expressed in highly varying meters and line lengths. Here as in the earlier volume, some of the poems were published under titles by which they are no longer known. The contents were as follows:

"How They Brought the Good News from Ghent to Aix." (16–.)

Pictor Ignotus. Florence, 16—.

Italy in England [later called "The Italian in England"]

England in Italy. (Piano di Sorrento.) [later called "The Englishman in Italy"]

The Lost Leader

The Lost Mistress

Home Thoughts, from Abroad

The Tomb at St. Praxed's (Rome, 15–.) [later called "The Bishop Orders His Tomb at St. Praxed's Church"]

Garden Fancies
   I. The Flower's Name
   II. Sibrandus Schafnaburgensis

France and Spain
   I. The Laboratory (Ancien Regime.)
   II. Spain—The Confessional

The Flight of the Duchess

Earth's Immortalities

Song ["Nay, but you, who do not love her"]

The Boy and the Angel

Night and Morning
   I. Night [later called "Meeting at Night"]
   II. Morning [later called "Parting at Morning"]

Claret and Tokay [later called "Nationality in Drinks"]

Saul [the first nine sections only, at the end of which is printed "(End of Part the First.)"]

Time's Revenges

The Glove (Peter Ronsard *loquitur*)

It will be noted that a number of these poems are complementary but, with the exception of three instances, are not, as in *Dramatic Lyrics*, given joint titles. Why this should be so is unclear. It may be that Browning no longer felt the need to emphasize the dramatic (as opposed to the personal) nature of the verses; it may be that he felt the yoking under one title to be too obvious. But the fact remains that several of the poems are related and are enhanced, as I propose to demonstrate, by being considered together. Indeed, all the poems gain from examination of them as related pieces having a common theme, which more often than not is expressed ironically.

Like *Dramatic Lyrics* the volume begins with a lyric narrative of adventure in war and on horseback. The anapestic lines of "How They Brought the Good News from Ghent to Aix" carry us with the rider on an urgent journey to bring the news that alone could save Aix. The poem has an unusual perspective in that the narrator makes his horse, Roland, and not himself the protagonist of the story, this being emphasized by the meter that almost suggests that the tale is being told from the horse's point of view. In the end all the narrator remembers is the last of the town's wine being poured down the horse's throat, "which . . . / Was no more than his due who brought good news from Ghent." In the end, in fact, Roland becomes the hero—not "which" but "who" brought the goods news to Aix.

"How They Brought the Good News" was eventually classified as a dramatic lyric. We might even call it a low-level dramatic monologue in that the selfless character of the speaker in this instance is obliquely revealed by what he says. But the romance quality of the poem is evident in the narrative, which stresses not the result but the process. Thus the narrator remembers every detail of his journey—the departure, what his fellows said, what the landscape was like, what he wore—but of his goal he can remember nothing save the state of his horse, the means by which the journey was made.

Loyal praise of a brave animal is inverted in the next poem to self-praise, at least self-defense, by a cowardly painter—not how *he* triumphed but why *I* failed. "Pictor Ignotus" is the monologue of an unknown painter of the Florentine High Renaissance who explains why he has not achieved the fame of the youth, presumably Raphael, who seems everywhere to be praised.[4] He could have done all the youth had done: he had the necessary talent and insight, nothing barred his way. Yet a voice spoke forbidding him to paint for the kind of worldly collector portrayed in "My Last Duchess." If then he is bested and his pictures die because he has shrunk from the new naturalism now fashionable, at least he has been able to dictate the terms of his defeat, having consciously and determinedly chosen to paint in the old style and thereby keep his art unsullied by the marketplace.

On first hearing, the apologia sounds convincing enough. We are in fact impressed by the artist who turns from the materialism of the Medicis and preserves a religious concern for his art. If there is a note of self-pity in his plea, it serves all the more to elicit our sympathy for this man of enormous potential but limited achievement. Yet on reflection we begin to wonder about two matters—namely, was he as talented as he says, and whose was the voice deflecting him from the fame he wished? In other words, judgment sets in when sympathy of the moment fades.

Claiming a God-given ability to perceive truth in the heavens, on the earth, and in man, he also makes pretense to the talent that would permit him to translate this truth to canvas, showing

> Each face obedient to its passion's law,
>   Each passion clear proclaimed without a tongue;
> Whether Hope rose at once in all the blood,
>   A-tiptoe for the blessing of embrace,
> Or Rapture drooped the eyes as when her brood
>   Pull down the nesting dove's heart to its place,

> Or Confidence lit swift the forehead up,
> And locked the mouth fast, like a castle braved.

We know from his descriptions that he would be showing these not embodied in real men and women but as personified abstractions in stylized form. And he too half faces up to his limitations when he asks, in the very next lines, "Men, women, children, hath it spilt, my cup? / What did ye give me that I have not saved?" The questions are not answered, but we see from the metaphor that whatever artistic gifts he possesses he has hoarded without ever expending them in art.

He has dreamed of fame, of sending his pictures forth "through old streets named afresh" in honor of him, and then in death would "not go to heaven, but linger here," on earth. The thought was thrilling; but then it grew frightful, " 'tis so wildly dear!" The expenditure of psychic energy would be simply too great: it would mean nothing less than becoming a new man, undergoing a rebirth. And is it worth it, after all? No, for "a voice changed it," this aspiration. The speaker does not tell us who spoke. He does not tell us for the very reason that he does not know. If he knew, then he could blame someone for his failure, and no apology to himself or to anybody else would be necessary. But he cannot seriously consider that the voice is his own because to do so would be tantamount to admitting to inadequacy.

Like so many of Browning's characters whom we have noticed, the painter attributes his limitations to fate, which in effect is the voice's authority. He was like a man looking through a door to the revels inside, the revels "of some strange House of Idols at its rites." Suddenly the world was changed for him. But he was afraid of what he saw, even afraid of himself. "Who summoned these cold faces which began / To press on me and judge me?" To enter would mean turning his back on the kind of art that he had perfected, doing violence to it and to himself. "They drew me forth," but "spite of me," like a nun "shrinking from the soldiery." Then the voice spoke and he went no farther. Fate intervened just in time. He can therefore urge that he did not transgress his own moral destiny: "they" drew him forth in spite of himself.

He and his pictures have been spared the "daily pettiness" of the collector who might purchase "our" work. Other artists may be willing to suffer the inanity of the material-minded virtuosos concerning "our pictures," but as for himself, "I chose my portion." If he is an unknown painter, it is because *he* has wanted to remain so. Fate, in the form of limitation of either skill or vision, has not barred the way; the responsibility, he says in a gesture of pride, is totally his: he has determined his own defeat.

The note of bravery wavers however: his heart "sinks" as he goes about his ordinary, "monotonous" business of painting the "endless cloisters and eternal aisles" with the "same" series of religious figures, all with "the same cold, calm, beautiful regard." In the end he poses as the pathetic but brave little soul who has consciously elected obscurity for himself and his art out of the highest principle. He knows his pictures will die, blackening and mouldering in the silence of the shrine, but at least he and they will be spared the merchant's traffic. Finally, he asks, is fame worth the debasement of principle and purity?

Throughout the monologue there are images of expansion and contraction, of blazing light and darkness, of expenditure and hoarding. Even the pictures he would paint reveal the same imagery: Hope rising to be embraced, Rapture drooping the eyes as when her brood pulls down the heart to its place, Confidence lighting up the forehead and locking the mouth. He paints, in other words, images of his own inhibiting will. Clearly every leaping up of his heart is checked by timidity and fear. Like his spiritual brother J. Alfred Prufrock, the unknown painter always settles down on the side of parsimony: "it" would not be worth the expenditure; the expense of spirit, whether in love or art, is lust in action.

The design of "Pictor Ignotus" is much like that of "My Last Duchess." The speaker inadvertently reveals his character by his utterance, which in this case is, as it is partially in the case of the earlier poem, a defense of, and apology for, himself. Where in the earlier monologue Browning employed rhymed couplets for a certain effect, he here uses alternative rhyme—*abab, bcbc* etc.—to suggest enclosure. Likewise, at the conclusion of the monologue, he introduces a further ironic note in a passage that epitomizes the speaker. Where the duke referred to Neptune taming a sea-horse, Pictor Ignotus asks: "Blown harshly, keeps the trump its golden cry? / Tastes sweet the water with such specks of earth?" These are of course the old Romantic questions: Is not the idea profaned when expressed in the imperfect medium of language? Is not the thought debased when translated into action? But here the questions, which the speaker intends as images of empty fame, are ironically expressed, as Herbert Tucker suggests,[5] in images of prophetic creativity. Gabriel's trumpet awakens the dead to new life; Shelley's west wind is to be a trumpet of prophecy. Moses strikes the rock to bring forth water from the earth; Browning himself uses the story in book three of *Sordello* to speak of the water of life that the multitude dispraises as dim oozings. By such means the poet himself intrudes, as it were, into his poem, to comment upon his creation, to make himself known, and to remind us that the monologue, for all its verisimilitude, is after all not life but art.

The same imagery of expansion and contraction is likewise used in the next two poems to yield an ironic effect. The first of the companion poems, "Italy in England," is the monologue of an Italian patriot now in exile in England recounting how a loyal *contadina* helped him escape the Austrian police. For three days he had been hiding in a recessed aqueduct, when he managed to attract the attention of a girl passing by. He was going to lie to her concerning why he was there; but finding her so artless he tells her the truth, asks for food and drink, and requests her to carry a message into Padua. She does all this and thereby helps him elude capture. Now, safely in England, he looks back over his last days in Italy long ago, and in doing so reveals how the intervening years have taken their toll of his youthful fervor and openness to spontaneous emotion.

During his long exile the monologist has become a professional patriot, so to speak, doing all those things, like raising money and eliciting statements of support, necessary for his cause. But in the process he has become a monomanic, has little "thought / Concerning—much less wished for—aught / Beside the good of Italy / For which I live and mean to die!" He is, in effect, dead to all save The Cause. He knows this, although he does not put it in exactly those terms and rationalizes it as the price one pays for such patriotism. Yet looking back over those few days just before he left Italy for good, he experiences something of the old emotion. For thinking what he might possibly wish for, if he pleased to spend three wishes on himself, he still turns to matters connected with The Cause for the first two, both of which, not unexpectedly, issue from hate: the bloody murder of Metternich and the slow death from a broken heart of his old friend Charles, who deserted The Cause. As for the third, he wishes to see the girl who rescued him, now grown into a married woman with children:

> know if yet that woman smiles
> With the calm smile—some little farm
> She lives in there, no doubt—what harm
> If I sat on the door-side bench,
> And, while her spindle made a trench
> Fantastically in the dust,
> Inquired of all her fortunes—just
> Her children's ages and their names,
> And what may be the husband's aims
> For each of them—I'd talk this out,
> And sit there, for an hour about,
> Then kiss her hand once more, and lay
> Mine on her head, and go my way.

Instead of such natural but homely joys that love can bring, he was wedded The Cause, which has sapped his soul's energy and made him dead to all natural joy. For an instant he is almost willing to admit that he wishes his life had been otherwise, but then the mania returns and in an *envoi* he says: "So much for idle wishing—how / It steals the time! To business now!"

Like Pictor Ignotus, the Italian in England refuses spiritual rebirth out of a mistaken sense of loyalty. And, as in the preceding monologue, Browning enters the poem, disguisedly, to try to make certain that we do not overlook what he intends. He does so here by infusing the poem with imagery of rebirth.

The story takes place during Holy Week. The speaker is a man with a price on his head and has a friend who betrays him. The girl comes to him in his "crypt." He pictures her as Mary is frequently represented iconographically, her foot on a snake, and he asks her to be the mediatrix between himself and the help he seeks in the Duomo, where as a type of Our Lady of Peace she is to ask "whence comes peace?" to which she may expect the reply "From Christ and Freedom." At the end of seven days—that is, on Easter—help comes through her aid and he rises from his hiding place and departs from Italy by sea.[6] There is never any hint of passionate love between the two, only selfless devotion on her part to a man in need and, on the part of both, to a common cause. " . . . I could not choose," says the speaker, "But kiss her hand and lay my own / Upon her head," the same gestures he would make again were his third wish granted. By his imagery Browning would have us see that the possibility of rebirth still remains: what is necessary is that the patriot for a while forgo his "business" in favor of more ordinary and purely human relationships. The poem depicts concisely the monomania and the bitterness of long political exile.

The companion monologue, "England in Italy," suffers from lengthiness and from the poet's lack of a clear conception of what he wanted it to be. Apparently Browning originally intended it as a description of the landscape around Naples, but then he added an ending concerning the Corn Laws, probably for two reasons: to give it a political slant so that it could more properly serve as a pendant to "Italy in England" and, secondly, to give the discursive stanzas a more pointed ending. Elizabeth Barrett wrote to the poet, after having seen first the manuscript and then the printer's proofs, that the ending "gives unity to the whole . . just what the poem wanted" (Kintner, 1:244).

The monologue is addressed to a small peasant girl frightened by the scirocco that has brought a storm of rain. The Englishman tries to comfort her by describing his impressions of the past day: the dryness, the churning seas, the flapping birdnets, the wine-making, his ascent of a mountain to view the sea below and the clear sky above—all images suggestive of death and rebirth and clearer vision. The wind has now come, the storm has passed, the festive celebration will soon begin. All this is described in 285 lines, at which point the speaker says, doubtless sensing the child's boredom, "'Such trifles' you say?" On this very day in England, Parliament is debating the Corn Laws, whether abolishing them be "righteous and wise." Why, they might just as well debate whether the scirocco should vanish in black from the skies!

The sentiment is noble, and the poem has been read as expressive of Browning's own political liberalism. If it is no more than that—description of Neapolitan landscape followed by an ejaculation of political liberalism—then it can make no claim to being a dramatic monologue. We must, however, recall that the poem is presumably intended as a companion to "Italy in England" and that we are expected to note certain similarities. This means that, at the very least, we must suspect an ironic intent. When we look carefully, we are puzzled by the speaker's claim to share Ulysses' secret: "He heard and he knew this life's secret / I hear and I know!" (227-28). Whatever the secret is—apparently it is that men should be free—the monologuist does little to help others realize it. Unlike the Italian in England, he is not forced into exile; on the contrary, he is a tourist fascinated by the quaint ways of Italian life and the oddity of the landscape. While "in my England at home, / Men meet gravely to-day" to debate the Corn Laws, he amuses himself with the "sensual and timorous beauty" (195) of southern Italy. Where the Italian exile has his country's freedom as his "business," the English tourist can give but a passing mention—and this to a child—of the most serious cause of starvation in England during the "hungry forties." The echo of Shelley's "Ode to the West Wind" that Browning so strongly intended is purely for ironic effect.

Loyalty to a cause is more forcefully the informing idea of the following poem, "The Lost Leader." The poet who was once in the glorious company of Shakespeare, Milton, Burns, and Shelley has broken from the vanguard and the freemen to sink to the rear and the slaves, although in the eyes of the world he is up front in the limelight for all to see. The apostate has gone and will never be welcomed back, being a "lost soul," the most serious charge Browning can make against anyone. But this Judas is lost only as a leader; his accomplished work remains and entitles him to be "pardoned in Heaven, the first by the throne!" It is not, I believe, so much Browning's devotion to the poetry of Wordsworth (who so obviously is the Lost Leader)[7] as his sense of irony that dictates the final turn in the poem.

"The Lost Mistress" is artificially linked to its companion by the adjective in the title. In tone it is entirely different. Where the speaker of the former poem was more than ready to shout invective and heap opprobrium upon the disloyal leader, the speaker of the second is more than gentle, making no charge against his unfaithful lady love. "The Lost Mistress" is a more interesting poem dramatically than its companion because here the speaker has a design upon his auditor, which is to elicit pity and show himself as the manly knight of infinite resignation. "All's over then..?" he asks. Surely this can hardly be, for his mistress's words of dismissal sound no bitterer than the sparrows' good-night twitter. Surely her farewell is but a signal for a slight transition in their relationship. She will not really send him away? He will appear as no more than a friend, claiming but ever so slightly more than mere friendship entitles him to.

We cannot know how the mistress interprets his pretty little speech, but we see that he enjoys his status as the rejected lover. In the first place, it is better to have loved and lost than never to have loved at all because in being the loser there are certain claims to distinction. In the second place, he enjoys playing the role of the martyr, enjoys abasing himself, enjoys the revel in self-pity: "Mere friends are we,—well, friends the merest / Keep much that I'll resign." The monologue is only twenty lines long but it manages to reveal the character of a rejected suitor who makes every effort to present himself in the most favorable light, to his auditor and to himself, as infinitely injured but eternally faithful. It is a sort of preliminary sketch of "Andrea del Sarto."

Loyalty of another kind is the theme of "Home-Thoughts, from Abroad," which was originally composed of three separate lyrics instead of the two that we now know. The beauties praised in "Oh, to be in England" are those quiet ones alluded to in the "The Lost Mistress." We have often noted, from *Paracelsus* onward, how for Browning the present moment takes on meaning only when viewed in terms of the future, as being ever in the process of becoming. We may note the same in this lyric.

> Oh, to be in England
> Now that April's there,
> And who wakes in England
> Sees, some morning, unaware,
> That the lowest boughs and the brush-wood sheaf
> Round the elm-tree bole are in tiny leaf,
> While the chaffinch sings on the orchard bough
> In England—now!

The "some morning" turns out to be "now," and the lines that were growing longer under the promise of a future morning end in a final "In England—now," the shortest line of the strophe.

For most poets these beautiful lines would be poem enough. For Browning, however, they must be redeemed from their April nowness by the coming May. Or to put it another way, the lyric moment is to be incorporated into a dramatic movement.

> And after April, when May follows,
> And the whitethroat builds, and all the swallows—
> Hark! where my blossomed pear-tree in the hedge
> Leans to the field and scatters on the clover
> Blossoms and dewdrops—at the bent spray's edge—
> That's the wise thrush; he sings each song twice over
> Lest you should think he never could recapture
> The first fine careless rapture!
> And though the fields are rough with hoary dew,
> All will be gay when noontide wakes anew
> The buttercups, the little children's dower,
> —Far brighter than this gaudy melon-flower!

The April-becoming-May is a month of rapid movement. Where the boughs and sheaf *are* in tiny leaf in the first strophe, the pear tree *leans* and *scatters*. Where April's chaffinch sings, the thrush of anticipated May sings his song twice over. Like the bird the poet of this lyric sings twice over so as to recapture the first moment, to bind his days together, to redeem the past from its pastness, to put futurity into the present. All *will* be gay when April becomes May. And because April possesses this quality of becoming, the flowers of the future-in-the-present are far brighter than *this* southern gaudy melon-flower here and now. It is not that we pine for what is not or that unheard melodies are sweeter than tonal ditties—attitudes of Romantic poets; rather, it is the pregnancy of the present that makes it meaningful. This is why the English April landscape of dainty, quiet beauties about to be the blossoms of May makes dull by comparison the gaudy beauties of the south, which, in this spring month, are already full-blown.

The second lyric of "Home-Thoughts"—"Here's to Nelson's memory!"—is a drinking song that sounds more like Thomas Hood than Browning and that the poet may have included so as to give his volume a certain topicality.[8] In the third of "Home-Thoughts," which takes place in the waters that inspired the preceding lyric, the speaker admonishes him who would help England to turn away from noisy earthly feats to silent prayer.

The irony is more pronounced in the next poem, "The Tomb at St. Praxed's." Officially a Christian, the speaker is actually an independent thinker who does not perceive that his speculations are often contrary to Christian doctrine. Like the soliloquizer of the Spanish cloister, he adheres to the outward forms of his religion but is almost totally oblivious to the meaning behind them. He begins his monologue with a quotation from Ecclesiastes—"Vanity, saith the preacher, vanity!"—which causes us to believe that we are about to hear a sermon on that text. But immediately we learn that the bishop, as the revised title of 1849 identifies him, is not in the pulpit but in bed. Yet in bed as in the pulpit, the bishop adopts a homiletic manner: "And as she died so must we die ourselves, / And thence ye may perceive the world's a dream. / Life, how and what is it?" The bishop is infected by a *déformation professionelle*: throughout his monologue he lapses into his homiletic style.

As he pleads with his sons for a magnificent tomb in which to be buried, he recalls his past (worldly) life, rehearses the recumbent posture of his effigy atop the desired tomb, and slips from time to time into his pulpit manner—all of which serve to point up the discrepancy between what as a Christian prelate he should be and what he actually is. Evidently unconcerned for the salvation of his soul, he is preoccupied with the tomb, which offers him a form of physical immortality. The most telling moral irony is expressed in the quotation from Job: "Swift as a weaver's shuttle fleet our years: / Man goeth to the grave, and where is he?" Where indeed? According to the bishop, in a beautiful tomb where he may gloat over his defeated rival. The bishop's greatest fear is not of the Last Judgment but of a cheap sepulcher.

As he continues to talk, his mind becomes muddled. At the beginning when he asked, "Do I live, am I dead?" he knew very well that, though dying, he was still very much alive and able, for perhaps the last time, to entreat his sons to bury him in proper fashion and to bargain with them concerning what they would be willing to give. At the end, however, when he asks the same question, he fancies himself already lying on his entablature atop the tomb, his sons' "ingratitude" having stabbed him to death.

In the case of the bishop of Saint Praxed's as in that of the Duke of Ferrara, the monologue serves no strategic prupose. The bishop knows that the more he talks, the less likely he is to get the tomb he wants. The sons have heard all this many times before and they whisper to Anselm that the old man's at it again. Why then does the bishop continue his monologue? For the same reason that the duke makes his indiscreet remarks to the envoy. The lyric impulse is so strong in each of them that they allow themselves to be carried away by the song of self, the song that they conceive not as condemning but as apologetic and justifying. In the bishop's own mind, he is an exemplary clergyman—"how I earned the prize!" He has met all the demands of religious formalism and been a Renaissance humanist to boot. What matter if he violated his priestly vow of celibacy or hated his brother clergyman? He has loved the blessed mutter of the Mass, felt the altar's candle flame, and tasted the strong incense smoke; he has lived with popes and cardinals and priests. What more could be expected of him? And now to crown his life, he must have a beautiful tomb as testimony not only to his Christian life but also to his superiority over his old rival, Gandolf. His sons may not give him what he deserves, but he wants to make clear that he has every right to it and is perfectly justified in whatever self-pity he may feel.

There is an obvious irony in all this. But the great irony is the poet's own intrusion into the monologue, an act that marks the monologue as a poem, calls attention to it as not merely the utterance of a Renaissance bishop but as a work of art. For Browning has designed the monologue as an exemplum, a sermon by example, on the text *Vanitas vanitatem,* the first line (in translation) of the monologue. "The Tomb at St. Praxed's" is thus a sermon unknowingly preached by the bishop; which is to say, the preacher proves his text by the revelation of his own character, and his plea for sympathy becomes a literary form—a sermon—that stands in judgment of him. A poet can hardly go further in achieving so subtly those reflections of the work of art in the work of art itself that characterize Romantic Irony. In brief, "The Bishop Orders His Tomb at St. Praxed's Church," the title by which it is now known, is a masterpiece. In future years Browning might add to the complexity of his dramatic monologues,[9] but he would never surpass the extraordinary ironic dimension of this poem.

The poems immediately following are of much smaller scale. "Garden Fancies" is composed of "The Flower's Name" and "Sibrandus Schafnaburgensis," both about language. In the first the speaker's lady has given to an inconspicuous flower without any obvious beauty "its soft meandering Spanish name: / What a name! was it love, or praise? / Speech half-asleep, or song half-awake?" Where "The Flower's Name" deals with the preservative power of language, the second deals with the uncreating word. The speaker recognizes the book by the author named in the title as the work of a pedant that may well be cast away. He places it in the crevice of the crotch of a plum tree, where it meets with all sorts of teeming animal life that mock the lifeless words. Finding this unquiet grave unfit, the speaker then takes the book to be buried on a bookshelf under other dead books by "A," "B," and "C" to "dry-rot at ease till the Judgment-day!"

The next two poems, with the joint title "France and Spain," are also concerned with language. In the first, "The Laboratory," words disguise the horror of the action: if the lady describes the poison with which she would kill her rival as beautiful, then it cannot be so bad to administer it. The lady, in fact, attempts by language to make murder a fine art. She is an innocent concerning the means to do her deed: "Which is the poison to poison her, prithee?" "And yonder soft phial, . . . —is that poison too?" And it is her very innocence, the quality of the ingenue, that gives a passionate intensity to her monologue and the hatred that it expresses.

Throughout her visit to the laboratory, the lady—wearing a mask of glass to ward off the noxious fumes as well as a mask of language to filter reality—acts as though she were inspecting a flower garden, asking the name of each and admiring its pretty color. This is, however, but the *vorspiel* to the main play. "Let death be felt and the proof remain; / . . . He is sure to remember her dying face!" she says, preparing the enactment of the drama that she is concocting. And for the man who has put together the requisite properties, she offers, with all the innocence and cold-bloodedness of a diva acting an ingenue: "Now, take all my jewels, gorge gold to your fill, / You may kiss me, old man, on my mouth if you will!"

In contrast to the dramatic monologue to which it is linked, "The Confessional" is more nearly a romance, the monologue of an imprisoned young woman who was tricked into revealing the secrets of her lover, a political revolutionary. The poem turns on the verb "to lie," in both its physical and linguistic meanings. Having lain with her lover, the girl is shocked to discover that his lips have "kissed / My soul out in a burning mist." She feels guilty not so much for the act of fornication as for the fact that physical love has supplanted religious love. Confessing her sexual transgressions to a priest, she is informed that she can "turn this love . . . / To lawful love, almost divine"; even further, she can be an angel to save the soul of her lover. All she has to do is ask of her paramour, when he "lies" upon her breast, his plans for political action, then steal off and reveal them to her confessor, who may then act to purge the lover's soul. Because her father confessor seemed full of "love and truth," she does as he wishes: her lover tells all, as she "lay listening in such pride," and she next morning trips off to the confessional "to save his soul in his despite." The result is that the young man is hanged. As the girl discovers his distorted body on the scaffold, she sees also, "lo,—on high—the father's face!" Now in prison, she turns her back entirely on religion. Clearly the truth for her is the physical "lying" of passionate lovers, not the "lying" of the Church.

There is a slight revelation of character in this confession, but it results more from the story than from the manner in which the story is told. The same is likewise true of "The Flight of the Duchess," which also shares the theme of loyalty. The poem seems to hesitate between the narrative and the dramatic modes. This was true of "Waring" of 1842, but as we saw, that poem finally comes down on the side of the dramatic. In the case of "The Flight of the Duchess," a much longer monologue recounting a more elaborate story, we can never be sure whether the interest should lie in *what* the speaker sees or *how* he sees. All commentators refer to it as narrative,[10] yet it has a dramatic setting and a dramatically portrayed speaker.

The monologue takes place in what seems to be a country tavern and is addressed to a long-suffering auditor who sits through 915 lines without saying a word. The speaker begins the story in a tone of beery confidence to his "friend," apparently a man he has never seen before. Now it may be that he has a design upon his auditor, for two matters, besides the story of the duchess, are very much on his tongue: drink, which he mentions at least twenty times, and friendship, which he praises frequently and which, to my ear at any rate, he protests too much. It may be that he tells the story of the duchess in hope of a free drink. If so, his hope seems to be unrealized because at the end he speaks of "no further throwing / Pearls before swine that can't value them: Amen"—which utterance may be intended to apply to the listener as well as to the duke.

We can have no assurance that we are to read the poem in this (dramatic) way—and I offer this interpretation unconfidently—because the poet has not, so far as I can see, given us enough clues. If it is merely a dramatic monologue *manqué,* the fault is perhaps owing to the difference between the original conception and the actual composition of the poem at a later date. Browning said that the idea of the poem grew out of a snatch of song he heard a gypsy singing. Some time soon thereafter he sat down to work on it but was called upon by a visitor and then other interruptions occurred so that he forgot the plan of the poem (Hood, *Letters,* p. 217). He told Miss Barrett that of "the real conception . . . not a line is written"

> —tho' perhaps after all, what I am going to call the accessories in the story are real though indirect reflexes of the original idea, and so supersede properly enough the necessity of its personal appearance,—so to speak: but, as I conceived the poem, it consisted entirely of the gipsy's description of the life the Lady was to lead with her future gipsy lover—a *real* life, not an unreal one like that with the Duke—and as I meant to write it, all their wild adventures would have come out and the insignificance of the former vegetation have been deducible only—as the main subject has become now. . . . (Kintner, 1:135)

It would appear, therefore, that having the story told by a retainer of the duke's household was an afterthought, which may account for the imperfect dramatic realization of the speaker.

The story itself is one common enough in Browning's later works—a woman rescued from a stultifying marriage to pursue a freer life of emotional fulfillment—but this is its first major expression. Commentators have argued that the poem was a calculated move in the poet's courtship of Elizabeth Barrett,[11] but as we have seen, something of the same pattern of movement is reflected in *Colombe's Birthday,* written and published before he even met his wife-to-be. Something happened to cause Browning to decide that he would admit the dialectic struggle between power and love to be irresolvable and that he would declare in favor of love, but showing it to retreat in the face of power. "The Flight of the Duchess" is the retelling of "My Last Duchess," the heroine this time, however, fleeing from the husband besotted by his family lineage. The gypsy woman who helps her escape assures her of "the thrill of the great deliverance," but such a life of love means to "retire apart" (671) from the ordinary world and all its responsibilities, as for Colombe and Valence it required retreat to flowery seclusion. In Browning's world love may no longer be a matter of pathology, but it is not one of healthy acceptance of the world. This is a point continually but unconsciously made by the narrator.

What the narrator proposes to recount is the duchess's tale "from beginning to end" (3). Yet it is the story of himself from start to almost finish. As far as the duchess is concerned, she does not even appear till line 133. The narrator then gives us a brief, straightforward, realistic account of the duke and of the duchess's unhappiness as his wife. But the realistic vein is soon transmuted as the old gypsy is metamorphosed from a crone into a stately woman who speaks with the sound of music and looks with beguiling eye to lend the duchess new life and transform her into a queen. Only at the end does the note of realism return, when he speaks of his dead wife and his duty to the duke. The world of the gypsies is but make-believe, one in which the fancied inhabitants live happily ever after, their story never coming to an end. The world of the huntsman, on the other hand, is all too real, lacking in picturesque adventure perhaps but not without its quiet pleasures, the domestic affections and loyalties that end (because being real they must end) only with death.[12] In romance the protagonist may depart into fancy to be a gypsy wanderer forever, but in the realistic tale, which is that of the huntsman, one "must stay till the end of the chapter" (861). In "The Flight of the Duchess," therefore, we have two versions of love and loyalty—one enclosed and the other open-ended—both of which we are in effect invited to see as true.

Like earlier works "The Flight of the Duchess" portrays characters self-consciously playing roles and speaking in accord with what they believe the scripts for those roles to be. The narrator presents himself as the plain man ready to tell a tale in an artistic fashion, even in verse, but limited by his halting manner—"More fault of those who had the hammering / Of prosady into me and syntax" (699–700). The duke is a product of Gothic Revival: a "middle-age manners adapter" (861) who talks and acts according to how "old books showed the way of it" and "how taught old painters in their pictures" (228, 231). In the cast of his little play, he is *The Duke,* his retainers are *Serfs, Thralls, Venerers, Prickers,* and *Verderers.* In reality he is effete, artificial, and anachronistic, so frozen in his role (and in a stultifying past) that his duchess, craving for real life, as Browning put it, cannot bear to live with him. Only in "Sibrandus Schafnaburgensis" does Browning so blatantly make fun of one of the characters in this volume.

"The Flight of the Duchess," although it has some of the same charming improvised air as "The Pied Piper," is not a successful poem because of its imperfectly realized narrator and because it is too long. It is, however, something of an experimental poem in that Browning employs in the opening lines a symbolic landscape.

> Ours is a great wild country;
> If you climb to our castle's top,
> I don't see where your eye can stop;
> For when you've pass'd the corn-field country,
> Where vineyards leave off, flocks are pack'd,
> And sheep-range leads to cattle-tract,
> And cattle-tract to open-chase,
> And open-chase to the very base
> Of the mountain where, at a funeral pace,
> Round about, solemn and slow,
> One by one, row after row,
> Up and up the pine-trees go,
> So, like black priests up, and so
> Down the other side again
> To another greater, wilder country,
> That's one vast red drear burnt-up plain,
> Branch'd thro' and thro' with many a vein

> Whence iron's dug, and copper's dealt;
> Look right, look left, look straight before,
> Beneath they mine, above they smelt,
> Copper-ore and iron-ore,
> And forge and furnace mould and melt,
> And so on, more and ever more,
> Till, at the last, for a bounding belt,
> Comes the salt sand hoar of the great sea shore,
> —And the whole is our Duke's country!
>
> (6–31)

The mixing of the agricultural and the industrial, the high and the low, the light and the dark, the open and the enclosed—all suggest the course the poem is to follow. This lovely piece of landscape painting is admittedly more or less forced on the huntsman's tale, but it is worthy of remark in that it shows Browning experimenting with more sophisticated modes of narration.[13]

In the first lyric of "Earth's Immortalities," the poet's grave—and by implication his reputation—"wants the freshness of its prime," the work of time having "softened down the crisp-cut name and date." In the second lyric the speaker, who may be the poet of the first, his initial line echoing the last word, "date," of the former,[14] notes how spring's garlands are severed by June's fever, which in turn is quenched in winter's snow—all in constant mockery of the words "Love me for ever!"[15] In "Song" ("Nay, but you, who do not love her"), the irony resides in a form of *praeterita*. In "The Boy and the Angel," the irony of God's need for the human is set forth in a simple lyric reminiscent of the manner of Blake.

The first lyric of "Night and Morning," now known as "Meeting at Night," is in the present tense and describes the lover's coming to meet his beloved, the rhythm and imagery suggesting tension and anticipation until the final coming to rest with "two hearts beating each to each." In the lyric now known as "Parting at Morning," which is one-third the length of the preceding one and which is related in the first person and in the past tense, there is no question of romantic love, as the speaker refuses to delude himself that rapture can sustain life: departing from the night's meeting, he declares "the need of a world of men."[16] "Claret and Tokay" are overly cute associations of certain wines with certain countries and are unworthy of mention save that they evince Browning's penchant for dramatizing everything, even bottles of claret and tokay.

"Saul" was printed as a fragment in 1845. It consisted of short half-lines instead of the anapestic pentameters with which we are now familiar, and it ended with the present section nine of the completed poem. These 102 lines, sung to the spiritually benumbed King Saul by the shepherd boy David, recall earth's beauties and bounties, great moments in Jewish history, his people's hymns of aspiration, the greatness of Saul's accomplishment—in short, all the things that Saul has to be thankful for. The matter and the manner of the song, largely a cataloguing of events and details, are doubtless borrowed from Christopher Smart, especially his "Song to David."[17] As it stands in 1845, the poem leaves us with the situation of a man who has everything to praise God for being unable to utter a word or even lift his eyes to heaven. Browning may not have been able to complete it either because after 102 lines he had exhausted the matter and manner of his model or because he had not in 1845 arrived at the stage of his religious development that would enable him to offer the Christian answer of the completed version.[18]

As a fragment (or even as a completed poem, for that matter), the monologue is generically unlike anything else in the 1845 volume. It is not a dramatic monologue because there is no revelation of character. It has a number of narrative elements, but clearly it is not primarily intended to tell a story. What it most nearly resembles is a Davidic psalm—and of course it would be very like Browning to have his David sing in the manner of the reputed author of Psalms.[19] In any case, the fragmentary "Saul" is a highly experimental poem, blending lyric, narrative, and dramatic elements in almost equal proportions. Browning recognized that some song of a different nature was required to bring Saul out of his lethargy and so complete the poem. The solution he eventually hit upon was to go beyond Psalms, as in the first nine sections he has gone beyond the Historical Books, to the Prophets; but that is a story for later telling, the completed poem not being published till 1855.

"Time's Revenges" deals with romantic love. On the one hand, the soliloquizer has a loyal friend who would go to any length of trouble for him but for whom he cares almost nothing. On the other hand, he has a ladylove who, although he has given up body and soul for her, not only would not help him in distress but would let him roast over a slow fire if this would procure her an invitation to a famous ball. In the end there is a balance of loyalties: his indifference to his friend is avenged by the indifference the lady shows toward him. Demanding obstacles to be erected and overcome so that he can prove himself "that sea / Of passion" which he "needs must be," the soliloquizer reminds us that every romantic lover is engaged in playing a role.

"Time's Revenges" is like a prelude to the next and last poem in the volume, for its ironies of loyalty and disloyalty are developed at greater length and with greater complexity in "The Glove." The poem is a dramatic monologue spoken by the French poet Pierre Ronsard at the court of Francis I. Browning makes daring use of him, for he has Ronsard report, accurately enough, the details of the central story yet be himself a not totally sympathetic or even reliable narrator. His use of the speaker is, then, slightly different from that of earlier dramatic monologues, for the speaker here tells a story in which he was not involved other than as a spectator and thus has no need to defend or apologize for himself where the details of that story are concerned. It is only when the speaker refers to himself and others in relation to him that we must be wary and carefully scrutinize what he has to say. In terms of genre this means that "The Glove" is a dramatic monologue incorporating a narrative that is the main business of the monologue. It is truly a *dramatic* romance. All this may be obvious enough, but I do not recall having read any commentary that questions the total reliability of the speaker and thus reads the poem as anything other than a narrative monologue or romance.

We have noted frequently the number of times that Browning calls attention to language as a mask for deception. In

"The Glove" he again cautions us, indirectly, to suspect ulterior meanings behind the words spoken by making rhetoric a dominant motif of the poem. Ronsard speaks as a buffoon, sounding like a cross between Samuel Butler and Thomas Hood; his words are rendered in fairly regular trimeter couplets all having feminine rhyme.[20] He accuses others of making "fine speeches like gold" (90), intending by the term to suggest the pretensions and triviality of the court. His harshest words, however, are reserved for the poet Clément Marot, whom he regards as a rival "whose experience of nature's but narrow, / And whose faculties move in no small mist" (46–47) and who is supposedly given to learned talk. Yet when the king asks for a verse, the best Ronsard can do is quote Ovid to the effect that "men are the merest Ixions" (14), whereupon the king interrupts to suggest that they go look at the lions. "Such," says Ronsard, "are the sorrowful chances / If you talk fine to King Francis" (17–18).[21] Further, he reports that when the lady departed after the glove episode, Marot stayed behind while he followed to ask "what it all meant" (119).[22] He goes up to her and says, "For I . . . am a Poet: / Human nature,—behooves that I know it!" (121–22). Surely such blatant posturizing (and such insipid rhymes) mark him as not much of a poet at all. Ronsard may not make "fine speeches like gold," but it may be because he is not capable of them. He may assume an ironic pose as a protest against the decadence of King Francis's court, but behind the pose there is little more than vacuity.

The lady's speech is rendered in somewhat irregular trimeter couplets all of male rhyme. Her speech sounds like human conversation instead of buffoonery. Although she holds views of mere words that seem to coincide with Ronsard's, we know that in her case they are not expressed simply for the benefit of others. The court is in fact depraved, from King Francis down. The talk is of superficialities or of views not truly held. Thus DeLorge wooed her with protestations of love and of his willingness to risk all danger for her sake. Too long she had heard "of the deed proved alone by the word" (124), so on the spur of the moment, as she reflected on what had been suffered by so many that the king might have a lion to look at as a sometime amusement, she decided to test DeLorge's words and threw the glove into the pit.

It is part of the irony of the tale that neither the lady nor Ronsard perceives that DeLorge's were not merely empty words. DeLorge had said that he would brave death if she commanded it, and when he leaps into the lion's pit to retrieve the glove she threw there, this is exactly what he does. The lady had thought to test his bravery or, rather, to discover the extent of his love by probing his courage. He proves his mettle, backs up word with deed, and does it, apparently, not only because the eyes of the court are upon him but also because of his regard for the lady and for the promises made to her. But her wanton disregard of his life causes him to question the object of that regard and, having fetched the glove, he gives public notice that he is through with her forever. The flinging of the glove into the lady's face is thus a symbolic act of praise and dispraise, of praise of himself for having endured the ordeal and dispraise of the one who forced such an ordeal upon him. As for the lady herself, she had every right to know whether her lover's protestations had any reality in deed. Yet from the trial she discovers his courage only to lose his love. It is worth noting that she makes no demands of her next lover to pass a similar test.

Objectively we have no reason to believe the lady more in the right than DeLorge. Most readers—all readers so far as I can find—see the right as belonging exclusively to the lady's side simply because the narrator says this is the way it should be. But as we have already noted, his is a flawed character, and we cannot accept what he says any more uncritically than we can accept what Browning's other narrators say. The king pronounces for the knight, saying, "'twas mere vanity, / Not love, set the task to humanity" (101–2). In a way his judgment is just as correct as Ronsard's, which is that the lady flung the glove so as "to know what she had *not* to trust to" (115). The fact that Marot does not go running after her the way Ronsard does also gives us additional reason for not fully accepting the speaker's view of the situation. This is again a case where, in Thirlwall's words quoted earlier, "characters, motives, and principles are brought into hostile collision, in which good and evil are so inextricably blended on each side, that we are compelled to give an equal share of our sympathy to each. . . . "

The story of the subsequent marriages of DeLorge and the lady to other people does not help us to come down finally on the side of one or the other. Ronsard says that the lady carried her shame from the court and married a youth of lower social status. The court foresees unhappiness in this mixed marriage, but "to that marriage some happiness" Ronsard "dared augur" (169–70). We wonder whether we can trust his prophecy any more than the court's.

As for DeLorge, he married a renowned beauty, who eventually became King Francis's mistress for a week. DeLorge, now serving the king not as knight but as courtier, is frequently "honored" with the commission to fetch his wife's gloves from her chamber while the king is in conversation with her. When DeLorge appears with the gloves, the king always tells the story of this modern Daniel in the lion's den and his wife always says that nowadays he brings the gloves and "utters no murmur" (188). Obviously Ronsard includes this story to show how DeLorge has been placed in the ignominious position of assisting the king to enjoy his wife's favor and, further, been subjected to pleasantries upon his discomfiture. DeLorge's marital distress may be a fact, but does this in any way validate the lady's wanton demand that he enter a lion's cage to retrieve her glove?

As we have already seen, Browning frequently arranges the final lines of a dramatic monologue as a summation of a character or situation. Here in the last two lines of "The Glove" he does more or less the same thing. "*Venienti occurrite morbo*! / With which moral I drop my theorbo," says Ronsard in farewell. This piece of macaronic verse is a fitting summation of the character who has told us the story. First, it suggests the "fine" writer *manqué*, one retreating into doggerel and burlesque to show his contempt for what he cannot do but nevertheless employing the learned language that he makes fun of his rival Marot for using. Second, the Latin proverb offered as the moral is not a particularly felicitous one.[23] "Go to meet the approaching ill"? Far more apropos as a moral would have been the scriptural counsel *Sufficit diei malitia sua*. Third, the theorbo, the lute with two necks, suggests the two contending strains of the narrative that merge into the song, the dramatic lyric, which is "The Glove."[24]

As a dramatic monologue recounting a tale of opposing loyalties, "The Glove" fittingly brings the *Dramatic Romances and Lyrics* to a close. Thematically all the poems—with the possible exception of "Claret and Tokay," which themselves may be about national loyalties—are concerned with many kinds of loyalties. In manner all are dramatic. In range of subject matter and prosody, they are enormously variegated. To this extent the 1845 poems bear a strong resemblance to the *Dramatic Lyrics* of 1842. The difference between the two volumes lies in the greater complexity of the *Dramatic Romances and Lyrics*. For here Browning makes his poems more allusive, more densely packed with different levels of meaning. In "The Bishop Orders His Tomb," for example, there is not only a perfect evocation of what Ruskin called the Renaissance spirit but also an implied comment on contemporary Anglo-Catholic ritualism. Or, to take another instance, "The Italian in England" is not only a celebration of the patriot typified by Mazzini[25] but a study of the stultifying effect of exile for the political revolutionary. A large number of the poems in *Dramatic Romances and Lyrics* deal with contemporary matters—the Corn Laws, the hunger and poverty of the 1840s, Puseyism, the laureateship, Austrian domination of Italy—of general concern in 1845. In short, the poet was turning toward a sociocultural scene to make meaning. But he was not thereby forgoing irony. For he gives us an ironic reading of society and history embodied in a form that only superficially is a little less extravagant than that of *Sordello* and *Pippa Passes*.

In *Dramatic Romances and Lyrics*, Browning perfected the dramatic monologue. Though hereafter he was to write other exquisite monologues, they were formally to be but variations on those in this collection. Perceiving the quality of Browning's achievement, Walter Savage Landor wrote and published, in the *Morning Chronicle* for 22 November 1845, one of the most generous compliments ever paid by one poet to another.

> There is delight in singing, tho' none hear
> Beside the singer: and there is delight
> In praising, tho' the praiser sit alone
> And see the prais'd far off him, far above.
> Shakespeare is not our poet, but the world's,
> Therefore on him no speech! and brief for thee,
> Browning! Since Chaucer was alive and hale,
> No man hath walkt along our road with step
> So active, so inquiring eye, or tongue
> So varied in discourse. But warmer climes
> Give brighter plumage, stronger wing: the breeze
> Of Alpine highths thou playest with, borne on
> Beyond Sorrento and Amalfi, where
> The Siren waits thee, singing song for song.

Landor recognized that by 1845 his friend had become "Browning," a name to be listed, along with Shakespeare and Chaucer, among the greatest English poets.

CHAPTER IX
LURIA AND *A SOUL'S TRAGEDY*

UPON COMPLETION OF *COLOMBE'S BIRTHDAY*, Browning had intended to "stop some things that were meant to follow, and begin again" (*Domett*, p. 106). Now that he had "begun again" and published *Dramatic Romances and Lyrics*, he returned to those pieces that were meant to follow. "I have one done here, 'A Soul's Tragedy,' " he told Elizabeth Barrett early in their correspondence (Kintner, 1:26). It but needed revision. Another he had been thinking about: "this darling 'Luria'—so safe in my head & a tiny slip of paper" (Kintner, 1:18). Yet however "darling" *Luria* might be in conception, the poet had little pleasure in the actual writing of it, and it was not finished till more than a year later. Even though he had lost interest in the drama as a literary form, Browning felt that he had to complete these two plays. They had to be "got rid of," he told Miss Barrett. Some things "I should like to preserve and print now, leaving the future to spring as it likes, in any direction,—and these half-dead, half-alive works fetter it, if left behind" (Kintner, 1:77, 451). And to his friend Alfred Domett, he wrote: "I felt so instinctively . . . that unless I tumbled out the . . . conceptions, I should bear them forever, and year by year get straiter and stiffer . . . , and at last parturition would be the curse indeed" (*Domett*, p. 127).

By 1845 Browning had written and published five plays for the theater, only two of which had been produced on the stage, and they with but indifferent success. He had had a serious falling out with Macready, and he had become convinced of the stupidity of theatrical folk in general. It "never entered into my mind," he wrote to a friend about Charles Kean and the possible production of *Colombe's Birthday*, "that anybody, even an actor, could need a couple of months to study a part, only, in a piece, which I could match with another in less time by a good deal" (Hood, *Letters*, p. 10). In addition, his growing aversion to the theater was encouraged by Miss Barrett, who frankly told him, "I have wondered at you sometime, not for daring, but for bearing to trust your noble works into the great mill of the 'rank, popular' playhouse, to be ground to pieces between the teeth of vulgar actors and actresses." "And what is *Luria*?" she asked hopefully, "A poem and not a drama?" (Kintner, 1:22).

Browning appears already to have made up his mind to quit writing for the theater by the time he began correspondence with Miss Barrett. In any event, answering her question he replied: "That 'Luria' you enquire about, shall be my last play..for it is but a play, woe's me!" (Kintner, 1:26). But, in extenuation, it was to be "for a purely imaginary Stage" (Kintner, 1:251). Moreover, though originally conceived "in the 'high fantastical' style," it was to be "very simple and straightforward," an antidote to "the general charge against me . . . of abrupt, spasmodic writing" (Kintner, 1:251, 281). The play was finished in February 1846, and although he had doubts about the wisdom of publishing *Luria* and *A Soul's Tragedy* together, he began reworking the earlier play upon completion of *Luria*. The two were published in April 1846 as the eighth and last number of *Bells and Pomegranates*, with a dedication to Walter Savage Landor stating that these two pieces were his "last attempts for the present at dramatic writing."

Echoing the preface to *Strafford*, in which he described his historical play as "one of Action in Character, rather than Character in Action," Browning said of *Luria*: "It is all in long speeches—the *action, proper*, is in them—they are no descriptions, or amplifications—but there..in a drama of this kind, all the *events*, (and interest), take place in the *minds* of the actors" (Kintner, 1:381). But if *Luria* and *Strafford* are alike in having psychological action as the central dramatic action, the general dramatic method of the two plays is, however, far different. Where the earlier is based on Elizabethan models, the later owes more to neoclassical drama, especially in its focus on one character and its observance of the unities of time, place, and action.[1] Moreover, with its long speeches and its dramatic emphasis upon one character, *Luria* reflects Browning's increasing dedication to the monologue form.[2] "I have a fancy that your great dramatic power would work more clearly &

audibly in the less definite mould," Elizabeth Barrett told him (Kintner, 1:30). Hereafter Browning was to heed her advice and his own inclination to work outside the formal drama.

As we have noted, tragedy does not easily accommodate Browning's kind of irony. The poet himself was perhaps more aware of this than ever while working on *Luria*. Describing his protagonist and his other characters, Browning admitted that "for me, the misfortune is, I sympathize just as much with these as with him" (Kintner, 1:26). Such divided loyalties could not easily be forced into tragedy, which calls for a hero clearly superior in nearly every way to those around him. It is perhaps not unduly fanciful to say that in *Luria* Browning undertakes to consider the very question that his aesthetic problem posed: What is the nature of the hero in a society (or a literary form) that does not accept him?

In *The Return of the Druses*, Browning had portrayed a hero who discovers his true heroism in trying to prove it to others. In *Luria*, on the other hand, he presents a hero whose noble deeds are obvious and whose greatness in battle is acclaimed by all yet who in all likelihood is to be refused the hero's laurels by those very persons whom he saves. Doubtlessly lurking in Browning's mind during the composition of *Luria* were not only his own thoughts about the lack of appreciation awarded him as a poet but also many ideas on the great man expounded by Carlyle, earlier in the decade, in the lectures *On Heroes and Hero-Worship*.[3] When a savior appears to a people standing on the brink of direst peril, what is his fate among those he saves?[4] Consideration of this question is the means by which Browning once again studies the dialectic of power and love.

Puccio calls Luria "the quiet patient hero" (4. 50) who hastened to the city's call "to save her as only he could" (1. 24). Domizia pronounces Luria the unselfconscious "saviour" (1. 264): "Such save the world which none but they could save, / Yet think whate'er they did, that world could do" (1. 355–56). Like all true heroes he was sent by God in response to an extreme need. "Time was for thee to rise, and thou art here," she tells him (4. 216). Luria has brought "new feeling fresh from God" for the people "to mould, interpret and prove right" (5. 264–65). His life reteaches what life should be, what faith, loyalty, and simpleness are—qualities once revealed in the Incarnation of Christ, but this so long ago that there is but a tradition of the fact, not a felt experience of the fact, "truth copied falteringly from copies faint." In Luria the people see the old truth return (5. 266–78).

Braccio, on the other hand, is highly suspicious of "those same great ones," finding that with all their "unconsciousness" they nonetheless never shrink from taking up whatever offices that involve "the whole world's safety or mishap / Into their mild hands [as] a thing of course" (1. 357–63). Holding society more important than any individual, Braccio says that Florence cannot tolerate so-called great men: they crave power and thus must somehow be subjugated to society immediately upon the victories achieved for the sake of society (3. 177–202, 256–70). Tiburzio, the Pisan general, is without illusions as to the fate of heroes. In saving Florence, Luria seeks "the sure destruction saviours find" (2. 185). Pisa would treat him in a similar way had the outcome of the battle been different (2. 231–37). But, in contrast to Braccio, Tiburzio believes in the superiority of the hero to the herd. For great men serve "as models for the mass" and thus "are singly of more value than they all." Hero worship is hence something like a religious duty because, as Carlyle said, history is a series of great men who bring authentic tidings from God. Lives of great men remind the mass that they too can make their lives sublime: "Keep but the model safe, new men will rise / To study it . . . " (5. 300–310).

While others put their faith in the hero, Luria holds by Florence as the embodiment of all that man can hope for. In fact, Florence "stands for Mankind" (2. 242). He "believes in Florence as the Saint / Tied to the wheel believes in God" (1. 108–9). Florence is for Luria, Browning told Miss Barrett, "his religion" (Kintner, 1:411). When Luria speaks of the city, he does so "as the Mage Negro King to Christ the Babe" (1. 382–83). Because he is "nearer Florence than her sons" and has made her the symbol of all that makes life worthwhile, the very thought that Florence can betray him is extremely unsettling. For if the city fails him, he has nothing left to believe in or fight for (2. 243–49). "What would be left, the life's illusion,— / What hope or trust in the forlorn wide world?" (4. 266–67).

Earlier we have noted the numerous instances in which a male lover submits to his "queen," whom he urges to exert her power over him. In *Luria* the hero still has the same need for power to be incarnated, but here it is a city-state that he devises to make "queen / Of the country" (5. 45–46).[5] He laments his new position of general officer who must stand aloof from battle, wishing instead to have remained a captain who has all the joy of the fight. In the inferior post he would have felt, in someone over him, "Florence impersonate," a "visible Head," and thus be able to take "life / Directly from her eye" (1. 277–84). Luria is, however, a Moor, not a Florentine; and although he has experienced the thrill of coming to Florence, being changed by her, and "feeling a soul grow . . . that restricts / The boundless unrest of the savage heart" (1. 321–24), the fact remains, says his friend Husain, that there stands a wall between their "expansive and explosive race / And those absorbing, concentrating men" of Florence. For Luria as for Browning's earlier heroes, the tension between expansion and contraction must remain unresolved. For all his love of Florence, he can never truly be a Florentine anymore than Othello, his prototype, can be a Venetian.[6]

Luria is not content, however, to remain simply a Moor in Florence; he and Florence must be one. "Incompleteness, incompleteness!" he wails (1. 238). Power and love, Luria and Florence—he would have all "decisive and complete" (1. 244). Thus he superimposes a Moorish design on the facade of the still incomplete Duomo, "his fancy how a Moorish front / Might join to, and complete, the body" (1. 124–25). But working against Luria's aspiration for wholeness are the forces of reality, personified in Braccio, who finds that "the Moorish front ill suits our Duomo's body" and thus commands, "Blot it out!" (1. 210–11).

The play dramatizes Luria's gradual discovery that the kind of Sordelloesque wholeness he aspires to is unattainable. What he learns is what Paracelsus learned just before his death: that in the state of becoming that characterizes all life, things can never remain the same, that one thing is always replacing another:

> e'en tho' better follow, good must pass,
> Nor manhood's strength can mate with boyhood's grace,
> Nor age's wisdom in its turn find strength,
> But silently the first gift dies away,
> And tho' the new stays—never both at once!
> (2. 272-76)

There is indeed a barrier between himself and Florence and the Florentines (3. 393–95). The East is distinguished by feeling, the North by thought. Instead of bringing the virtues of the East to the North, he should have chosen the reverse "mission" of bringing the North to the East, "giving Thought's character and permanence / To the too-transitory Feelings there— / Writing God's message in mortal words!" (5. 250–52).

But even though he doubts the validity of his own role, he never allows himself to question his conception of Florence. For if the union of love and power cannot be realized in his own life, at least he must guard, as a necessity of his own psychic well-being, the idea that somewhere they are indeed joined. Time after time he has opportunity to investigate Florence's intentions with respect to him, and just as often he refuses to inquire further lest his ideal collapse into a meaningless illusion. In the end he decides that it would not serve his soul to destroy its allegiance to its highest dream. He kills himself so that Florence, the city in which he has placed all his faith and which has become the spiritual basis of his life, will not prove, in its execution of him, other than what he believed her to be. Taking a phial of poison, he drinks to the salvation of the city and the maintenance of his dream of her: thus "*we* Florentines" can serve "*our* Florence" (4. 306, 304; emphasis added). The irony of loyalty, a constant theme in all Browning's plays, here becomes pure absurdity.

Luria is fully aware that mankind can stand only so much reality, which means that he is conscious of the unreality of many of his actions and those of others. This in turn means that he sees himself as acting a role in a play, a conviction that he shares with the other characters. The basic play may have been written elsewhere and by someone else, but it is Braccio who is seen by Luria and the others as the *metteur en scène* and reviser of the script. "What you created," Luria says to him, "see that you find food for" (1. 337). In *Luria* as in *Colombe's Birthday*, papers and documents are not only theatrical properties but also parts of the text, Braccio here providing most of them to keep the action going.

The text begins with this stage direction: "*Braccio, as dictating to his Secretary*"; and with this bit of dialogue: Braccio asking Puccio to read over the commissary's account of the soldier's report. As the dialogue develops, Puccio notes that the report does not contain any praise of Luria, the new commander of the Florentine forces, whereupon Braccio incorporates this into his text. When Puccio departs, however, Braccio, according to the stage directions, "*slowly tears the paper into shreds.*" The action in these first fifty lines is emblematic of the action of the entire play, its scripts, and (borrowing a word from *Colombe's Birthday*) rescripts. Braccio constantly writes and revises, yet all the while recognizing the absurdity of his reports, which are mere exercises in the art of fiction, means by which he manipulates his readers of the Florentine Signory to act in the way he wants. All these "proofs," he says, "weigh with me less than least; as nothing weigh!" He alters his text so as to prevent certain results and to bring about others: "I go! / On what I know must be, yet while I live / Will never be" (1. 185–89).

The extraordinary aspect of these constant inquiries and reports is that all the characters seem to know that Braccio is setting down words that do not accurately reflect their past actions but that will determine how they act in future. Luria, for example, comes unexpectedly upon Braccio discoursing with his secretary, Jacopo: "it was in that paper / What you were saying!" Braccio frankly admits, "I censure you to Florence: will you see?" But Luria refuses to read it because if he did so Braccio would simply write another to mention "that important circumstance" (1. 217–24). In a more prominent instance, Tiburzio presents Luria with one of Braccio's captured dispatches to read. "And act on what I read?" (2. 240). He refuses to read it because to do so would mean following a script, even though the script means that certain actions will be eventually imposed upon him. Although he has "the means / Of knowing what his reward will be" (2. 317–18), he tears the letter up. This is in Luria's mind doubtless an act of defiance and assertion of free will, yet even he knows that, whatever his action in this instance, the script remains in a duplicate copy and that, willy-nilly, he must act in accord with it. All the characters have a sense of fate at work in their lives that predestines them to the enactment of roles assigned them, either with or against their wills. All may declare, as Puccio does, that they refuse to live "on orders, warrants, patents and the like" (5. 101), but they nevertheless feel that they have little scope for evasion of the words that control their actions.

Even though Luria wishes to be Florentine, he is consigned by Braccio to the role of "our inevitable foe," no matter how much he may engage in "mere dissimulation" of another role (1. 155, 374). Luria cannot be allowed to show himself as a victorious Florentine general; it would be a serious miscasting of the part: "the black face, the barbarous name, / For Italy to boast her show of the age, / Her man of men!" (1. 389–91). Domizia likewise agrees that such casting of the role is more than slightly amiss: "black faces in the camp / Where moved those peerless brows and eyes of old!" (2. 51–52).

His friend Husain argues that Luria is being forced to play a certain role: "They use thee"; they "fashion thee anew"; they say, "here shalt thou move" (2. 84, 113, 121). And Luria, recently become aware that the Florentines will never accept him in the part he wants to play, agrees that "an alien force like mine / Is only called to play its part outside / Their different nature" (2. 85–87). Now that he has acted that role, he will depart from the stage: "my use is over, . . . 'tis best I go" (2. 97–98). Whatever his desires to the contrary, he will remain "the Moor" (3. 398). "So at the last must figure Luria then!" (4. 248).

Where Braccio plays the schemer who revises the script to suit his convenience—the type of wily Florentine epitomized by Machiavelli—his secretary, Jacopo, is merely the amanuensis and witness of the action: "I observe / The game, watch how my betters play" (4. 4–5). Puccio realizes that he himself is but a kind of puppet whose strings are pulled by Braccio (4. 6–11). "I am," he tells the commissary,

> as you have made me, and shall die
> A mere trained fighting hack to serve your end;
> With words, you laugh at while they leave your mouth,
> For my life's rules and ordinance of God!
> (4. 64–67)

Domizia, who seeks vengeance against Florence for the harm done her family, regards herself as a talented player of the role of intriguer, but in reality her part is allotted to her by Braccio, who has had her posted to the camp so that he can oversee her actions (1. 172–75).

The last act brings a reversal in the roles of the principals. Luria himself comes to the conclusion that his "natural" role is his best: "I, born a Moor, lived half a Florentine; / But, properly punished, can die a Moor" (5. 209–10). Domizia, forswearing the use of Luria as an agent of her vengeance, is now become "another woman" (5. 184) who gives her love to him. Puccio turns against his puppeteer and vows no longer to live according to how the strings are pulled but be his own man and follow Luria into exile or death (5. 100–12). Jacopo will no longer "move with Braccio as the masterwind" but "must move" with Luria (5. 172–74). Braccio himself tells "in just a word the whole": his past errors and his new belief in Luria as one as capable of the exercise of love as of power (5. 321–33).

Browning said that "the last act throws light back on all" (Kintner, 1:411). Doubtless he meant that the reversal in act five is designed to point up the ironic difference between the way things are and the way they could be. In the grand scheme of things, there is gradual progress in the "soul" of mankind, and one day it may be that human potentialities for good will be realized. "All now is possible," Braccio tells Luria, only at that very moment to discover that the general is dead. Luria himself makes the better judgment: "If one could wait! The only fault's with Time: / All men become good creatures...but so slow!" (5. 180–81). To try to hurry the process—for the "lesser," as Luria calls it, to ape the "greater"—is, in existential and theatrical terms, to play a role for which one has no natural talent and thus to be miscast.

Miss Barrett was puzzled by the last act. She lamented Luria's suicide as unheroical, for example. "But you are a dramatic poet & right perhaps, where, as a didactic poet, you would have been wrong" (Kintner, 1:406). Browning replied that if the character is properly drawn, Luria stands "in such a position as to render any other end impossible without the hurt to Florence which his religion is, to avoid inflicting . . . : his aim is to prevent the harm she will do herself by striking him—so he moves aside from the blow—But I know there is much to improve and heighten . . . " (Kintner, 1:411). Apparently the poet had at this time not yet decided to have Florence's judgment of his hero made known. It is, of course, an additional irony for the protagonist to learn that his dream of Florence that he kills himself to preserve is not a dream after all, that in fact his suicide is pointless; but such an ending is uncharacteristically Browningesque. Ever since *Paracelsus* the poet had taken an ambiguous attitude towards the nature of destiny in the near future. As "a dramatic poet" he had shown that it is the condition of human existence for man not to know the truth of his "religion." But evidently, whether because of the influence of Miss Barrett or not, Browning was becoming "a didactic poet" and thereby reducing the ironic tensions of his work.

There are, nevertheless, tensions that are as much in evidence here as in the earlier works. The difference is that here Browning comes down more in favor of one position than of the other and leaves us with none of those tantalizing questions that occur at the end of even so late a play as *Colombe's Birthday*, in which power is left to travel its weary way without love and love is left to live in seclusion without social responsibility. In *Luria* the conflict between feeling and reason, a form of the contention between love and power, is resolved, and there is no question that the resolution is not the correct one. Puccio decides for the "glowing eye . . . / To glance straight inspiration to [his] brain" (5. 102–3). Jacopo, who "used to hold by the instructed brain," finds that "the heart leads surelier" (5. 172, 174). Domizia renounces scheming for "new feeling" (5. 265). Braccio admits "his old great error" of placing all his faith in man's power of reason. Luria says in his "own East" the people are "nearer God" and feel "the everlasting minute of creation" (5. 228–33). Feeling is of course transitory and hence needs "thought's character and permanence" (5. 251–52), but there is no doubt that feeling is superior to thought. In the end the play is unequivocal in pronouncing that though the "completeness" for which Luria, like Sordello, was seeking may not be attainable, the best form of "incompleteness" lies in the recognition of the superiority of feeling to reason, of the individual to society, of love to power.

The play is, as Elizabeth Barrett characterized it, complete (Kintner, 2:569); it is fully enclosed and therefore least like Browning, who had shown plainly, time after time over the past eleven years, that completeness can be achieved only at the cost of vitality. Through act four *Luria* proceeds along typical Browningesque lines, though without a character like D'Ormea, Guendolyn, or Guibert to point up the ironies of the action. But then act five, with its wholesale conversions, brings matters to the rounded close of tragedy. Browning recognized that it was wrong: the play, he said, "is a pure exercise of *cleverness* . . . —clever attempted reproductions of what was conceived by another faculty, and foolishly let pass away" (Kintner, 1:551). While writing the tragedy, he had Elizabeth Barrett foremost in his mind and apparently tried to write the kind of ("didactic") play she would like: "I say . . . in excuse to myself,—unlike the woman at her spinning-wheel, 'he thought of his *flax* on the whole far more than of his singing'—more of his life's sustainment, of dear, dear Ba . . . , than of these wooden figures—no wonder all is as it is!" (Kintner, 1:551).[7]

A Soul's Tragedy, the second piece in the last number of *Bells and Pomegranates*, is almost totally different from *Luria* in structure, theme, and mode. Composed of two parts (later called acts) like *King Victor and King Charles*, and dealing with a protagonist without principles or illusions, it is, in spite of its name, not a tragedy but a comedy. Unlike *Luria*, *A Soul's Tragedy* has, Browning told Miss Barrett, "no trace of you . . . —you have not put out the black face of *it*—it is all sneering and disillusion" (Kintner, 1:451). Though, as we shall see, the play may contain more of Miss Barrett than Browning consciously knew, it nonetheless stands in sharpest contrast to the first in the pamphlet and indeed at times seems almost a parody of it.

In *A Soul's Tragedy* heroes and heroism are matters not of serious concern but for quiet amusement. The populace are only too willing to proclaim anyone who even appears heroic as "our saviour," "thrice-noble saviour" (1. 377, 2. 5–6). "Come forth to counsel us, our chief, our king," they say. "Come and harangue us in the market-place!" (1. 387, 390). No wonder that Ogniben appears humming "Why do the people clamor?" (2. 95). The acclaimed savior, however, is a fraud, and the real hero is unrecognized. Only when a wise man comes to view the situation is the charlatan sent packing.

Chiappino is proclaimed a hero simply because he acts like one. For years he wore the "coarse disguise" of the beaten man beset by troubles from all sides (1. 338). His "tongue was tied" because of the position in which he found himself, while others of "slight, free, loose and incapacious soul" might give their tongues "scope to say whate'er [they] would" (1. 188, 170–71). In fact, silence is the only possession that he can lay claim to (1. 20–21). His "part" is to play the martyr as others enjoy the "parts" of the privileged (1. 135). It is, however, he himself who writes the script for the play enacted, as he recites his fancy of what the world says about himself and Luitolfo (1. 58–89), what Luitolfo tells the provost and Luitolfo's report of the interview (2. 212–14), what the city will say concerning his banishment (1. 221–27), and what Luitolfo will say upon his return to the house (1. 275–89). But suddenly when he sees the opportunity to portray the strong man, he ceases to be a "mere accomplice" (1. 356) and becomes the chief actor: "I am master here," he twice says (1. 337, 352). Now in a new part, "I can't be silent..I must speak..or sing— / How natural to sing now" (1. 360–61). "Here they come, crowds! . . . If they would drag one to the market-place / One might speak there!" (1. 371, 374–75). And that is precisely where he is invited to address them and speak the words appropriate for their "saviour." Hereafter Chiappino interests himself only in "performance" and "public appearance" (2. 298, 371). As we shall see, "profession" and "principle" are of no importance for such "performing natures" (2. 311).

Part one is called "The Poetry of Chiappino's Life." Because of this designation and because of the title of the play itself, commentators on the work see it as the tragedy "about a great mind and soul turning to ill."[8] It may be that Chiappino's taking the blame for the attack on the provost is altruistic, but this seems unlikely in that there is no evidence anywhere earlier of altruism in Chiappino's nature. He takes Luitolfo's place because he wants to exhibit himself as the doer of heroic deeds. Better to receive "men's vengeance" than to be at best a "mere accomplice" in exile (1. 355–56). Part one is the poetry of Chiappino's life because in it he is given the chance to "speak..or sing" at last (1. 360).[9] Finally he has a proper stage on which to perform. To be sure, there is the opportunity even in this deception for the "soul" to grow, but Chiappino does not avail himself of it.

Part two is called the "Prose" of Chiappino's life because in it the would-be singer is shown to be but a noisy speaker of empty rhetoric. It is Ogniben who appears singing, "thro' the streets humming a '*cur fremuêre gentes*' " (95). Where Chiappino's is a song of self, Ogniben's is the song of ironic humor. Chiappino claims to possess a "soul that can perceive / The outward and the inward, nature's good / And God's" (1. 262–64). The claimed wholeness of insight leads him to speak "in praise of a pure Republic" and "a perfect State" (2. 138, 240) and of Eulalia as the female embodiment of beauty, virtue, and wisdom whom he will love forever. Yet when offered the provostship, he accepts with alacrity, justifying his action by arguing that he changes no principles, only adapts them. And when Eulalia charges that he does not love her as he claimed, he replies that his "soul's capacity for love widens—needs more than one object to control it,—and being better instructed, will not persist in seeing all the component parts of love in what is only a single part,—nor in finding the so many and so various loves united in the love of a woman" (2. 264-70). In the character of Chiappino, all avowed love yields at the drop of a hat to a craven wish for power; profession but serves as a mask for performance.

It is the "humour" of Ogniben to unmask Chiappino's professions and show them up for what they really are. "I help men to carry out their principles," he says. "If they please to say two and two make five, I assent, if they will but go on and say four and four make ten" (2. 365-68). He judges people by what they might be, not are or will be; thus inverting the cliché, he values men not by their performances but by what they profess. And acting on this premise, he proceeds to show that Chiappino fails more in profession than in performance, however reprehensible that performance might be. "Observe, I speak only as you profess to think and so ought to speak—I do justice to your own principles, that is all" (2. 480-82). For, ironically, it is Chiappino's fault to profess too much. He aspires to a *pure* republic when obviously in sixteenth-century Italy such a government has no hope of realization; he can only love "a woman that could understand the whole of me" when, says Ogniben, such a one who could "comprehend you" must necessarily be "not merely as great as yourself, but greater considerably" (2. 349-50, 339-43). His professions exceed the possibility of performance and thus he must fail, whereas Luitolfo, who professes only "standing stockishly, plodding soberly, suffering . . . with due patience" (2. 641-44), succeeds.

Unexpectedly and ironically it is the "prose" part of Chiappino's life that contains the amusing good sense of Ogniben, whom Browning characterized to Miss Barrett as "a man of wide speculation" with "universal understanding of men and sympathy with them" (Kintner, 2:579).[10] Ogniben speaks only in prose, yet clearly his prose is much wiser than Chiappino's verse. He touches on almost all the ideas dear to his author's heart: the futility of aspirations for wholeness and completeness, progress through contradiction, the eventual unfolding of the good, the changing nature of truth, the importance of point of view in the evaluation of a person, event, or object, the inadequacy of language to express truth. But Browning feared that the essential seriousness of Ogniben might be overlooked, and in one version of the play, he had the legate deliver "a huge kind of sermon" on "the belief in a future state . . . [which] modifies every feeling derivable from this present life" (Kintner, 1:546, 2:579). Miss Barrett agreed that this was a felicitious omission, but Browning still felt that a "proper objection" could be made "to the immediate, *first* effect of the whole—its moral effect,—which is dependent on the contrary supposition of its being really understood, in the main drift of it" (Kintner, 1:455).

Hitherto, I believe, the poet would not have been so interested in the moral effect as the *first* effect. Now, however, he was unwilling to allow the morality of the work to emerge from an understanding of its irony. He therefore felt it necessary to have his spokesman define the moral boundaries of irony. Thus Ogniben praises "discovering much good on the worse side" but then goes on to say "that the same process should proportionately magnify and demonstrate to you the much more good on the better side!" Thus he approves that "a large nature should sympathize with every form of intelligence" but maintains that one should "preserve the proportions of [one's] sympathy." Thus he applauds the ability to "descry beauty in corruption where others see foulness only" but insists that one should also "see a redoubled beauty in the higher forms, where already everybody sees no foulness at all" (2. 461–75).[11] In such passages Ogniben (as well as Browning) becomes more of a moralist than an ironist. He seems to change roles, which movement prompts Chiappino to ask: "Do you begin to throw off your mask?" (2. 594). Indeed, at the end he is not so much the man who loves "composing differences" (2. 108) by employing a kind of Socratic irony as the homilist who puts the finishing touch to a sermon on the text "Let who thinketh he standeth take heed lest he fall" (2. 653–54).

Ogniben's rhetorical irony leads to an ending in which all loose strands are tied up. The lovers Luitolfo and Eulalia are reunited, and the deceiver departs "out of sight" (683). Power rests with Ogniben, who commands "unlimited obedience to

Rome's authority in my person" (600–601). Love and power are left in separate hands, but here there is no suggestion that, as in *Colombe's Birthday*, one without the other will be diminished. Luitolfo and Eulalia will live happily ever after, neither ever having wanted power in the first place; they are content to be "undivided, whatever be [their] fortune" (647–48). Love is enough. In the case of power, the former provost, who apparently had misued power, is overthrown; and its present representative is a benign and wise priest, for whom sexual love was never a question and whose last words are a benediction: "And now gives thanks to God, the keys of the Provost's Palace to me, and yourselves to profitable meditation at home." The sermon is ended; the play is fully enclosed.

Elizabeth Barrett was full of admiration for *A Soul's Tragedy:* "Why it is full of hope for both of us, to look forward & consider what you may achieve with that combination of authority over the reasons & the passions. . . . " She objected only that Ogniben seemed "too wise for a crafty worlding" (Kintner, 2:569). Clearly it was the thought and the morality of part two that appealed to her. It may or may not be that Browning gave it the strong moral twist at the end to please her.[12] But it is evident that as he was bidding farewell to the formal drama he was becoming a poet less willing to allow his work to unfold in the same ironic fashion that had characterized his poetry since the time of *Sordello*. "If I had not known you *so far* THESE works might have been the *better*," Browning told his future wife. "If you take a man from prison and set him free..do you not probably cause a signal interruption to his previous all-ingrossing occupation, and sole labour of love, of carving bone-boxes, making chains of cherry-stones, and other such time beguiling operations—does he ever take up that business with the old alacrity?" His plays had, he says by implication, been but time-serving. Now he is ready for more serious enterprise, to begin "Ploughing, building (castles . . . , no bone-boxes now)" (Kintner, 2:580).

One can hardly regret that Browning gave up writing formal drama. Indeed, one is inclined to view the plays as a distraction from what the poet should properly have been about—writing poems. For though there are some excellent parts in nearly every one of the seven plays, none of them—I am, of course, excluding *Pippa Passes*—is entirely successful. But the reason for their failure is not, I think, the one usually offered—that they are lacking in action or plot.[13] This might have been a relevant objection in the early Victorian period, when audiences were yet unaccustomed to psychological action as the basic dramatic action. But nowadays, when Beckett's and Pinter's plays are standard pieces in the theatrical repertory everywhere, who cares about the kind of action, "Character in Action," which Browning's dramas so obviously and admittedly lack? No, this can no longer be a valid objection. What is wrong with them in my opinion is that they are cast in the wrong mold, tragedy.

As we have many times observed, Browning's way of seeing things was essentially ironic—that is, seeing at least two, usually contradictory, sides of every question. Tragedy, on the other hand, demands that there be *a* way in which to view a man and his actions; its meaning is largely unproblematical, at least on the literal level of story and plot. Also, tragedy necessarily entails sedateness, a subordination of comic elements to a grave and solemn ending.[14] Irony, however, calls for laughter, the laughter that results from the perception of the incongruity of things in a state of becoming. It may deal with serious matters, but in effect it is always comic.[15]

Browning himself came to recognize that he could not fit his ironic view of life into a tragic mold. Arthur E. DuBois is right, I think, when he says that *A Soul's Tragedy* is "a conscious rebellion against tragedy as a type of drama."[16] In that play the one who suffers the "tragedy," Chiappino, is replaced as protagonist by the cosmic humorist, Ogniben, who changes the whole mode of the drama. Browning had, I believe, come finally to realize that his talent was for the human comedy. Had he not been disillusioned by the theater, its actors and managers, he might have become a great playwright. Had he not moved to Italy and had he continued writing for the stage, he might have given the English theater the kind of ironic comedies that it did not enjoy till Shaw appeared some fifty years later. Browning had all the qualifications—far more, in fact, than Shaw. He did not, alas, ever hit on the right theatrical form.

AFTERWORD

IN CASTING A BACKWARD GLANCE OVER Browning's earlier work, I want now to confront directly the problem that, I believe, lies at the heart of almost all commentary on the young Browning and that Philip Drew has articulated when asking "why Browning is alone among the poets of his century in adopting a dramatic form for the bulk of his work."[1] The answer most frequently offered by his critics and biographers is that he was compelled by the fear of self-exposure to hide behind a dramatic mask and so protect himself from revelation of certain characterological defects.[2] A second answer is that he wished to avoid the subjectivity that he saw as vitiating much Romantic poetry.[3] A third answer is that the objectivity and impersonality provided by the dramatic mode were necessitated, in Browning's case as well as that of fellow poets, by the lack of an effective ethos that would admit personal assertion.[4] There is no doubt an element of truth in all three answers. But I think there is still a better answer—namely, Browning was a dramatic poet because, unlike his contemporaries, he was essentially an ironist. If this sounds like question-begging, let me explain what I mean.

For Browning art is imperialistic: it aims to embrace and absorb everything; it is power. The artist "would be all, have, see, know, taste, feel all"; he wishes "to create, and rule, and call / Upon all things to minister to [him]" (*Pauline*, 275–78). Like Aprile he desires "to perfect and consummate all" (*Paracelsus*, 2.475) and like Sordello to have it "All at once" (*Sordello*, 2.626). Yet art is also love and evokes a contrary impulse: the desire to represent to others what the artist sees and feels, which means that the artist must subdue himself to that which can be represented. If he does not do this, then he will, like Aprile and Sordello, end up doing nothing.[5] An artist who aspires to be a "whole poet" must be both a "seer" and a "fashioner" (*Essay on Shelley*).

Browning's art is therefore both egotistically sublime and

negatively capable, subjective and objective at once.[6] "The world and all its action, as a show of thought," Walter Pater said of him, "that is the scope of his work."[7] His art is the external medium into which the truths acquired by the soul have been objectified. It exists first for him and for his use. While ostensibly characterizing individuals of every type, it is actually the means by which the poet has defined himself. Art is, then, a mediation between the self and the infinite.[8] Or to put it another way, it is the drama of the becoming soul.

The idea of the drama as the form capable of uniting the subjective and the objective modes of poetic faculty did not originate with Browning. Schlegel had called for a *Universalpoesie* that would join the opposites of lyric and epic, that would be epic in undertaking to mirror the whole world surrounding it but lyric in refracting the world through the medium of a single mind; but, he said, as "yet no form has thus far arisen appropriate to expressing the author's mind so perfectly, so that artists who just wanted to write . . . have by coincidence described themselves" (*Athenaeum* Fragment No. 116). Henry Crabb Robinson did, however, specifically cite drama as the means by which the epic and lyric, the objective and subjective could be combined:

> The epic is marked by this character of style,—that the poet presents his *object* immediately and directly, with a total disregard of his own personality. He is, as it were, an indifferent and unimpassioned narrator or chronicler. . . . The opposite class of poetry is the *lyric*, in which the poet gives mainly objects as they are reflected in the mirror of his own individuality. . . . These same classes, designated generally, as the *objective* and and *subjective*, were called by Schiller the naive and sentimental, and they have also been named the real and the ideal. In general, modern poets belong to the subjective class. . . . The dramatic poet must unite the powers of both in an equal degree. In the plan of his drama, in the relation of the characters to each other, all in subordination to the purpose of the work, he must have the epic impartiality; but in the execution, he is lyric.[9]

Other voices as well cried out during the 1830s for a poetry displaying the psychology of human character, a poetry that would inevitably have to be dramatic.[10]

But even though the idea did not originate with Browning,

he nevertheless was highly conscious of attempting something new. The note appended to *Pauline* speaks of the poem as a "singular" production in a new genre. The preface to *Paracelsus* calls that work "novel" in its genre and "difficult" in its form. The preface to *Strafford* refers to the play as following a new method of presentation of character and action. The narrator in the opening lines of *Sordello* represents himself as a maker of "quite new men" and a setter-forth of "unexampled themes." In the Advertisement to *Dramatic Lyrics,* the poet felt compelled to explain the novelty of the dramatic pieces of that volume. Throughout his poetry and letters of the period 1833–46, there is a consciousness of difference and distinction, of doing something new. It is no wonder that, because his was, as John Forster called it, "a new genius for dramatic poetry,"[11] his readers frequently found him obscure and unintelligible.

Dramatic poetry does not, of course, always take what Browning referred to as "the vulgar or more obvious form of drama,—scene & dialogue."[12] It assumes, as we have noted, many forms. Once having determined that his poetry would be the drama of self-enactment, Browning had to search for those forms that would permit ever-fresh origination and display the continuing development of soul. Since every "performance" represents an advance in soul-making, the poet was under compulsion to discover new media for each successive "performance."[13] Partly as the result of the drama, the dramatist was greater than his poem. As Sordello learned to his dismay, he could never achieve a poem that would contain all of him. Or as Browning said of himself, his poetry was far from being the "completest expression of my being" (Kintner, 2:725).

Art like other aspects of life must be viewed as a continuing struggle for freedom within form, as the artist seeking a progressive enfranchisement of his soul from limiting embodiments. And even though there is always an increasing ascendancy of content over form,[14] the artist must constantly search for media "answering to and indicative of the process of the informing spirit" *(Essay on Shelley)*. Eventually, in the new kind of synthetist art envisioned in *Sordello,* there will be a "sympoetry" in which form will disappear almost entirely. This does not, however, mean the death of art, only an increasing transparency of form. Browning's aesthetics as well as his metaphysics reflects a belief in the gradual evolution of soul, not to perfectability but to ever more advanced states.

It is this manifestation of his philosophy of becoming in drama that most obviously sets Browning off from his Romantic predecessors, whose greatest achievements were in the lyric mode.[15] Where they sought for an organic form fully matching content, Browning always insists on the disequilibrium between the two.[16] For him all embodiment is a type of evil in that it conceals and limits the good beneath: body, whether it be genre, verse form, language, or human corporeality, is the prison house of soul. Art represents the releasing of soul from body, but only into a less restrictive form—into a more comfortable temporary prison, as it were, that significantly is not fully enclosed. For Browning all life is a progressive struggle of the soul for freedom within form. This is why the drama of the soul is enacted in such different forms in Browning's earlier verse, why no other nineteenth-century poet employed so many various genres during a comparable thirteen-year period.

This revel of dramatic forms, to alter slightly a term used by Geoffrey Hartman,[17] is matched in Browning's earlier work by a revelry of character portrayal. Seemingly so different in personality and in personal and historical circumstances, his characters nevertheless share certain common qualities. First, they are caught at moments of crisis in their lives, when their souls may advance or stand still.[18] Second, they are conscious of their literary status, aware of being *dramatis personae*. Third, they court an ideal to which, however faulty it is shown to be, they for the most part remain steadfastly loyal. These characteristics combine to mold dramatic characters with whom we are asked to feel sorrow or joy but from whom we also are invited to detach ourselves because they are shown to be unworthy of our complete empathy. We see, in effect, two sides of Browning's characters; and furthermore, behind the dramatic form in which they are displayed, we also see the playwright, who manages—whether by form, as in "The Bishop Orders His Tomb," or by symbol, as in "My Last Duchess," or by manner of narration, as in *Sordello*—to reveal himself as the maker of the proceedings.

In his forms and in his characters, then, Browning the ironist revels. It is, however, in his language and in his consideration of language, whether explicitly or implicitly, that he seems to revel most of all. For his works are not so much dramas as dramatic *poetry*. Ultimately he is less interested in both character in action and action in character than in the dramatic language that ultimately conveys both plot and character. What fascinates Browning is what his characters say and the way in which they say it. As he remarked to Elizabeth Barrett concerning *Luria,* "Whatever comes of it, the 'aside,' the bye-play, the digression, will be the best, and the true business of the piece" (Kintner, 1:411). And as George Bernard Shaw observed years later, "Browning, when the mere action of his plays flags, lifts and prolongs apparently exhausted situations by bursts of poetry."[19] Not what his characters do or even what they are—these are of less interest to the poet than what they say. And this is because he himself was always aware that in letting them speak he was in fact speaking for them, using them to define and advance himself. "Energetic extroversion," Peter Conrad remarks of the Romantic Ironist, "is his mask for moody introversion."[20] The mannered interruption of dialogue in the plays,[21] the constant return to the nature of language in *Sordello,* the frequent allusions to documents and scripts, the fragmented speech of the monologists, the undulated speech of Pauline's lover and Paracelsus, the infinite deferrals and reconsiderations of decisions and actions—all point to Browning's central concern with language and its ironies. For Browning language is re-presentation of imaging; it is "the stuff / That held the imaged thing"; and he laments its inability to do more than re-present, mediate, or substitute, to allow scarcely "a tithe / To reach the light" (*Sordello,* 2.570–73). As an embodiment language inevitably conceals that which it pretends to reveal. Language, in short, is a phenomenal system that at best permits hints, tokens, and broken glances of the noumenal world. Here also Browning is in sharp disagreement with his Romantic predecessors who believed, to quote Shelley's *Defence of Poetry,* that "to be poet is to apprehend the true and the beautiful, in a word, the good which exists in the relations subsisting, first between existence and perception and secondly between perception and expression."[22]

In pointing out Browning's difference from the English Romantics in his insistence on the dramatic mode and in his theory and practice of form and of language, I do not, however, wish to represent Browning as one who was totally unlike his immediate predecessors. As we have seen, he conceived of poetry as an engine ever in process of construction and dismantlement. Like the Romantic poets he believed in the creative ego, which employs a constructive mind to shape chaotic material. But where for the Romantics the ego is a manifestation of the Absolute Ego—Nature, Mind, Power, Being—for Browning the ego is self-creating. Like the Romantics he makes meaning by reference to transcendental categories. But where they appealed to a stable transcendental order, Browning recognizes only a transcendental process by which man is still becoming man and God still becoming God. Where romantic poetry is allegorical, visionary, and mythic, Browning's early work glorifies self-activity and finds meaning in the empirical and in time.

It would be wrong to consider Browning's as a rejection rather than a revision of Romantic metaphysical and aesthetic modes, for he remains a seer, a "subjective" poet. Like the Romantics he places his faith in what Wallace Stevens calls "the magnificent cause of being, / The imagination, the one reality / In this imagined world" ("Another Weeping Woman"). He exalts philosophy and literature as authentic discourses. But he is also a maker and fashioner, an "objective" poet. He is a maker-see—the "whole" poet. He does not reject Romantic idealism, but he injects into it a strong strain of realism.[23] Although, again like Wallace Stevens, he insists that "things are as I think they are / And say they are," he nevertheless maintains that "I am a native in this world / And think in it as a native thinks" ("The Man with the Blue Guitar"), his "instinct for earth" as great as his "instinct for heaven" ("An Ordinary Evening in New Haven"). Browning insists on the actual and the temporal: his subject is men and women in history, characters like those in *Pippa Passes* who can change their minds and their whole ways of life in a moment. As the poet said of himself in later life, "By a law of the association of ideas—*contraries* come into the mind as often as *similarities*—and the peace and solitude readily called up the notion of what would most jar them."[24] For him and for his characters, each moment is pregnant with possibilities. This does not mean, however, that they live in possibility, which would be the very kind of inaction Browning so often deplores; on the contrary, the characters whom we are asked to approve—Paracelsus, for example—act decisively, sin boldly. Their chief problem lies in determining which course of action to follow. What is needed, as Browning says in *Sordello,* is some "moon" or "star" to light the way.

Now, it is his conception of this "moon" that makes Browning so difficult to come to grips with. What does it mean? Or to put the question within the framework I have been using, what does it indicate about his irony? By way of uncovering the answer, let me briefly consider Browning in light of what I understand to be the two chief contemporary theories of literary irony. The first, championed by Wayne C. Booth,[25] insists that irony is rhetorically functional and that beneath every ironic surface there is to be discovered a stable center of meaning. The other, proposed by Paul de Man,[26] maintains that the interpretation of an ironic text is impossible because there is no stable center of meaning, "meaning" being an illusion of the conscious mind imprisoned in its own linguistic system but desiring release into "metaphysics." Where Booth reconstructs, de Man deconstructs. Where then is the young Browning?

The answer is, I believe, in neither one camp nor the other but in both. For Browning sees each separately obviating possibility—the possibility of becoming. When modern deconstructionists insist on the death of meaning, they reify a meaning that precludes others. And when reconstructionists declare that a statement of meaning may be recovered, they too lapse into dogma and affirm meaning as something fixed and final. What concerns Browning is not so much meaning as the possibility of meaning. As Mrs. Orr remarked concerning his religious belief, it "held a saving clause, which removed it from all dogmatic . . . grounds of controversy: the more definite or concrete conceptions of which it consists possessed no finality for even his own mind; they represented for him an absolute truth in contingent relations to it" (*Life,* p. 436). For him meaning is neither absent nor fixed: it is always becoming, realizing itself and being realized in different styles, forms, and perspectives. Which is to say, it is provisional—a fiction perhaps, but an enabling fiction, a guiding "moon" or "star." That is, I think, Browning's chief semantic irony—one we have noted in all his work from *Pauline* to the last of the *Bells and Pomegranates*—and from it all his other semantic ironies spring. Meaning in Browning's earlier poetry is nearly always problematical, and to appreciate it we as readers must be extraordinarily agile.

As he was bringing the *Bells and Pomegranates* series to a close in 1846, Browning was about to begin a new kind of life—in marriage and in Italy. "My whole scheme of life . . . was long ago calculated," he wrote to his bride-to-be, "and it supposed *you,* the finding such an one as you, utterly impossible" (Kintner, 1:193). But having found her, he must change, in many ways. As for poetry, "I mean to take your advice and be quiet awhile and let my mind get used to its new medium of sight—, seeing all things . . . thro' you: and then, let all I have done be the prelude and the real work begin" (Kintner, 1:455). Seeing all things through Elizabeth's eyes would indeed make a difference. It can, I believe, be plausibly argued that, with the exception of *Christmas-Eve and Easter-Day,* the poems of his middle years prior to *The Ring and the Book* are the least characteristic of this poet dedicated to the philosophy of becoming. It would be possible, I think, to maintain that Browning's marriage to Elizabeth Barrett marked a period when the poet contented himself, artistically at least, more with being than becoming. But whatever the case, the fact remains that during the years of his marriage Browning wrote less and in a less formally experimental fashion than at any other period of his life. Where during the thirteen years prior to his marriage he published twelve separate volumes of verse, during the fifteen years of his married life he published only three.

Browning did not cease to be an ironist during his middle

years, but his irony is more limited. Seeing through his wife's eyes necessarily gave him a new perspective: he became more conscious of his "mission of humanity" (Kintner, 1:493). I do not mean to imply that the great monologues of the 1850s and 60s are reducible to their moral content, but I do think it fair to say that they have more moral design upon the reader than do the earlier poems. Admittedly there are ironies galore in "Cleon," "Karshish," "Abt Vogler," and the others, but they are ironies that by and large point to some fixed meaning. Only later, when he returns to England, does the old sense of irony return strongly, never so wonderfully zanily as in the case of *Sordello* but boldly and paradoxically nevertheless. Where during the years of his wife's influence he worked mainly with one form, the dramatic monologue, upon coming back to London he began again the formal experimentation of the ironist who, aware of the principle of becoming and the inadequacy of any form to serve for more than one occasion, always seeks new vehicles to embody new ideas. *The Ring and the Book* reintroduces radically ironic notions of art that continue in the poet's work, with some fluctuation, until his death in 1889.[27]

Being an ironist does not, of course, preclude being a moralist. As I have tried to demonstrate, from the beginning Browning's earlier work is nearly always concerned with moral problems. But they are not rendered as such; it is the moral drama—the dialogue—that he invites us to witness and enjoy. He does not, like Shelley, present us with a world of perfect order where nature is redeemed. There is nothing in him of an apocalyptic imagination that is unleashed in visions, dreams, trance, or madness, as in Tennyson, say. The young Browning is more like Balzac in that he pressures the phenomenon to make it yield meaning. His historical characters, for example, are nothing—or almost nothing—until he resuscitates them, molds them anew, as he says in *Sordello*. What he aims to do is to deal with fact—to turn, twist, contort it, if need be—and make the fact yield the vision and thereby persuade us that fact and vision are so interconnected that they cannot be distinguished. That is the essence of Browning's drama—the drama of the body and the soul—and it is ultimately, if incidentally,[28] a moral drama. All life, the young Browning would have us see, all life is significant. And it is the function of the maker-see to uncover it, to make us experience the becoming of an object, to defamiliarize the object dulled for us by habitualization, by lifting it out of the field of ordinary perception and placing it within a network of relationships that constitute the work of art. His instruction to us is that which Henry James offered to young novelists: "Try to be one of the people on whom nothing is lost."[29] And he does this by being both "subjective" and "objective"—a "whole poet"—in a word, an ironist.[30]

NOTES

Abbreviations

BIS	*Browning Institute Studies*
CE	*College English*
DeVane, *Handbook*	*A Browning Handbook*
Domett	*Robert Browning and Alfred Domett*
Griffin and Minchin	*The Life of Robert Browning*
Hood, *Letters*	*Letters of Robert Browning Collected by Thomas J. Wise*
Irvine and Honan	*The Book, the Ring, & the Poet*
Kintner	*The Letters of Robert Browning and Elizabeth Barrett Barrett, 1845–1846*
New Letters	*New Letters of Robert Browning*
NLH	*New Literary History*
Orr, *Handbook*	*A Handbook of the Works of Robert Browning*
Orr, *Life*	*Life and Letters of Robert Browning*
PBSA	*Publications of the Bibliographical Society of America*
PQ	*Philological Quarterly*
RES	*Review of English Studies*
SBHC	*Studies in Browning and His Circle*
SiR	*Studies in Romanticism*
SP	*Studies in Philology*
TSLL	*Texas Studies in Literature and Language*
UTQ	*University of Toronto Quarterly*
VNL	*Victorian Newsletter*
VP	*Victorian Poetry*
VS	*Victorian Studies*
Yes	*Yearbook of English Studies*

Introduction

1. For a concise statement of the traditional view of Shelley's influence on the young Browning, see William Clyde DeVane, *A Browning Handbook*, pp. 9–10; hereafter cited in the text as DeVane, *Handbook*. Recent studies argue for the ironic nature of Romantic discourse and the Romantics' acceptance of doubt and disharmony. The most recent of these are David Simpson, *Irony and Authority in Romantic Poetry* (Towtowa, N.J.: Rowman and Littlefield, 1979); Anne K. Mellor, *English Romantic Irony*; and Tilottama Rajan, *Dark Interpreter: The Discourse of Romanticism* (Ithaca, N.Y.: Cornell University Press, 1980).

2. A more detailed consideration of philosophical irony may be found in Mellor, *English Romantic Irony*, pp. 7–14.

3. "Irony is," said Schlegel, "a clear consciousness of an eternal agility, of the infinitely abundant chaos." *Athenaeum* Fragment No. 69, in Friedrich Schlegel, *Dialogue on Poetry and Literary Aphorisms*, p. 155; hereafter cited in the text by journal and fragment number.

4. The terms were popularized in Germany at the end of the eighteenth century and imported into England during the second decade of the nineteenth century. For an account of their use in English critical vocabulary, see M. H. Abrams, *The Mirror and the Lamp*.

5. Elizabeth Barrett remarked to Browning early in their correspondence: "You have in your vision two worlds—or to use the language of the schools of the day, you are both subjective & objective in the habits of your mind." *The Letters of Robert Browning and Elizabeth Barrett Barrett*, 1:9; hereafter cited in the text as Kintner.

6. Speaking of Browning's religious opinions, Mrs. Sutherland Orr observed: "No one felt more strongly than he the contradictions involved in any conceivable system of Divine creation and government. No one knew better that every act and motive which we attribute to a Supreme Being is virtual negation of His existence. He believed nevertheless that such a Being exists. . . . " Further, "The Evangelical Christian and the subjective idealist philosopher were curiously blended in his composition." Mrs. Sutherland Orr, *Life and Letters of Robert Browning*, pp. 436, 374; hereafter cited in the text as Orr, *Life*.

7. For a brief account of the three Victorian poets' reactions to the notion of their age as one of transition, see Patricia Ball, *The Central Self*, pp. 198–99.

8. For a discussion of possible ways in which Browning's career may be divided, see P. J. Keating, "Robert Browning: A Reader's Guide," in *Robert Browning*, ed. Isobel Armstrong (London: G. Bell, 1974), p. 323.

9. Quoted in D. C. Muecke, *The Compass of Irony*, p. 192.

Chapter One

1. The earliest reviewers were of the same opinion. For example, the reviewer for the *Atlas*, 14 April 1833, said that the "author is in the confessional." This view of the poem has led critics to formulate a theory of Browning's poetical development to the effect that, stung by adverse comments of the reviewers and especially by John Stuart Mill's marginal comments in his copy of *Pauline*, which Browning saw, the young poet turned from the confessional to the dramatic mode. The most recent critic to classify *Pauline* as a confessional lyric is Eleanor Cook in her book *Browning's Lyrics*, pp. 12–13. For revised estimates of Browning's reactions to Mill's comments, see Masao Miyoshi, "Mill and *Pauline:* The Myth and Some Facts," *VS* 9 (1965): 154–63; O. P. Govil, "A Note on Mill and Browning's *Pauline*," *VP* 4 (1966): 287–91; Michael A. Burr, "Browning's Note to Forster," *VP* 12 (1974): 343–49.

2. Roma A. King, Jr., *The Focusing Artifice*, p. 3. See also Michael Hancher, "The Dramatic Situation in Browning's 'Pauline'," *YES* 1 (1971): 149–59.

3. Most commentators claim that *Alastor* was the model for *Pauline*. "Even the casual reader can now see that *Alastor* is the poetic model upon which Browning's poem was formed" (DeVane, *Handbook*, p. 44). Ian Jack, *Browning's Major Poetry*, p. 20, suggests *Epipsychidion* as the model, as does William H. Gilbert in his doctoral dissertation "Browning's *Pauline:* The Case for Shelley's Influence" (Duke University, 1975).

4. Browning's friend Joseph Arnould, writing to their mutual friend Alfred Domett in New Zealand, called *Pauline* "a strange, wild (in parts singularly magnificent) poet-biography: his own early life as it presented itself to his own soul viewed poetically: in fact, psychologically speaking, his 'Sartor Resartus.' " *Robert Browning and Alfred Domett*, p. 141; hereafter cited in the text as *Domett*.

5. Why is the woman named Pauline? H.-L. Hovelaque, *La Jeunesse de Browning*

(Paris: Presses Modernes, 1932), pp. 121–25, suggests a parallel between *Pauline* and Balzac's *Louis Lambert,* which has a character called Pauline. Another possibility is that the name was intended to suggest the speaker's "conversion," St. Paul's being the archetype. Moreover, we know that Browning conceived the poem after seeing a performance of *Richard III.* In the play Richard habitually swears by St. Paul, an oath not found elsewhere in Shakespeare. See Geoffrey Carnall, "Shakespeare's Richard III and St. Paul," *Shakespeare Quarterly* 14 (1963): 186–88.

6. "I believe that in what follows he alludes to a certain examination of the soul, or rather his own soul, which he formerly carried out so as to discover the series of objectives that he could possibly attain."

7. *Letters of Keats,* ed. Hyder E. Rollins (Cambridge, Mass.: Harvard University Press, 1958), 2:102–3.

8. For the latest and best account of Browning's formative years, see John Maynard, *Browning's Youth.* Maynard's book is not, however, a biography in the usual sense; it focuses on such matters as Browning's reading, his assimilation of what he read, what he gained from family relationships. For a more usual kind of biography relating the facts of the subject's life, see William Irvine and Park Honan, *The Book, The Ring, and the Poet;* hereafter cited as Irvine and Honan.

9. For a study of the Romantic visionary poet and the nature of his discourse, see M. H. Abrams, *Natural Supernaturalism.*

10. Morse Peckham places *Pauline* in its relation to Romantic tradition in his essay "Browning and Romanticism."

11. Philip Drew, *The Poetry of Browning,* argues that Browning's whole conception and mode of poetry stem from a rejection of the Romantic tradition. See especially chapter 3.

12. Harold Bloom, *The Anxiety of Influence* and *Poetry and Repression.*

13. The best study of the dynamics of Browning's psychological response to Shelley may be found in Herbert F. Tucker's *Browning's Beginnings.* The story of Browning's discovery of Shelley's poetry is most authoritatively treated in Frederick A. Pottle, *Shelley and Browning.* Negative views of Browning's revision of Shelley's poetry may be found in Roland A. Duerksen, *Shelleyan Ideas in Victorian Literature* (The Hague: Mouton, 1966), chapter 2, and in Bloom's *The Anxiety of Influence,* p. 69. Richard C. Keenan, "Browning and Shelley," *BIS* 1 (1973): 119–45, provides a brief survey of Browning's changing later views on Shelley. Keenan is careful to point out that Browning's revised estimate of Shelley the man did not obviate his continued admiration for Shelley's poetry. C. Willard Smith studies the poet's star imagery in *Browning's Star-Imagery* (Princeton, N.J.: Princeton University Press, 1941) but reaches conclusions different from mine.

14. The final revised text of 1888–89 is perhaps clearer on the relationship between self-love and love for Pauline: "Why else have I sought refuge in myself, / But from the woes I saw and could not stay? / Love! is not this to love thee, my Pauline?" (687–89).

15. The near-tautology suggests the speaker's haziness and lack of conviction.

16. The poet's father gave him a copy of Mandeville's *The Fable of the Bees,* which apparently had been in the Browning household for some time, on 1 February 1833, less than a month after *Pauline* was completed. Mandeville's book is an "edition" of a poem, "The Grumbling Hive," surrounded by all sorts of editorial paraphernalia. I think it probable that Browning took *The Fable* as his model. See Maynard, *Browning's Youth,* pp. 330–33.

17. The note in French has evoked a number of adverse critical comments. Some

regard it as an excrescence; others see it as a safety device, a disclaimer on the part of the poet of all that is weak or extravagant in the confession. W. J. Fox, in his review of *Pauline* in the *Monthly Repository* for April 1833, thought the note "the chief blemish" on the poem. J. S. Mill crossed it out in his copy as an excrescence. Pottle, *Shelley and Browning*, p. 41, says that the note "certainly does not serve the purpose for which it is ostensibly inserted; that of making the poem easier to understand." Mrs. Sutherland Orr, *A Handbook to the Works of Robert Browning*, p. 20, views it as a disclaimer. (Hereafter this work is cited in the text as Orr, *Handbook*.) Park Honan sees the note as an artistic safety device that "provides Browning with a perfect excuse for . . . weakness and, at least theoretically, makes *Pauline* virtually invulnerable to critical attack" ("Browning's *Pauline*: The Artistic Safety Device," *VNL* No. 18 [Fall 1960], p. 23). Masao Miyoshi, "Mill and *Pauline*: The Myth and Some Facts," p. 163, says that the note, "for all its ironic spirit, is the author's disclaimer." K. W. Grandsen, "The Uses of Personae," in *Browning's Mind and Art*, ed. Clarence Tracy (Edinburgh: Oliver and Boyd, 1968), p. 52, regards the note as "a curious attempt at dissociation from what is clearly a very personal poem." I have not discovered anyone who regards the note as an essential part of the work.

18. I am aware that I have not made mention of the letters "V.A.XX." which come just before the beginning of the poem. Browning later explained these as follows: "V.A.XX. is the Latin abbreviation of *Vixi Annos*—'I was twenty years old'—that is, the imaginary subject of the poem was of that age" (*Letters of Robert Browning Collected by Thomas J. Wise*, p. 256). If we did not have Browning's explanation, we would doubtless regard these letters as referring to the speaker of the confession, perhaps his initials. (Hereafter the letters collected by Wise will be cited in the text as Hood, *Letters*.)

19. J. Hillis Miller, *The Disappearance of God*, p. 95.

20. See A. Dwight Culler, "Monodrama and the Dramatic Monologue." For a consideration of *Pauline* as a monodrama, see Robert Preyer, "Robert Browning: A Reading of the Early Narratives."

21. In a penciled note in a copy of *Pauline* once in the possession of John Stuart Mill and now in the Forster and Dyce Collection in the Victoria and Albert Museum. The full note may most conveniently be found transcribed in DeVane, *Handbook*, p. 41. For a full account of Mill's comments, see William S. Peterson and Fred L. Standley, "The J. S. Mill Marginalia in Robert Browning's *Pauline*: A History and Transcription," *PSBA* 66 (1972): 135–70.

Chapter Two

1. See Joseph W. Donahue, *Dramatic Character in the English Romantic Age*, for a discussion of early nineteenth-century acting styles.

2. A. W. Schlegel, *A Course of Lectures on Dramatic Art and Literature*, quoted by Terry Otten, *The Deserted Stage*, p. 5.

3. Lectures of 1818, quoted by Otten, p. 7.

4. John Henry Newman, *Poetry, with Reference to Aristotle's Poetics*, ed. A. S. Cook (Boston: Ginn, 1891), p. 2.

5. Donahue, p. 345.

6. *Table Talk* (27 April 1823), in *The Complete Works of Samuel Taylor Coleridge*, ed. W. G. T. Shedd (New York: Harper, 1884), 6:265.

7. *Letters of Keats* 1:192.

8. *Poetry, with Reference to Aristotle's Poetics*, pp. 25–28.

9. "The Two Kinds of Poetry," in John Stuart Mill, *Literary Essays*, ed. Edward Alexander (Indianapolis: Bobbs-Merrill, 1967), p. 71.

10. *Blackwood's Magazine* 38 (1835): 829, 837 n.

11. *London Magazine* 8 (1823): 85.

12. Philarète Chasles, "De l'art dramatique et du théatre actuel en Angleterre," *Revue des Deux Mondes* 22 (1840): 122-50.

13. Writing to John Kenyon on 1 October 1855, Browning expressed his belief that "lyric is the oldest, most natural, most *poetical* of poetry, and I would always get it if I could: but I find in these latter days that one has a great deal to say, and try and get attended to, which is out of the lyrical element and capability—and I am forced to take the nearest way to it: and then it is undeniable that the common reader is susceptible to plot, story, and the simplest form of putting a matter 'Said I,' 'Said He' & so on." The letter is in the Houghton Library, Harvard University. I am quoting from Eleanor Cook, *Browning's Lyrics*, p. xv.

14. Hallam Tennyson, *Alfred Lord Tennyson: A Memoir* (London: Macmillan, 1897); 2:113 n.

15. W. Hall Griffin and Harry Christopher Minchin, *The Life of Robert Browning*, p. 72; hereafter cited in the text as Griffin and Minchin.

16. In his note Browning says that when someone styled him "Luther alter," Paracelsus replied, "And why not?"

17. A passage inserted later into the text makes this clearer. Paracelsus says to Festus:

> You and I, wandering over the world wide,
> Chance to set foot upon a desert coast.
> Just as we cry, "No human voice before
> Broke the inveterate silence of these rocks!"
> —Their querulous echo startles us; we turn:
> What ravaged structure still looks o'er the sea?
> Some characters remain, too! While we read,
> The sharp salt wind, impatient for the last
> Of even this record, wistfully comes and goes,
> Or sings what we recover, mocking it.
>
> (4. 439-48)

18. Mark D. Hawthorne, "*Paracelsus* Once Again: A Study in Imagery," *BIS* 3 (1975): 57, observes that Paracelsus failed because "he wanted a static end without taking the dynamic means into consideration."

19. Roma A. King, Jr., *The Focusing Artifice*, p. 19.

20. See, for example, Robert Langbaum, *The Poetry of Experience*, pp. 78-80.

21. F. E. L. Priestley, "The Ironic Pattern of Browning's *Paracelsus*."

22. Gerald L. Bruns, "The Formal Nature of Victorian Thinking," maintains that it is specifically the appeal to time that sets off Victorian meaning-making from that of the Romantics.

23. Evaluation of *Paracelsus* has varied widely over the near century and a half since its first publication. At the end of the last century, Edward Berdoe, whom some regarded as "the greatest authority on Browning we have" (Raymond Blathwayt, "Browning and His Teaching: A Talk with Dr. Edward Berdoe," *Great Thoughts from Master Minds* 41 [1904]: 312), was of the opinion that *Paracelsus* is "the work that posterity will probably estimate as Browning's greatest" (Edward Berdoe, *The Browning Cyclopaedia*, 7th ed. [Lincoln, England: George Allen, 1912], p. 322). In this cen-

tury, on the other hand, critics reviewing Browning's career have by and large rushed hastily past it to get to the dramatic monologues of the 1840s and 50s.

Chapter Three

1. *The Diaries of William Charles Macready: 1833–1851,* 1:389.
2. Ibid. 1:362, 355.
3. *Autobiographical Notes of the Life of William Bell Scott,* ed. W. Minto (London: James R. Osgood, McIlvaine, 1892), 1:124–25.
4. Terry Otten, *The Deserted Stage,* p. 109. Denis Donoghue, *The Third Voice: Modern British and American Verse Drama* (Princeton, N.J.: Princeton University Press, 1959), p. 21, says that Browning "was an experimental dramatist, trying to clarify and exploit ideas of drama which Macready would have found bewildering." For Browning as an experimental dramatist, see James P. McCormick, "Robert Browning and the Experimental Drama."
5. For a study of Browning as an ironic dramatist, see Arthur E. Dubois, "Robert Browning, Dramatist." H. B. Charlton, "Browning as Dramatist," considers Browning's dramatic failures when dealing with men in groups.
6. Eleanor N. Hutchens, "The Identification of Irony."
7. Connop Thirlwall, "On the Irony of Sophocles," pp. 489–90. I can find no reference to Thirlwall's essay in Browning's published correspondence. Browning may have been acquainted with this particular issue of the *Philological Museum* because it contained an Imaginary Conversation by Landor, the writer who had an enormous influence on the young poet ("Robert always said that he owed more as writer to Landor than to any contemporary," reported his wife [*The Letters of Elizabeth Barrett Browning,* ed. F.G. Kenyon (New York and London: Macmillan, 1897), 2:354]). The first volume of the *Museum* (1832) also contained one of Landor's Imaginary Conversations.
8. Cf. Irvine and Honan, p. 71: "Pym and Strafford suggest not so much a political rivalry as the high-flown estrangements and cross-purposes of conventional romantic love."
9. One must not, however, overlook the demands that W. C. Macready placed on Browning for an actable play with as wide appeal as possible. He may well have insisted on a larger role for Lady Carlisle. Certainly Helen Faucit, who acted the part of Carlisle, objected during rehearsal (and revision of the text) to the poverty of her part. See *The Diaries of William Charles Macready, 1833–51,* vol. 1, entries for October 1836 to May 1837.
10. Just before writing *Strafford,* Browning had satirized Calvinistic doctrines of election and reprobation in "Johannes Agricola in Meditation," published in *Monthly Repository,* N. S., 10 (1836): 45. It is salutary to remember this fact because it is often said that Browning's sympathies in the play are with Pym and the Puritans. See, for example, DeVane, *Handbook,* pp. 70–71.

Chapter Four

1. I can discover only three commentators who have previously associated Browning's name with Romantic Irony. C. N. Wenger, *The Asthetics of Robert Browning,* p. 128, says that Browning "in his theory . . . usually supports . . . part of the romantic irony theory" that holds the world to be an expression of the self in that the poet creates it out of his imagination and bodies it forth in his art. Browning "frequently

supports the whole ironical attitude of the extreme romaticists such as Friedrich Schlegel." Michael Mason, "The Importance of *Sordello,* p. 148, says: "Closely connected with this [view of poetry as an act of cooperation between poet and audience] is a fascinating notion that the poet who 'looks forth' to his audience in this way is somehow dispassionate, aloof from his work, this being a mere chance reflection of the underlying context of the poet's whole life. This is a view that echoes so-called 'romantic irony,' but Browning seems to be original in voicing it in this country." In "Robert Browning's *Paracelsus:* A Study in Romantic Irony," *Northwest Missouri State College Studies* 33 (1972): 1–33, Charles Leo Rivers associates Romantic Irony with Browning's practice in *Paracelsus.* This discursive essay is reprinted in Rivers's *Robert Browning's Theory of the Poet, 1833–1841,* Salzburg Studies in English Literature, No. 58 (Salzburg: At the University Press, 1976). Rivers says (p. 73 of the book) that Browning "shows himself to be a romantic ironist by assuming towards his subject ideas and an impartial, detached attitude similar to God's." Although she does not speak specifically of Browning as a Romantic Ironist, E. S. Shaffer in her book *"Kubla Khan" and The Fall of Jerusalem: The Mythological School in Biblical Criticism and Secular Literature, 1770–1880* (Cambridge: At the Cambridge University Press, 1975) discusses the relationship between Browning's "A Death in the Desert" and the Higher Criticism, which is, she maintains, a form of Romantic Irony (pp. 8, 191–224).

2. The most masterful studies in English of Romantic Irony are D. C. Muecke, *The Compass of Irony,* and Anne K. Mellor, *English Romantic Irony,* which discusses Romantic Irony in relation to works by Byron, Keats, Carlyle, Coleridge, and Carroll. Part of Mellor's book was published as "On Romantic Irony, Symbolism, and Allegory" in *Criticism* 21 (1979): 217–29. Janice L. Haney studies the nature of Romantic Irony in English literature particularly as it relates to *Sartor Resartus* in " 'Shadow-Hunting' ." Leonard P. Wessell, Jr. studies the metaphysics of Schlegel's irony in "The Antinomic Structure of Friedrich Schlegel's Romanticism." I gratefully acknowledge my indebtedness to all four. I have drawn most liberally on Janice Haney's splendid essay, not only in this chapter but in the book as a whole.

3. Quoted by Wessell, p. 667.

4. See A. E. Lussky, *Tieck's Romantic Irony,* pp. 69–70.

5. Characterizing Romantic Irony, Alan R. Thompson says: "To combine extreme objectivity and immanence . . . is to resemble God Himself. And this state of godlike self-division and self-consciousness is Romantic irony" (*The Dry Mock: A Study of Irony in Drama* [Berkeley: University of California Press, 1948], p. 64).

6. See Maynard, *Browning's Youth,* pp. 274–77.

7. See C. R. Tracy, "Browning's Heresies," *SP* 33 (1936): 610–25, and O. P. Govil, "Browning's 'Literary Father,' " *Indian Journal of English Studies* 9 (1968): 1–17.

8. See Charles Richard Sanders, "The Carlyle-Browning Correspondence and Relationship," *Bulletin of the John Rylands Library* 57 (1974–75): nos. 1 and 2.

9. Its main Victorian competitor is *Sartor Resartus.* See Mellor's book and Haney's essay mentioned in note 2 above.

10. See Lionel Stevenson, "The Key Poem of the Victorian Age," in *Essays in American and English Literature Presented to Bruce R. McElderry, Jr.,* ed. Max F. Schulz, with William T. Templeman and Charles R. Metzger (Athens, Ohio: Ohio University Press, 1967), pp. 260–89. Stevenson sees the technique of *Sordello* as a response to the popularity of prose fiction. He characterizes *Sordello* as "a poem about a poet writing a poem about a poet writing poems" and compares it with *Sartor Resartus,* a treatise "about a philosopher writing a treatise about a philosopher writing a treatise" (p. 278).

11. *Dialogue on Poetry*, p. 96, and fragments from the *Lyceum* and *Ideen* quoted by Hans Eichner, *Friedrich Schlegel* (New York: Twayne, 1970), p. 64.

12. See *New Letters of Robert Browning*, pp. 11, 57; hereafter cited in the text as *New Letters*. For the German Romantics' appreciation of *Don Quixote*, see Robert Wagner, *Romanticism and the Romantic School in Germany* (New York: Appleton, 1910), and Lussky, p. 133.

13. Browning added elucidatory page-headings to the revised edition of *Sordello* in 1863. This is the heading for the beginning passage of the poem. Mark D. Hawthorne, "Browning, *Sordello*, and Don Quixote," *MLN* 92 (1977): 1033–37, notes some similarities between the poem and Cervantes' novel.

14. J. Hillis Miller, "Narrative Middle," p. 386, maintains: "Schlegel's theory of irony as 'permanent parabasis' . . . suspends, interrupts, and pulverizes the narrative line altogether. It abolishes any conceivable center, finite or infinite, visible or invisible. . . . If irony is parabasis, it is the one master trope which cannot be graphed as a line. . . . All irony in narrative is one form or another of that doubling in the storytelling which makes its meaning undecidable, indecipherable, unreadable, unreadable even as the 'allegory of unreadability.' All narrative is therefore the linear demonstration of the impossibility of linear coherence."

15. See Stevenson and Daniel Stempel, "Browning's *Sordello*: The Art of the Makers-See," *PMLA* 80 (1965): 554–61.

16. See Robert R. Columbus and Claudette Kemper, "*Sordello* and the Speaker: A Problem in Identity," *VP* 2 (1964): 251–67.

17. But he also indicates his distance from the narrator when, in the revised edition of the poem, he has the narrator interrupt the poet's musing to chide: "Only, do finish something!" (3. 731).

18. Paul Elmer More observed that "the narrative is in reality a long confession of Sordello to himself who is conscious of a hostile power without" ("Why Is Browning Popular?" [1905], reprinted in *The Browning Critics*, ed. Boyd Litzinger and K. L. Knickerbocker [Lexington: University of Kentucky Press, 1967], p. 107). Alan J. Chaffee, "Dialogue and Dialectic in Browning's *Sordello*," treats the poem as psychoanalytic discourse, the narrator being the analyst and Sordello the analysand.

19. Betty Miller, *Robert Browning: A Portrait*, pp. 23–28, 47–49.

20. Barbara Herrnstein Smith, *Poetic Closure*, pp. 140–41, notes how "poetry cannot attempt to be faithful to the minutiae of interior verbalization—not if it is to be poetry. The fact that our thoughts are not intended for any audience—that they do not seek to instruct or delight anyone, or even to express anything—is reflected in the very structure of thinking. But the structure of a poem, at least when it functions as art, is controlled at every point by its ultimately expressive design: its effect, that is, upon the potential reader."

21. For accounts of Browning's reading, see Maynard, *Browning's Youth*, and John Woolford, "Sources and Resources in Browning's Early Reading."

22. Walter J. Ong, *Interfaces of the Word*, p. 224.

23. Speaking of *Sordello*, Michael Mason says: "The concept of 'Genius' is most persistently deflated in the person of the hero. The most important constituent of this new, unideal figure of the poet is reliance on his audience; poetry is not the effusion of genius, but a dynamic co-operation of audience and poet; gone is the old notion of poetry as the overheard solitary audience, still expressed by Mill in 1833" "The Importance of *Sordello*," p. 148.

24. "Epoist," "analyst," and "synthetist" are the designations Browning provided in the headnotes for the 1863 edition of *Sordello*.

25. J. C. F. von Schiller, *Über naive und sentimentalische Dichtung*, quoted by Abrams, *The Mirror and the Lamp*, p. 238.

26. The last half of the second line is quoted from the 1863 edition. In 1840 the words following the ellipsis are "but enough!" In the quotation above I have retained the 1840 reading in the first line.

27. The term "Maker-see" is a complex pun. Such a poet is, to use Browning's own designations in the *Essay on Shelley*, both a fashioner—that is, a maker—and a seer. He sees and he shapes what he sees so as to cause others to see what he has seen. Such a poet is, then, both "objective" and "subjective."

28. Quoted in *The Diary of Alfred Domett, 1872–1885*, ed. E. A. Horsman (London: Oxford University Press, 1953), pp. 52–53.

29. Michael G. Yetman, "Exorcising Shelley Out of Browning: *Sordello* and the Problem of Poetic Identity," *VP* 13 (1975): 90, finds Palma "an ideal stimulus" for Sordello's turn to humanitarian action. Elissa Schagrin Guralnick, "Archimagical Fireworks: The Function of Light-Imagery in *Sordello*," *VP* 13 (1975): 120, says of Palma: "Bright and whole in her existence, she is, like vision itself, incomprehensible and inexplicable. Eluding reason, she teases imagination and perception to grasp the essence of her totality and thus proves herself the worthy paramour of a visionary soul like Sordello."

30. *Complete Works of Robert Browning*, 2: 326. Stewart Walker Holmes, "Browning's *Sordello* and Jung: Browning's *Sordello* in the Light of Jung's Theory of Types," *PMLA* 56 (1941): 783, 786, sees Palma as "passion's votaress" who is displaced by the beggar-maid, the symbol of humanity. Columbus and Kemper, "*Sordello* and the Speaker," p. 261, say that when Sordello most needs her, Palma "prates about how best to use Sordello in the political arena. Love there is deaf; it too fails Sordello."

31. See W. O. Raymond, *The Infinite Moment and Other Essays in Robert Browning*, chapter 3, for a discussion of the interplay between love and power in *Paracelsus*.

32. Guralnick, "Archimagical Fireworks," pp. 121–22, says of him: Salinguerra "is defined by the very light of truth and wholeness he would seem to scorn. Indeed, one senses that had the soldier ever freed himself from the Romano cause in which he loses his identity, he might well have approached Sordello's near impossible ambition to become a star; for this is a man unique in his potential brilliance."

33. Browning explained to Edward Dowden that Sordello's character was "enervated" by the impulse to "thrust in time eternity's concern": "This is indicated in the passage where these words occur, and the rest of the poem is an example of the same" (Hood, *Letters*, p. 92).

34. Cf. this passage from Hegel: "Consciousness . . . seems . . . to be unable to determine the purpose of its action before action has taken place; but before action occurs it must, in virtue of being consciousness, have the act in front of itself as entirely its own, i.e. as a purpose. The individual, therefore, who is going to act seems to find himself in a circle, where each moment already presupposes the others, and hence seems unable to find a beginning, because it only gets to know its own original nature, the nature which is to be its purpose beforehand" (G. W. F. Hegel, *The Phenomenology of Mind*, trans. J. B. Baillie [New York: Harper and Row, 1967], p. 422). For a study of the problem of action in nineteenth-century British literature, see my essay "The Nineteenth-Century Cult of Inaction," *TSL* 4 (1959): 51–61.

35. Browning wrote to Elizabeth Barrett in December 1845: "Yesterday I was reading the 'Purgatorio' and the first speech of the group of which Sordello makes one struck me with a new significance, as well describing the man and his purpose and fate in my poem." He then quotes a passage from Dante, which, he says, "is just my

Sordello's story" and which he then translates: "And sinners were we to the extreme hour; / Then, light from heaven fell, making us aware, / So that, repenting us and pardoned, out / Of life we passed to God, at peace with Him / Who fills the heart with yearning Him to see" (Kintner, 1: 336).

36. There are many different interpretations of the passage on Power and Love. See, for example, Holmes, "Browning's *Sordello* and Jung"; Earl Hilton, "Browning's *Sordello* as a Study of the Will," *PMLA* 69 (1954): 1127–34; Thomas J. Collins, *Robert Browning's Moral-Aesthetic Theory, 1833–1855*, p. 60; Lawrence Poston III, "Browning's Career to 1841." Tucker, *Browning's Beginnings*, p. 90, writes: "The substantive identities of the powers must remain in doubt because Browning's interest lies not in substances but in dynamics of relationship. . . . Both powers are invoked at 'need' and are needed at a point of failure where love is 'descried': 'Or may failure here be success also when induced by love?' (headnotes, 6.569, 598). The 'divine' first power is 'still' with a fixity like Shelley's in *Pauline* and 'incomprehensible' like Festus' 'inscrutable' God. . . . The 'Human' second power is a totally distinct, deputized mediator. Despite its apparent secondariness, however, this mediating power is an indispensable go-between. . . . The two powers taken together prescribe for the soul the single course of salvation through deferment; and they do so through a Browningesque play of mutual dependence in which each needs the other and the first and last in importance tend to change places."

37. Quoted by René Bourgeois, *L'Ironie romantique*, pp. 30–31.

38. I have borrowed a number of ideas in this paragraph from Bourgeois and from Ingrid Strohschneider-Kohrs, *Die romantische Ironie in Theorie und Gestaltung*.

39. Although not addressing himself to the question of Romantic Irony, what Geoffrey Hartman has to say in his essay "Romanticism and 'Anti-Self-Consciousness'," in *Romanticism and Consciousness*, ed. Harold Bloom (New York: Oxford University Press, 1970), pp. 46–56, is pertinent. Hartman speaks of art as the only means by which the nineteenth-century poet could bridge the gap between the self and the external world. Browning himself was to speak more directly of art as serving this function in the last book of *The Ring and the Book*.

40. See Bourgeois, pp. 34–35.

41. See Mark D. Hawthorne, "Browning's *Sordello*: Structure through Repetition," *VP* 16 (1978): 205.

42. See Ong, *Interfaces of the Word*, p. 297.

43. J. H. Harper, "'Eternity Our Due': Time in the Poetry of Robert Browning," in *Victorian Poetry*, ed. Malcolm Bradbury and David Palmer (London: Arnold, 1972), p. 64, observes that Browning recognizes the possibility of simultaneity as "an intolerable negation of essential human desires."

44. See Mason, "The Importance of *Sordello*," p. 137.

45. Herbert F. Tucker, Jr., "Browning, Eglamor, and Closure in *Sordello*,"*SBHC* 4 (1976): 68.

46. For example, Thomas J. Collins, "The Poetry of Robert Browning," p. 333, writes that "there can be no question that the reviews of *Sordello* led him, as it were, to pull in his poetic horns." In this essay Collins is more sympathetic to Browning's aims and accomplishments in *Sordello* than he earlier was in *Browning's Moral-Aesthetic Theory*.

47. *Poetry* 10 (1917): 113.

48. Isobel Armstrong, in her essay "Browning and the 'Grotesque Style'," has some excellent comments on the style of *Sordello*. She notes Browning's ability to render "the structure of experience as a fluid, unfinished *process* on which we continually try

to impose a shape, an order" (p. 97) and observes how the "grammar, assisted by the breaks in the lines, constantly creates and dispels illusions of meaning and relationship and requires a continuous reorientation and adjustment to its direction" (p. 102).

49. Irvine and Honan use the term to apply to the dramatic monologues. To them it means "techniques which present description, narration, or reflection from the point of view of a limited, individual consciousness" (p. 117). The term has a long history in Browning criticism. Stopford A. Brooke, *The Poetry of Robert Browning* (London: Ibister, 1902), p. 10, said, for example, that Browning "was impressionist long before Impressionism arrived."

50. See Irving Massey, *The Uncreating Word: Romanticism and the Object* (Bloomington: Indiana University Press, 1970), pp. 31–32.

Chapter Five

1. Thomas J. Collins advances the idea that "Pippa represents the creation of an ideal poet-figure . . . , the chastened and romantic version of a poet who can do all things for all men" (*Robert Browning's Moral-Aesthetic Theory, 1833–1855,* p. 86). As will soon become evident, though I agree with Collins that Pippa represents a poet-figure, I espouse a different idea concerning the effectiveness of her function.

2. Only in the collected edition of 1849, for which Browning made many changes in the text, was *Pippa* subtitled "*A Drama.*"

3. Irvine and Honan, p. 95, find Pippa's description of the dawn "as so many different things at once—a cauldron of boiling light that overflows the world with divine love, a breast that flickers, a chalice to be drunk—that one gives up consistency in despair."

4. Pippa is the same age as Phene, who has just married, and only a year younger than Luigi, who rushes off to commit regicide. Pippa's views of life are not, therefore, to be attributed to extreme youth, as a number of commentators suggest the case to be.

5. The marble statue of Canova's that Jules so adores is the *Psichefanciulla*, which represents Psyche as a young girl with a butterfly. In treating Phene in this new fashion, he will be adding the butterfly, an image of the soul occurring frequently in Browning, to the girl whom he has already idolized as Psyche-come-to-life. During the interlude preceding the Jules-Phene episode, the art students talk of one of their number who was in love with himself and had a woman fall in love with him, too, whereupon he takes himself and the poem he is writing off to Trieste "out of pure jealousy." About the poem Bluphocks writes an epitaph: "Here a mammoth-poem lies, / Fouled to death by butterflies" (1. 293–300). It is in such seemingly casual but important ways that Browning interweaves the images in his poem to underscore meaning without resorting to a chorus figure.

6. The idea of love and bondage is suggested in this episode by Italy's political bondage to Austria and Luigi's love of his country because of her enslavement. See 3. 39–50.

7. The outcome of this episode is left unclear. Is the Monsignor to return to Pippa her rightful inheritance, or is he to keep Maffeo gagged and thus unable to tell about Pippa's existence so that the Church will receive the money?

8. A number of commentators have addressed the problem whether Pippa's New Year's hymn represents the poet's own thoughts. Indeed, for years it was held that Pippa's "God's in his heaven— / All's right with the world!" represented the height of Victorian optimism. By now this view is seldom advanced, at least in print. Looking at

the New Year's hymn from another angle, Margaret Eleanor Glen [Cook] maintains nonetheless that the hymn provides the theme of the whole poem: "God is working out His purposes as He wills through men whether they strive for or against these purposes. Men are in the hands of God, be they conscious or unconscious of it." Thus Mrs. Cook concludes that the poem portrays "the irony of God's ways when regarded from man's point of view" ("The Meaning and Structure of *Pippa Passes*," *UTQ* 24 [1955]: 412, 426). This position has been questioned, correctly in my estimation, by E. Warwick Slinn, who asks which character in the play represents man's view and how the reader can know that he is seeing God's ways from God's point of view. Slinn argues that the notion that all are God's puppets is ironic because the characters seem to be the puppets of their own views of themselves (" 'God a Tame Confederate'.") For other views see Dale Kramer, "Character and Theme in *Pippa Passes*," *VP* 2 (1964): 241–49; Jacob Korg, "A Reading of *Pippa Passes*," *VP* 6 (1968): 5–19; and Marvin P. Garrett, "Language and Design in *Pippa Passes*," *VP* 13 (1975): 47–60.

9. There are intriguing hints of an episode, which exists only in germ, concerning Bluphocks and Pippa. The girls on the street in the interlude between episodes three and four have been employed to pass Bluphocks off as a rich Englishman in love with Pippa. That Pippa is clearly fascinated is shown in the epilogue when she says, "it had done me / . . . surely no such mightly hurt / To learn his name"—that foreigner "with blue eyes and thick rings / Of English-coloured hair" (4. 256–61). If Bluphocks's design had succeeded, Pippa would have proved the natural "slave" in the relationship. The idea of Pippa—pure innocence, a highly manipulable puppet—being joined to Bluphocks—pure evil, the arch-manipulator—must have been for Browning a tempting one to develop, and, of course, one he did develop in *The Ring and the Book*.

10. In his revisions of the poem, Browning emphasized the notion that men assume that they can know God's ways and that their actions are in accord with his will. Slinn deals at length with the characters' self-conceived ideas of themselves working God's ways as they are displayed in the revised text.

11. Slinn, " 'God a Tame Confederate,' " p. 171, writes: "In drawing attention to itself through its use of excessive coincidence, the design makes the work both a totality and an obvious artifice: as totality, the design embraces the ironies in private illusion and social intrigue, and as artifice it sustains the reader's detachment, reminding him of his own participation as an ironic observer." Roma A. King, Jr., *The Focusing Artifice*, p. 53, remarks that the play's movement is "continuous and circular rather than horizontal."

12. The most sophisticated examination of *Pippa* as a transitional work is E. D. H. Johnson, *The Alien Vision of Victorian Poetry*, pp. 86–91.

13. In a later poem, *Balaustion's Adventure* (1871), Browning has his protagonist explicitly declare that "poetry is power" (line 236). This is repeated in the poem devoted to "Balaustion's Last Adventure," *Aristophanes' Apology* (1875; line 5582). Critics have frequently noted that Browning's plays deal with power, political power. Herbert Tucker is the first, however, to suggest that in Browning political power may be taken as a figuration of poetic power.

14. Browning himself said in February 1845 that he liked *Pippa* better than anything he had yet done (Kintner, 1: 27). Reviewers at the time, however, cared little for it.

15. Browning does not, however, provide a historical background. He chose the subject not for its historical interest—as he says in the Advertisement, it was an "event without consequences"—but for, apparently, its possibilities for psychological investigation.

16. In the Advertisement, Browning in fact speaks of "the fiery and audacious temper, unscrupulous selfishness, profound dissimulation, and singular fertility in resources, of Victor" in contrast to "the extreme and painful sensibility, prolonged immaturity of powers, earnest good purpose and vacillating will, of Charles."

17. J. Hillis Miller, *The Disappearance of God*, pp. 130–31, observes that "the plays study the question of *power*, political rather than magical or poetical power, but still power."

18. Mary Rose Sullivan, "Browning's Plays: Prologue to *Men and Women*," *BIS* 3 (1975): 18, in tracing the theme of illusion and false ideals in Browning's plays, notes: "His protagonists invariably *refuse* to accept the fact of betrayal: blinding themselves to the irrefutable evidence, they cling stubbornly to the idol, rather than admit his human imperfection."

Chapter Six

1. *A Victorian Vintage, Being a Selection . . . . From the Diaries of . . . Sir Mountstuart E. Grant Duff*, ed. A. Tilney Bassett (London: Methuen, 1930), p. 181. We know that Browning destroyed many of his early poems; see Griffin and Minchin, p. 43, and Maynard, *Browning's Youth*, pp. 4, 179.

2. The late Geoffrey Tillotson remarks: "Browning restored literature to its origins as a thing recited. . . . Many things . . . that look like defects do not sound like them" (Geoffrey Tillotson, *A View of Victorian Literature* [Oxford: Clarendon Press, 1978], p. 365).

3. For general remarks on the companion poems, see Nancy B. Rich, "New Perspectives on the Companion Poems of Robert Browning," *VN*, No. 36 (Fall 1969), pp. 5–9, and William E. Harrold, *The Variance and the Unity*. There is also a dissertation on the subject, which I have not seen: John J. Roberts, "The Comparison Poems of Robert Browning," Tulane University, 1972.

4. See Robert Langbaum, *The Poetry of Experience*; Park Honan, *Browning's Characters*, pp. 104–25; Philip Drew, *The Poetry of Robert Browning*, pp. 12–38; Michael Mason, "Browning and the Dramatic Monologue," in *Robert Browning*, ed. Isobel Armstrong, pp. 231–68; Ralph W. Rader, "The Dramatic Monologue and Related Lyric Form."

5. Most critics have paid little attention to Browning's repeated rearrangement of his poems. Ian Jack, however, in his book *Browning's Major Poetry*, finds the classifications useful guides and discusses the poems under such headings. See also Lawrence Poston III, "Browning Rearranges Browning."

6. See Arthur E. Dubois, "Robert Browning, Dramatist," p. 629.

7. Vladamir Jankélévitch, *L'Ironie, ou la bonne conscience*, p. 23.

8. There is a sprawl of critical opinions on the poem. I shall mention only two of the more recherché: B. R. Jerman, "Browning's Witless Duke," *PMLA* 72 (1957): 488–93, sees the duke as a stupid nobleman who in speaking of a second-rate realistic picture of a photogenic woman gives himself away to his auditor; Thomas J. Assad, "Browning's 'My Last Duchess,'" *Tulane Studies in English* 10 (1960): 117–28, sees the duke as a tough-minded realist who has had to deal with a silly sentimental woman who could not make distinctions between men and mules or men and trees.

9. Langbaum, pp. 82–85; Rader, pp. 138–39. In his study of prose fiction, Wolfgang Iser speaks of the reader as two persons: "the alien 'me'," the one who involves himself imaginatively in the fiction, and "the real 'me'," the one who is firmly rooted in the present and in his own sense of himself as a person (*The Implied Reader* [Balti-

more: Johns Hopkins University Press, 1974], p. 293). As I understand Iser, these two aspects of reading pretty much correspond to what Langbaum calls sympathy and judgment. G. G. Sedgewick maintains that all forms of drama involve both the sympathy and the judgment (or detachment) of the viewer or listener and that this makes for an ironic situation that he calls "general dramatic irony": "The very theatre itself . . . is a sort of ironic convention whereby a spectator occupying a good seat, as it were, in the real world is enabled to look into a world of illusion and so to get 'a view of life from on high.' . . . The peculiar pleasure of the theatre, then, is the spectacle of a life in which, it is true, we do not interfere but over which we exercise the control of knowledge. And this spectacle, when it pleases or holds us, we do not view with the 'swelling or pride' of superiority but with a sort of paradoxical sympathy; for, though it is *sympathy*, it is likewise *detached*. . . . *The whole attitude of the interested spectator is ironic*; by the very fact that he is such a spectator, he is an ironist" (*Of Irony, Especially in Drama*, 2d ed. [Toronto: University of Toronto Press, 1948], pp. 32–33.)

10. "Through the Metidja to Abd-el-Kadr," "Waring," and "The Pied Piper" were written in 1842 (Griffin and Minchin, p. 128).

11. John V. Hagopian, "The Mask of Browning's Countess Gismond," *PQ* 40 (1961): 153–55; John W. Tilton and R. Dale Tuttle, "A New Reading of 'Count Gismond'," *SP* 59 (1962): 83–95; Sister Marcella M. Holloway, "A Further Reading of 'Count Gismond'," *SP* 60 (1963): 549–53; Frank Allen, "Ariosto and Browning: A Reexamination of 'Count Gismond'," *VP* 11 (1973): 15–25.

12. Dorothy M. Mermin, "Speaker and Auditor in Browning's Dramatic Monologues," *UTQ*, 45 (1976): 139, observes of the characters in Browning's plays: "Their obsessive concern with what they have or haven't said, will or won't say, generally retards the action and is often the centre of the plot."

13. Ian Jack, on the other hand, finds that "the whole tone of the poem" indicates that "the only lie the Countess tells occurs when she fibs about the subject of her conversation." Jack says that her children have been playing in the distance as she tells her story and then "mother-like, she changes the subject when the younger of her children comes running up" (*Browning's Major Poetry*, p. 88).

14. William Cadbury, "Lyric and Anti-Lyric Forms: A Method for Judging Browning," *UTQ* 34 (1964–65): 49–67, maintains that the poem fails because we cannot catch in the speaker's tone a proof of personality clear enough to let us judge her or her story. "We are, then, convinced of her innocence, not through knowledge of her character, but through Gauthier's admission of guilt, which is a result of the narrative of the poem, not of its drama" (p. 53).

15. C. H. Herford, *Robert Browning*, p. 136, observes that Browning's "intellectual thirst for the problematic, and his ethical thirst for the incomplete, combined to hurry him away to moments of suspense, big with undecided or unfulfilled fate." In similar vein Patricia Ball, *The Central Self*, p. 219, says: "Browning's sense of climax is commonly a point of unfulfilled expectation or speculation."

16. The echo of the last scene of *Othello* is probably intentional and ironic: the serenader is in effect his own murderer.

17. See, for example, Irvine and Honan, pp. 119–20. Santayana perceived the steamy eroticism of the last speech but then commented: "We are not allowed to regard these expressions as the cries of souls blinded by the agony of passion and lust. Browning unmistakably adopts them as expressing his own highest intuitions" (George Santayana, "The Poetry of Barbarism," in *Interpretations of Poetry and Religion* [New York: Scribner's, 1900], p. 194). How "we are not allowed" and how we know that "Browning unmistakably adopts them" as his own we are not informed.

18. I have discovered subsequent to writing this that a club is also the setting envisioned by Philip Drew, *The Poetry of Browning*, p. 286.

19. For example, William Lyon Phelps, *Robert Browning: How to Know Him* (Indianapolis: Bobbs-Merrill, 1919) pp. 116–24. W. O. Raymond, *Infinite Moment*, pp. 218–19, speaks of "the good moment" that the two lovers do not seize and as a result their lives are "irretrievably marred."

20. Clyde S. Kilby, "Browning's *Cristina*," *Explicator* 2 (November 1943): item 16, has also questioned the truth of the speaker's statement. Marylyn J. Parins, "Browning's 'Cristina': The Woman, the Look, and the Speaker," *SBHC* 7 (1979): 33, finds the speaker "naive, idealistic, impetuous, and probably foolish."

21. Alice Chandler, "'The Eve of St. Agnes' and 'Porphyria's Lover'," *VP* 3 (1965): 273–74, notes similarities in plot, phrasing, and theme. These may result from an unconscious influence or they may be intentional, Browning aiming "to take one of the archetypal works of the romantic imagination and, as a conscious experiment, use physical realism and psychological insight to re-explore its possibilities" (p. 274). As my text should suggest, I believe that Browning uses a romantic situation, which he may well have got from Keats, to show it up for what it is (or what he felt it is): namely, the reality of "romantic" love is madness and death.

22. There has been some disagreement as to whether the lover kills Porphyria because he loves her or hates her. Langbaum holds that he kills her in order to hold the good moment, "is a criminal because he loves" (*Poetry of Experience*, p. 203). Max K. Sutton, "Language as Defence in 'Porphyria's Lover'," *CE* 31 (1969): 280–89, maintains that the speaker hated Porphyria. David Eggenschwiler, "Psychological Complexity in 'Porphyria's Lover'," *VP* 8 (1970): 39–48, agrees with Sutton. C. R. Tracy, "*Porphyria's Lover*," *MLN* 52 (1937): 579–80, sees the act as an illustration of Browning's philosophy of seizing the moment.

Chapter Seven

1. G. K. Chesterton, *Robert Browning*, p. 51.

2. Honan, *Browning's Characters*, pp. 66–67, shows how Browning attempted to differentiate the speech of the Europeans from that of the Druses and to combine the two styles in Djabal's speech.

3. In the nineteenth as well as in the seventeenth century, the spectacle of heroic drama was part of its appeal. In *The Return of the Druses,* there are crowd scenes, exotic costumes, violent action, frequent entrances and exits, all doubtless designed to make the play more appealing on the stage. H. B. Charlton, "Browning as Dramatist," pp. 48–49, applauds the spectacular scenes but finds the tragedy of the chief characters poorly integrated into the political concern of the play. I believe, however, that we misconceive Browning's purpose in his plays if we see them as plays about politics. For a healthy antidote to Charlton's views of the dramas, see Lawrence Poston III, "Browning's Political Skepticism."

4. For an account of the quarrel between the two, see Joseph W. Reed, "Browning and Macready."

5. Macready's lack of sympathy with Browning's dramatic efforts is suggested by the many changes that he made in the text of *A Blot*. The manuscript of the play, showing the excisions and revisions proposed by Macready, is in the Beinecke Rare Book and Manuscript Library at Yale University. Details are given by Reed, "Browning and Macready."

6. Opinions of the play are widely varied. I here offer three. Dickens was given the

play to read in manuscript by John Forster, who apparently showed Dickens's remarks to Macready but, surprisingly, not to Browning. Dickens wrote: "Browning's play has thrown me into a perfect passion of sorrow. To say that there is anything in its subject save what is lovely, true, deeply affecting, full of the best emotion, the most earnest feeling, and the most true and tender source of interest, is to say that there is no light in the sun, and no heat in blood. It is full of genius, natural and great thoughts, profound and yet simple and beautiful in its vigour. I know nothing that is so affecting, nothing in any book I have ever read, as Mildred's recurrence to that 'I was so young—I had no mother.' I know no love like it, no passion like it, no moulding of a splendid thing after its conception, like it. And I swear it is a tragedy that MUST be played: and must be played, moreover, by Macready . . . " (quoted in John Forster, *Life of Charles Dickens* [London: Chapman and Hall, 1872-74], 2:25). As to Dickens's opinion of the play and why Forster never showed it to Browning, see Gertrude Reese, "Browning and *A Blot*," *MLN* 63 (1948): 237-40; and Harry Stone, "Dickens, Browning, and the Mysterious Letter," *Pacific Coast Philology* 1 (1966): 42-47. Percy Lubbock was of the opinion that "the sombre beauty of the treatment only exposes pitilessly the hopeless absurdity of the plot" ("Robert Browning," *The Quarterly Review* 217 [1912]: 445). A more recent and representative opinion is the following: "It is difficult to imagine how the fastidious author of these plays [prior to *A Blot*] and *Dramatic Lyrics* could have descended so low" (F. E. Halliday, *Robert Browning: His Life and Work* [London: Jupiter Books, 1975], p. 59).

7. See Terry Otten, "*A Blot in the 'Scutcheon* and the *Pièce Bien Faite*: An Artistic Dilemma," *Research Studies* (Washington State University) 36 (1968): 214-22.

8. For a consideration of the melodramatic element in the play that Browning attempted to shape into a tragedy, see Donald S. Hair, *Browning's Experiments with Genre*, pp. 57-65.

9. Tresham also sees others in terms of roles. For example, when he apprehends Mertoun, he says that the young man bears himself "exactly as in curious dreams I've had / How felons, this wide earth is full of, look / When they're detected . . . " (3. 1. 59-61).

10. The word *name* occurs seventeen times in the play, significantly more than in any other work earlier than *The Ring and the Book*.

11. "Oh, thought's absurd," he says in soliloquy. Better to "yield my reason up" (2. 80,86).

12. Tresham has taught his code of honor even to his servants. If Gerard had cared a bit less about "the pitifullest thing / That touched the House's honor"—"that this was right, nor that was wrong" (1. 1. 85-92)—he would have kept his mouth shut and so averted the tragedy.

13. The play is so lacking in focus that to many modern readers it is not even evident that Tresham is the protagonist. Donald Hair, for example, feels it necessary to show that it is not the deaths of the two lovers but Tresham's suffering which "could alone make the play worthy of such a name" as tragedy (*Browning's Experiments with Genre*, p. 59). Dickens apparently saw the play as the tragedy of Mildred and Mertoun. See his letter to Forster quoted in note 6, above.

14. The song he sings is even less integrated into the play than the child's song in the last act of *Strafford*. Furthermore, it is verse as poor as any Browning ever wrote.

15. One could multiply the questions concerning what Lounsbury calls "the untruthfulness of the play as a representation of real life" (Thomas R. Lounsbury, *The Early Literary Career of Robert Browning* [London: Fisher Unwin, 1912], p. 141).

16. The hardships of the "hungry forties" are almost certainly reflected in the sufferings of the workers at Cleves.

17. I am, of course, excluding *Pippa* from consideration as a "theatrical piece."

18. In *King Victor and King Charles,* Polyxena was "to serve in place / Of monarch, minister and mistress" (1. 1. 70–71) till Charles was confirmed as King.

19. For example:

Valence.   she no whit depends
        On circumstance; as she adorns a throne
        She had adorned..
Berthold.   ..A hovel—in which book
        Have I read that of every queen that lived?
                                                              (4. 130–33)

20. Possibly the name "Valence" is meant to suggest decisiveness in contrast to Guibert's ambivalence.

21. Counterpart to Guibert in insight and ironic detachment among the prince's retinue is Melchior, although he is not so well integrated into the action of the play as Guibert.

22. For Valence the agent for the conclusion of the conflict is, of course, Colombe. In lines that Browning added in 1849, doubtless influenced by his marriage some three years earlier, Valence sees woman as the mediatrix between God and man:

There is a vision in the heart of each
Of justice, mercy, wisdom, tenderness
To wrong and pain, and knowledge of its cure:
And these embodied in a woman's form
That best transmits them, pure as first received,
From God above her, to mankind below.
                                                                (2. 263–68)

In these lines there seems to be a resolution to the conflict, power incarnating itself (in woman) as love.

Chapter Eight

1. Elizabeth Barrett's letters to Browning are full of remarks about the poems of the 1845 volume. In addition, she wrote fifty-six manuscript pages about them and the two plays that were to follow. A somewhat inaccurate transcription is printed in *New Poems by Robert Browning and Elizabeth Barrett Browning,* and reprinted in the Macmillan Edition of Browning's works, *The Complete Poetical Works of Robert Browning, New Edition with Additional Poems First Published in 1914.* Eleven of the fifty-six pages were inexplicably omitted and have never been printed. See Kintner, 1: 134 n. 1.

2. Richard Hengist Horne, *A New Spirit of the Age* (London: Smith, Elder, 1844), 2: 170.

3. They are "The Italian in England," "The Englishman in Italy," "The Flight of the Duchess," "The Boy and the Angel," "Time's Revenges," and "The Glove." "Pictor Ignotus" and "The Bishop Orders His Tomb at St. Praxed's Church" were subsumed by the heading "Men and Women." The rest were classified as "Dramatic Lyrics."

4. DeVane believes that the poem embodies a cultural-historical type: it is Browning's conception of how the unknown painters "of those pale, formal, monastic series—Virgin, Babe, and Saint—might defend themselves in the face of the great vogue for the newer, more vulgar, painters who depict the expressions of contempo-

rary human beings" (*Handbook*, p. 155). This was first questioned by Paul F. Jamieson, "Browning's 'Pictor Ignotus, Florence, 15—,'" *Explicator* 11 (1952): item 8. Jamieson sees the speaker not as a type but as a failed painter who would have liked fame but found exposure to the crowd and to criticism unendurable. Jamieson suggests that "the youth" is Raphael. J. B. Bullen, "Browning's 'Pictor Ignotus' and Vasari's 'Life of Fra Bartolommeo di San Marco,'" *RES* 23 (1972): 313–19, identifies the speaker of the poem as Fra Bartolommeo, whose history Browning learned from Vasari's *Lives of the Painters* and who was a painter of great talent but limited achievement. Michael H. Bright, "Browning's Celebrated Pictor Ignotus," *ELN* 13 (1976): 192–94, argues that Bullen has missed "the central point Browning is making. The whole idea of the poem, as the title makes clear, is that the painter is unknown" (p. 194). In a later essay, "Browning's 'Pictor Ignotus': An Interpretation," *SBHC* 4 (1976): 53–61, Bright admits that the speaker could have done all he says but that the true reasons for his forswearing fame were his fear of idolatry and his less justifiable fear of unsympathetic criticism. In contrast to Bullen and Bright, Richard D. Altick, "'Andrea del Sarto': The Kingdom of Hell Is Within," in *Browning's Mind and Art*, ed. Clarence Tracy (Edinburgh: Oliver and Boyd, 1968), pp. 18, 24, maintains that the unknown painter's claim to artistic talent is unsupported and that the painter is thus rationalizing to his own satisfaction his refusal to compete.

5. *Browning's Beginnings*, p. 170.

6. I am endebted to Bernadine Brown, "Robert Browning's 'The Italian in England,'" *VP* 6 (1968): 179–83, for the suggestion of the religious overtones in the poem.

7. See Hood, *Letters*, pp. 166–67; Orr, *Life and Letters*, p. 123; and DeVane, *Handbook*, pp. 159–62.

8. James F. Loucks, "The Dating of Browning's 'Here's to Nelson's Memory,'" *SBHC* 4 (1976): 71–72, suggests that the poem was prompted by the recent donation of the coat Nelson wore when he was wounded at Trafalgar to the Greenwich Hospital. Loucks says that the poem could have been written so late as the autumn of 1845, when the poet was readying the volume for publication.

9. Browning spoke of it as "just the thing for the time—what with the Oxford business, and Camden society and other embroilments" (*New Letters*, pp. 35–36), referring to the Tractarians and the concern over John Henry Newman's recent conversion to the Roman Catholic Church. Ruskin was of the opinion that there is "no other piece of modern English, prose or poetry, in which there is so much told, as in these lines of the Renaissance spirit,—its worldliness, inconsistency, pride, hypocrisy, ignorance of itself, love of art, of luxury, and of good Latin" (*Modern Painters*, vol. 4, chap. 20, in *The Works of John Ruskin*, ed. E. T. Cook and Alexander Wedderburn [London: George Allen, 1903–12], 6: 449). See Robert A. Greenberg, "Ruskin, Pugin, and the Contemporary Context of 'The Bishop Orders His Tomb,'" *PMLA* 84 (1969): 1588–94.

10. See, for example, Robert Felgar, "Browning's Narrative Art," *SBHC* 3 (1975): 82, who says that Browning uses a dramatically imagined participant or onlooker in this poem to give the reader "a sense of immediacy, of almost being there."

11. See Frederick Palmer and Edward Snyder, "New Light on the Brownings," *Quarterly Review* 269 (1937): 48–63, and DeVane, *Handbook*, pp. 175–76.

12. Mrs. Orr, *Handbook*, p. 276, says of the narrator: "He is a jovial, matter-of-fact person, in spite of the vein of sentiment which runs through him; and the imaginative part of his narrative was more probably the result of a huntsman's breakfast which found its way into his brain." Here as elsewhere Mrs. Orr is more perspicacious than many of Browning's commentators who belittle her.

13. The technique is reminiscent of Tennyson, particularly of such poems as "Oenone," in which the opening lines descriptive of the landscape prefigure, in their suggestive detail, the action of the poem. For Browning's love of Tennyson's early poems, see *Domett*, pp. 40–41, and the many references to Tennyson in Kintner.

14. Mrs. Orr, *Handbook*, p. 293, also notes the close relationship of the two lyrics: "The words: 'love me for ever,' appeal to us from a tombstone which records how Spring garlands are severed by the hand of June. . . . "

15. Browning said that he intended the refrain to be "a mournful comment on the short duration of the conventional 'For Ever'" (quoted in Macmillan Edition, p. 1350).

16. Browning said that the man is the speaker in both parts of the poem and that "it is *his* confession of how fleeting is the belief (implied in the first part) that such raptures are self-sufficient and enduring—as for the time they appear" (quoted in Macmillan Edition, pp. 1350–51).

17. See DeVane, *Handbook*, pp. 255–57.

18. That the fragmentary nature of "Saul" is owing to an impasse in Browning's religious life is advanced by William Clyde DeVane, *Browning's Parleyings: The Autobiography of a Mind* (New Haven, Conn.: Yale University Press, 1927), pp. 116–18; A. W. Crawford, "Browning's *Saul*," *Queen's Quarterly* 34 (1927): 448–54; and, later, Collins, *Robert Browning's Moral-Aesthetic Theory, 1833–1855*, pp. 91–92. Arguing that the first nine stanzas are as Christian in outlook as the stanzas of the second part completed seven years or so later are W. David Shaw, *The Dialectical Temper*, pp. 224–25; Ward Hellstrom, "Time and Type in Browning's 'Saul,'" *ELH* 33 (1966): 370–89; and Elizabeth Bieman, "The Ongoing Testament in Browning's 'Saul,'" *UTQ* 43 (1974): 151–68.

19. J. S. McClatchey, "Browning's 'Saul' as a Davidic Psalm of the Praise of God: The Poetics of Prophecy," *SBHC* 4 (1976): 62–83, is, I believe, the first to note this as the genre of the poem.

20. Cadbury, "Lyric and Anti-Lyric Forms: A Method for Judging Browning," p. 52, contends that the speaker of the poem "has no interest in lying to us, and so we can question what he says only by asking his relationship to it. Why, we ask, does he remain in a court, the depravity of which he sees so clearly? . . . He remains precisely because of the operation of the humorous irony which is the tone of the poem. His defence against depravity, his ironic wit, makes particularly vivid the necessity for less ironic souls to get out." David Sonstroem, "'Fine Speeches Like Gold,' in Browning's 'The Glove'," *VP* 15 (1977): 85–90, maintains that Ronsard's substitution of buffoonery for a lofty style is for the sake of deflation of the court, showing its pretensions and trivialities.

21. Ronsard also sums up the moral of his story in a Latin tag.

22. The historical Ronsard and Marot were bitterly divided on the subject of religion. During the religious wars Ronsard was committed to an extreme royalist and Catholic position. He was noted for attacking his opponents, especially in his *Discours*, whom he dismissed as traitors and hypocrites. Marot, on the other hand, was a Protestant who was imprisoned for his beliefs and who finally fled from France. If we apply this biographical information to the poem, then the action becomes doubly ironic.

23. George Saintsbury, "Browning," reprinted in *The Browning Critics*, ed. Litzinger and Knickerbocker, p. 28, agrees that "the moral is mainly rubbish" and, in addition, that "Marot *was* a poet."

24. Louise Schutz Boas, "Browning's 'The Glove'," *Explicator* 2 (1943): item 13,

claims that by the theorbo Browning meant to refer to DeLorge's two actions in fetching the gloves for the two different ladies.

25. Mrs. Orr, *Handbook*, p. 306 n., says that Mazzini told Browning how he had read the poem to his fellow exiles in England to show how an Englishman could sympathize with them.

Chapter Nine

1. Robert Brainard Pearsall, *Robert Browning* (New York: Twayne, 1974), p. 45, maintains that the play is based on Greek models. Like them *Luria* observes the dramatic unities, has no action on stage, "and the emphasis is firmly placed on the Greek values of stagecraft, solitude, and irony."
2. Browning's lack of interest in the characters other than Luria is suggested by the fact that he does not even supply certain narrative details about them that the audience finds necessary. For example: How does Domizia function in the camp? Why is she supposed to be there? Is she Luria's mistress?
3. Irvine and Honan, p. 186, find the influence of Carlyle clearly discernible in the play.
4. In *Sordello*, 3. 819–33, Browning had spoken out plainly on the matter in reference to poets.
5. The language in which he speaks of Florence is highly erotic, especially in the passage l. 321–30.
6. Browning to Miss Barrett: "Luria is a Moor, of Othello's country, and devotes himself to something he thinks Florence, and the old fortune follows . . . " (Kintner, 1:26).
7. Taking Browning's characterization of the style of the play, "high fantastical," as his point of departure, Donald S. Hair, *Browning's Experiments with Genre*, pp. 69–70, says: "Fantasy may either be presented entirely for its own sake . . . , or to serve a didactic intention. . . . If fantasy is presented entirely for its own sake, it is free from moral instruction, or is at least morally neutral. If fantasy is used for a didactic purpose, the poet is anything but neutral. It can be shown, I think, that Browning tried to have it both ways; that as an artist he used fantasy with didactic intention, but that as a man he remained uncommitted to his own conceptions. This discrepancy between the artist and the man reflected the uncertainty of Browning's beliefs in 1845, and in particular the uncertainty of his attitude toward Christianity. . . . Browning's imagination was sufficiently involved in his subject that he did not wish to leave the play incomplete, but at the same time he could not honestly say that he believed in what he was creating. He portrayed Luria, then, in a 'high fantastical' manner, which allowed him to characterize Luria as a Christ-like figure while he himself remained morally neutral."
8. In May 1842 Browning wrote to Domett that he would soon print *The Return of the Druses* and "finish a wise metaphysical play (about a great mind and soul turning to ill)" (*Domett*, p. 36). DeVane, *Handbook*, p. 190, believes this unfinished play to be *A Soul's Tragedy*, and others have followed DeVane—for example, Ian Jack, *Browning's Major Poetry*, p. 69. I personally see no indication anywhere of Chiappino as either a great mind or a great soul. His name, I feel certain, derives from the diminutive of the obsolete Italian word *chiappo*, which means "unexpected advantage."
9. Mary Rose Sullivan, "Browning's Plays: Prologue to *Men and Women*," p. 33, takes a contrary view of the role of language in the play: Browning here "abandoned action almost entirely to concentrate on the final stage of moral degeneration, the

flight into rhetoric. Returning to a central idea of *Pippa Passes*, that only words used lyrically, to express felt experience, can be trusted, he exhibits a morally ruined man using rhetoric to corrupt others."

10. In Italian his name means something like "every good."

11. Browning was aware of his own tendency toward special pleading and the seeming amorality of his views. He wrote to Miss Barrett that he could easily be misunderstood: " . . . I *seemed* to speak against; and only seemed—because that is a way of mine which you must have observed; that foolish concentrating of thought and feeling, for a moment, on some one little spot of a character or anything else indeed, and—in the attempt to do justice and develop whatever may seem ordinarily to be overlooked in it,—that over vehement *insisting* on, and giving an undue prominence to, the same—which has the effect of taking away from the importance of the rest of the related objects which, in truth, are not considered at all" (Kintner, 1: 343).

12. As to her influence on the play, see Kintner, 2:576, 580.

13. Irvine and Honan's remarks are representative: "Browning was fascinated by motives, but seemed scarcely interested in how motives produced action or how one action must be linked logically and psychologically with another. He could depict character in isolation—even at a moment of crisis—but he could not easily bring one character into dynamic relation with another. In short, he understood the private drama of passions and ideas occurring in the mind, but not the public drama of men acting and conflicting in the great world of politics and business" (p. 71). Paul de Reul, *L'Art et la pensée de Robert Browning* (Brussells: Maurice Lamertin, 1929), p. 71, speaks more specifically about Browning's concentration on one character: "Le poète se projette avec une belle force pénétrante dans les consciences [de ses caractères], mais il n'explore qu'une ame à la fois, trop profondément pour saisir l'action des ames entre elles ou le choc des ames et des événements." Further (p. 299) he says that "Browning, comme Sordello, parvient à s'oublier dans ses personages, mais à mesure qu'il pénètre en chacun d'eux, il perd contact avec leur vie collective."

14. A. W. Schlegel found it impossible to relate the ironic and the tragic: "No doubt, wherever the proper tragic enters everything like irony immediately ceases; . . . the subjection of mortal beings to an inevitable destiny demands the highest degree of seriousness" (*Lectures on Dramatic Art and Literature*, quoted by D. C. Muecke, *Irony*, p. 19). In his essay "De l'essence du rire," Baudelaire insists that irony is always accompanied by "le sentiment du comique."

15. See Muecke, *Irony*, pp. 33–36. In *Joseph the Provider*, chapter six, Thomas Mann has Joseph speak of the necessity for serenity when one confronts the ambiguities and paradoxes of existence: "It is all too exciting and solemn for words! And just because it is so solemn it must be treated with a light touch. For lightness, . . . flippancy, the artful jest, that is God's very best gift to man, the profoundest knowledge we have of that complex, questionable thing we call life. God gave it to humanity, that life's terribly serious face might be forced to wear a smile" (H. T. Lowe-Porter translation, quoted by Muecke, pp. 35–36).

16. Arthur E. DuBois, "Robert Browning, Dramatist," p. 642.

Afterword

1. Philip Drew, *The Poetry of Browning*, p. 38.
2. So far as I can discover, Francis R. Duckworth, *Browning: Background and Conflict* (London: Ernest Benn, 1931), pp. 183–213, is the first to advance this theory. Betty Miller pretty much builds her whole biography of the poet (*Robert Browning: A*

Portrait) around the theory. J. Hillis Miller, in his chapter on Browning in *The Disappearance of God*, argues that the poet uses the dramatic mode to conceal an inner vacuity. Irvine and Honan, Browning's latest biographers, are more guarded in their speculations, but they too seem to subscribe to the theory that Browning turned to the dramatic mode in order to conceal something about himself; see especially p. 32.

3. Drew, *The Poetry of Browning*, p. 38, and chapter 3, "Browning and the Rejection of the Romantic Tradition."

4. Robert Langbaum, *The Poetry of Experience*, p. 158.

5. Friedrich Schlegel observes: "As long as the artist invents and is inspired, he remains in a constrained state of mind, at least for the purpose of communication. He then wants to say everything, which is the wrong tendency of young geniuses. . . . Thus, he fails to recognize the value and dignity of self-restraint, which is indeed for both the artist and the man the first and the last, the most necessary and the highest goal. The most necessary: for wherever we do not restrain ourselves, the world will restrain us; and thus we will become its slave. The highest: for we can restrain ourselves only in those points and aspects where we have infinite power, in self-creation and self-destruction" (*Lyceum* Fragment No. 37).

6. In her book *The Central Self*, Patricia Ball studies the dual impulses of the egotistical sublime and negative capability in works of the major Romantic and Victorian poets; she is not, however, concerned with the ironic implications. The section dealing with Browning may be found on pp. 198–220. E. Warwick Slinn, " 'God A Tame Confederate'," considers the ironies of the egotistical sublime in *Pippa*.

7. Walter Pater, *Essays from "The Guardian"* (London: Macmillan, 1920), p. 43.

8. Browning said that "all the arts are mediators, between the soul and the infinite." They are "Mediators, messengers, projected from the soul to go and feel for Her, out there" (quoted by C. N. Wenger, *The Aesthetics of Browning*, pp. 163, 217).

9. "Goethe's Works—No. 9, and Last," *Monthly Repository*, N.S., 7 (1833): 281–82.

10. See especially the reviews of Tennyson's *Poems, Chiefly Lyrical* by W. J. Fox in the *Westminster Review* for January 1831 and by Arthur Henry Hallam in the *Englishman's Magazine* for August 1831. Fox writes: "The most important department in which metaphysical science has been a pioneer for poetry is in the analysis of particular states of mind." Hallam says: "These expressions of character are brief and coherent. . . . They are like summaries of mighty dramas."

11. John Forster, "Evidences of a New Genius for Dramatic Poetry," *New Monthly Magazine and Literary Journal* 46 (1836): 289–308.

12. Letter to John Kenyon, 1 October 1855, in Houghton Library, Harvard University; quoted by Eleanor Cook, *Browning's Lyrics*, p. xv.

13. Browning frequently referred to his poems as though they were plays in which he himself acted. See, for example, "One Word More" and the prefatory note to the 1888 edition of *Pauline*, in which he refers to the work as the "first of my performances."

14. Robert Preyer, "Two Styles in the Verse of Robert Browning," *ELH* 32 (1965): 79, observes: "The poems have the look of constantly being on the point of overleaping their formal structure." Wenger, *The Aesthetics of Robert Browning*, p. 163, notes that for Browning "the truths of art are never represented as though contented and at home in their forms, but rather as though projecting out of, overflowing, and transcending their mediums. Accordingly, the reconciliations he would have discoverable in art are those sufficient only to indicate the necessity of life in forms while the spirit makes its progress toward an eventual escape."

15. Walter Jackson Bate, *The Burden of the Past* (New York: Norton, 1972), p. 114,

in considering the accomplishments of the Romantics and the problems that they left to their successors, writes: "Thus the romantic poets themselves confronted for the first time and left to their followers the problem of attaining the scope and diversity of a major expression within an essentially lyrical habit of mind and for an audience that—by the later nineteenth century—had come to expect, and still expects, lyricism."

16. It is worthwhile recalling that when Browning refers to artistic form and literary history he more often than not employs the metaphor of the machine, as for example in books 2, 3, and 5 of *Sordello* and in the *Essay on Shelley.*

17. Geoffrey Hartman, "History Writing as Answerable Style," *NLH* 2 (1970): 73–83.

18. Walter Bagehot, "Wordsworth, Tennyson, and Browning; or Pure, Ornate, and Grotesque Art in English Poetry" (1864), reprinted in *Literary Studies* (London: Longmans, 1879), ed. Richard Holt Hutton, 2:375, says of Browning's "grotesque" art: "It takes the type, so to say, in *difficulties*. It gives representation to it in its minimum development, amid the circumstances least favourable to it, just while it is struggling with obstacles, just where it is encumbered with incongruities."

19. Quoted in Maisie Ward, *Robert Browning and His World: Two Robert Brownings?* (New York: Holt, Rinehart & Winston, 1969), p. 205.

20. Peter Conrad, *Shandyism: The Character of Romantic Irony* (Oxford: Basil Blackwell, 1978), p. 183.

21. Harold Orel, "Browning's Use of Historical Sources in *Strafford*" in *Six Studies of Nineteenth-Century English Literature and Thought*, ed. Harold Orel and George J. Worth, University of Kansas Humanistic Studies, No. 35 (Lawrence: University of Kansas Publications, 1962), p. 36, notes "the irritating mannerism whereby one speaker finishes the sentence of an earlier speaker, and in turn has his sentence finished for him by a third speaker."

22. In *Shelley's Prose: or, The Trumphet of Prophecy*, ed. David Lee Clark (Albuquerque: University of New Mexico Press, 1954), p. 279.

23. Cf. James Fotheringham, *Studies of the Mind and Art of Robert Browning*, 3d ed. (London: Horace Marshall and Son, 1898), p. 85: "His creed as thinker and his governing conception as poet are the same—real idealism. No man holds more deeply and no poet has given more forcible expression to a conviction of the higher issues of life—to the belief in the reality of a life and order more perfect and more beautiful than the actual world. But the way to it is through the realities of this world and not through dreams and fine sentiments." In somewhat similar vein G. Wilson Knight, *Neglected Powers: Essays on Nineteenth and Twentieth Century Literature* (London: Routledge and Kegan Paul, 1971), p. 246, observes of Browning: "He offers exactly what the Romantics, apart from Byron, lacked, while lacking what they offer. Browning gives us humanity with comparatively little emphasis on either nature . . . or on the transcendent, except in so far as it can be felt to flower from human instincts, passions and purposes."

24. *Learned Lady: Letters from Robert Browning to Mrs. Thomas FitzGerald, 1876–1889*, ed. Edward C. McAleer (Cambridge, Mass.: Harvard University Press, 1966), p. 152. Haakon M. Chevalier, *The Ironic Temper: Anatole France and His Time* (New York: Oxford University Press, 1932), p. 79, says that irony "characterizes the attitude of one who, when confronted with the choice of two things that are mutually exclusive, chooses both. Which is but another way of saying he chooses neither. He cannot bring himself to give up one for the other, and he gives up both. But he reserves the

right to derive from each the greatest possible passive enjoyment. And this enjoyment is Irony."

25. Wayne C. Booth, *A Rhetoric of Irony*.

26. Paul de Man, "The Rhetoric of Temporality," pp. 173–209; "Nietzsche's Theory of Rhetoric," *Symposium* 28 (1974): 33–51; "Action and Identity in Nietzsche," *Yale French Studies* 52 (1975): 16–30; "The Purloined Ribbon," *Glyph* 1 (1977): 28–49; *Allegories of Reading: Figural Language in Rousseau, Nietzsche, Rilke,* and *Proust*

27. Thomas J. Collins, "The Poetry of Robert Browning," argues that the dramatic monologues of the 1840s, 1850s, and 1860s were a deviation from the path marked out by Browning in *Sordello* and that he resumed the route he had intended to follow in *The Ring and the Book* and the later poems.

28. C. N. Wenger, *The Aesthetics of Robert Browning*, p. 240, notes that Browning "requires that the functioning of art among men generally must always be only a secondary end for the artist, for unless the artist works primarily towards his own development and salvation, he is soon equalled by those who benefit by his services and so ceases to be of further use or significance. It is for this reason that the poet puts his stress in aesthetics so much more upon the artist and his work than upon the appreciation and effects of art. . . . "

29. Henry James, "The Art of Fiction," reprinted in *The Future of the Novel,* ed. Leon Edel (New York: Vintage Books, 1956), p. 13.

30. In the second letter that she ever wrote to him, Elizabeth Barrett stated that the most salient characteristic of Browning's art was his ability to be both subjective and objective: "You have in your vision two worlds—or to use the language of the schools of the day, you are both subjective and objective in the habits of your mind. . . . Thus, you have an immense grasp in Art; and no one at all accustomed to consider the usual forms of it, could help regarding with reverence and gladness the gradual expansion of your powers" (Kintner, 1:9). For an account of modern or Romantic Irony as the necessary combination of subjective and objective elements, see D. C. Muecke, *The Compass of Irony,* chapter 7, especially pp. 196–97, 211–12. In a later book, *Irony*, p. 78, Muecke says of Romantic Irony: "Ironic literature . . . is literature in which there is a constant interplay of objectivity and subjectivity, freedom and necessity, the appearance of life and the reality of art, the author immanent in every part of his work as its creative vivifying principle and transcending his work as its objective 'presenter.' " Michael Mason, "The Importance of *Sordello*," p. 149, says that "Browning, in effect, made the historical concept of objective and subjective poetry, in a revised form, a live issue, not a long-solved one. In this way he was perhaps the only writer at the time who, by taking his stand firmly on the actual nature of poetic composition, was able to relate the exhilaration of a new psychological poetry to the chastening fact of a climate of moral uncertainty."

SELECTED BIBLIOGRAPHY

WORKS BY BROWNING
(ARRANGED CHRONOLOGICALLY)

Editions

Complete Works of Robert Browning. Ed. Charlotte Porter and Helen A. Clarke. Camberwell Edition. 12 vols. New York: Thomas Y. Crowell, 1898.

The Works of Robert Browning. Ed. Frederick G. Kenyon. Centenary Edition. 10 vols. London: Smith, Elder, 1912.

New Poems by Robert Browning and Elizabeth Barrett Browning. Ed. Sir Frederick G. Kenyon. London: Smith, Elder, 1914.

The Complete Poetical Works of Robert Browning, New Edition with Additional Poems First Published in 1914. Ed. Augustine Birrell. New York: Macmillan, 1915.

The Complete Poems of Robert Browning with Variant Readings and Annotations. Ed. Roma A. King, Jr., et al. 5 vols. to date. Athens: Ohio University Press, 1969–.

Individual Works (First Publication)

Pauline; A Fragment of a Confession. London: Saunders and Otley, 1833.
"Eyes Calm Beside Thee." *Monthly Repository*, N.S. 8 (October 1834): 712.
Paracelsus. London: Effingham Wilson, 1835.
"A King Lived Long Ago." *Monthly Repository*, N.S. 9 (November 1835): 707–8.
"Johannes Agricola." *Monthly Repository*, N.S. 10 (January 1836): 45–46.
"Porphyria." *Monthly Repository*, N.S. 10 (January 1836): 43–44.
"Still Ailing, Wind? Wilt Be Appeased or Not?" *Monthly Repository*, N.S. 10 (May 1836): 270–71.
Strafford: An Historical Tragedy. London: Longman, Rees, Orme, Brown, Green, & Longman, 1837.
Sordello. London: Edward Moxon, 1840.
Bells and Pomegranates. No. I.—Pippa Passes. London: Edward Moxon, 1841.
Bells and Pomegranates. No. II.—King Victor and King Charles. London: Edward Moxon, 1842.
Bells and Pomegranates. No. III.—Dramatic Lyrics. London: Edward Moxon, 1842.
Bells and Pomegranates. No. IV.—The Return of the Druses. London: Edward Moxon, 1843.

Bells and Pomegranates. No. V.—A Blot in the 'Scutcheon. London: Edward Moxon, 1843.

Bells and Pomegranates. No. VI.—Colombe's Birthday. London: Edward Moxon, 1844.

Bells and Pomegranates. No. VII. Dramatic Romances & Lyrics. London: Edward Moxon, 1845.

Bells and Pomegranates. No. VIII. And Last. Luria; and A Soul's Tragedy. London: Edward Moxon, 1846.

Introductory Essay. In *Letters of Percy Bysshe Shelley*, pp. 1–44. London: Moxon, 1852.

Letters

Robert Browning and Alfred Domett. Ed. Frederick G. Kenyon. London: Smith, Elder, 1906.

Letters of Robert Browning Collected by Thomas J. Wise. Ed. Thurman L. Hood. London: John Murray, 1933.

New Letters of Robert Browning. Ed. William Clyde DeVane and Kenneth Leslie Knickerbocker. London: John Murray, 1951.

The Letters of Robert Browning and Elizabeth Barrett Barrett, 1845-1846. Ed. Elvan Kintner. 2 vols. Cambridge, Mass.: Belknap Press of Harvard University Press, 1969.

BIOGRAPHIES, STUDIES, AND CRITICISM

Abrams, M. H. *The Mirror and the Lamp: Romantic Theory and The Critical Tradition.* New York: Oxford University Press, 1953; rpt. New York: W. W. Norton, 1958.

———. *Natural Supernaturalism: Tradition and Revolution in Romantic Literature.* New York: W. W. Norton, 1971.

Armstrong, Isobel. "Browning and the 'Grotesque Style'." In *The Major Victorian Poets: Reconsiderations*, ed. Isobel Armstrong, pp. 92–123. London: Routledge and Kegan Paul, 1969.

Ball, Patricia. *The Central Self: A Study in Romantic and Victorian Imagination.* London: Athlone Press, 1968.

Bloom, Harold. *The Anxiety of Influence: A Theory of Poetry.* New York: Oxford University Press, 1973.

———. *Poetry and Repression: Revisionism from Blake to Stevens.* New Haven, Conn.: Yale University Press, 1976.

Booth, Wayne C. *A Rhetoric of Irony.* Chicago: University of Chicago Press, 1974.

Bourgeois, René. *L'Ironie romantique.* Grenoble: Presses Universitaires, 1974.

Bruns, Gerald L. "The Formal Nature of Victorian Thinking." *PMLA* 90 (1975): 904–18.

Chaffee, Alan J. "Dialogue and Dialectic in Browning's *Sordello*." *Texas Studies in Literature and Language* 23 (1981): 52–77.

Charlton, H. B. "Browning as Dramatist." *Bulletin of the John Rylands Library* 23 (1939): 33–67.

Chesterton, G. K. *Robert Browning*. London: Macmillan, 1903.

Collins, Thomas J. "The Poetry of Robert Browning: A Proposal for Reexamination." *Texas Studies in Literature and Language* 15 (1973): 325–40.

―――. *Robert Browning's Moral-Aesthetic Theory, 1833–1855*. Lincoln: University of Nebraska Press, 1967.

Cook, Eleanor. *Browning's Lyrics: An Exploration*. Toronto: University of Toronto Press, 1974.

Culler, A. Dwight. "Monodrama and the Dramatic Monologue." *PMLA* 90 (1975): 366–85.

DeVane, William Clyde. *A Browning Handbook*. 2d ed. New York: Appleton-Century-Crofts, 1955.

Donahue, Joseph W. *Dramatic Character in the English Romantic Age*. Princeton, N.J.: Princeton University Press, 1970.

Drew, Philip. *The Poetry of Browning: A Critical Introduction*. London: Methuen, 1969.

Dubois, Arthur E. "Robert Browning, Dramatist." *Studies in Philology* 33 (1936): 626–55.

Griffin, W. Hall, and Harry Christopher Minchin. *The Life of Robert Browning*. 3d ed. rev. London: Methuen, 1938; rpt. Hamden, Conn.: Archon Books, 1966.

Hair, Donald S. *Browning's Experiments with Genre*. Toronto: University of Toronto Press, 1972.

Haney, Janice L. " 'Shadow-Hunting': Romantic Irony, *Sartor Resartus*, and Victorian Romanticism." *Studies in Romanticism* 17 (1978): 307–33.

Harrold, William E. *The Variance and the Unity: A Study of the Complementary Poems of Robert Browning*. Athens: Ohio University Press, 1973.

Herford, C. H. *Robert Browning*. New York: Dodd, Mead, 1905.

Honan, Park. *Browning's Characters: A Study in Poetic Technique*. New Haven, Conn.: Yale University Press, 1961.

Hutchens, Eleanor N. "The Identification of Irony." *ELH* 27 (1960): 352–63.

Irvine, William, and Park Honan. *The Book, The Ring, and the Poet*. New York: McGraw-Hill, 1974.

Jack, Ian. *Browning's Major Poetry*. Oxford: Clarendon Press, 1973.

Jankélévitch, Vladamir. *L'Ironie, ou la bonne conscience*. 2d ed. Paris: Presses Universitaires de France, 1950.

Johnson, E. D. H. *The Alien Vision of Victorian Poetry: Sources of the Poetic Imagination in Tennyson, Browning, and Arnold*. Princeton, N.J.: Princeton University Press, 1953.

King, Roma A., Jr. *The Focusing Artifice: The Poetry of Robert Browning*. Athens: Ohio University Press, 1968.

Langbaum, Robert. *The Poetry of Experience: The Dramatic Monologue in Modern Literary Tradition*. New York: Random House, 1957.

Lussky, A. E. *Tieck's Romantic Irony*. Chapel Hill: University of North Carolina Press, 1932.

Macready, William Charles. *The Diaries of William Charles Macready: 1833–1851*. Ed. William Toynbee. London: Chapman and Hall, 1912.

de Man, Paul. *Allegories of Reading: Figural Language in Rousseau, Nietzsche, Rilke, and Proust*. New Haven, Conn.: Yale University Press, 1980.

———. "The Rhetoric of Temporality." In *Interpretation: Theory and Practice*, ed. Charles S. Singleton, pp. 173–209. Baltimore: Johns Hopkins University Press, 1969.

Mason, Michael. "The Importance of *Sordello*." In *The Major Victorian Poets: Reconsiderations*, ed. Isobel Armstrong, pp. 125–51. London: Routledge and Kegan Paul, 1969.

Maynard, John. *Browning's Youth*. Cambridge, Mass.: Harvard University Press, 1977.

McCormick, James P. "Robert Browning and the Experimental Drama." *PMLA* 68 (1953): 982–91.

Mellor, Anne K. *English Romantic Irony*. Cambridge, Mass.: Harvard University Press, 1980.

Miller, Betty. *Robert Browning: A Portrait*. London: John Murray, 1952.

Miller, J. Hillis. *The Disappearance of God: Five Nineteenth-Century Writers*. Cambridge, Mass.: Harvard University Press, 1963; rpt. New York: Schocken Books, 1965.

———. "Narrative Middle: A Preliminary Outline." *Genre* 11 (1978): 375–87.

Muecke, D. C. *The Compass of Irony*. London: Methuen, 1969.

———. *Irony*. London: Methuen, 1970.

Ong, Walter J. *Interfaces of the Word*. Ithaca, N.Y.: Cornell University Press, 1977.

Orr, Mrs. Sutherland. *A Handbook to the Works of Robert Browning*. 6th ed. London: G. Bell, 1927.

———. *Life and Letters of Robert Browning*. London: Smith, Elder, 1891.

Otten, Terry. *The Deserted Stage: The Search for Dramatic Form in Nineteenth-Century England*. Athens: Ohio University Press, 1971.

Peckham, Morse. "Browning and Romanticism." In *Robert Browning*, ed. Isobel Armstrong, pp. 47–76. London: G. Bell, 1974.

Poston, Lawrence, III. "Browning's Career to 1841: The Theme of Time and the Problem of Form." *Browning Institute Studies* 3 (1975): 79–100.

———. "Browning's Political Skepticism: *Sordello* and the Plays." *PMLA* 88 (1973): 260–70.

———. "Browning Rearranges Browning." *Studies in Browning and His Circle* 2 (1974): 39–54.

Pottle, Frederick A. *Shelley and Browning: A Myth and Some Facts*. Chicago: Pembroke Press, 1923.

Preyer, Robert. "Robert Browning: A Reading of the Early Narratives." *ELH* 26 (1959): 531–48.

Priestley, F. E. L. "The Ironic Pattern of Browning's *Paracelsus*." *University of Toronto Quarterly* 34 (1964): 68–81.

Rader, Ralph W. "The Dramatic Monologue and Related Lyric Form." *Critical Inquiry* 3 (1976): 131–51.

Raymond, W. O. *The Infinite Moment and Other Essays in Robert Browning.* 2d ed. Toronto: University of Toronto Press, 1965.

Reed, Joseph W. "Browning and Macready: The Final Quarrel." *PMLA* 75 (1960): 597–603.

Schlegel, Friedrich. *Dialogue on Poetry and Literary Aphorisms.* Trans. Ernst Behler and Roman Struc. University Park: Pennsylvania State University Press, 1968.

Shaw, W. David. *The Dialectical Temper.* Ithaca, N.Y.: Cornell University Press, 1968.

Slinn, E. Warwick. " 'God a Tame Confederate': The Reader's Dual Vision in *Pippa Passes*." *University of Toronto Quarterly* 45 (1976): 158–73.

Smith, Barbara Herrnstein. *Poetic Closure: A Study of How Poems End.* Chicago: University of Chicago Press, 1968.

Strohschneider-Kohrs, Ingrid. *Die romantische Ironie in Theorie und Gestaltung.* Tübingen: M. Niemeyer, 1960.

Thirlwall, Connop. "On the Irony of Sophocles." *Philological Museum* 2 (1833): 483–537.

Tucker, Herbert F., Jr. *Browning's Beginnings: The Art of Disclosure.* Minneapolis: University of Minnesota Press, 1980.

Wenger, C. N. *The Aesthetics of Robert Browning.* Ann Arbor, Mich.: George Wahr, 1924.

Wessell, Leonard P., Jr. "The Antinomic Structure of Friedrich Schlegel's Romanticism." *Studies in Romanticism* 12 (1973): 648–69.

Woolford, John. "Sources and Resources in Browning's Early Reading." In *Robert Browning*, ed. Isobel Armstrong, pp. 1–46. London: G. Bell, 1974.

INDEX

Abrams, M. H., 258, 259, 265
Aeschylus, 181; *Oresteia* 182, 183
Altick, Richard D., 274
Anglo-Catholicism, 228, 274
Apollo (in *Sordello*), 81, 83, 87, 88, 92, 97
Aristotle, 31, 260
Agrippa, 10, 26
Armstrong, Isobel, 266–67
Arnold, Matthew, 7
Arnould, Joseph, 258
Assad, Thomas J., 269
Athenaeum, 199
Atlas, 258

Bagehot, Walter, 279
Bate, Walter J., 278–79
Baillie, Joanna, 33
Ball, Patricia, 258, 270, 278
Balzac, Honoré de, 255; *Louis Lambert*, 259
Bards and visionaries, 13, 14, 25, 38, 87–88, 90, 93–95, 113, 122
Barrett, Elizabeth, 7, 14, 119, 201, 202, 210, 219, 230, 231, 232, 233, 239, 240, 241, 243, 244, 245, 251, 254, 255, 258, 262, 265, 273, 276, 277, 280
Baudelaire, Charles: "De l'essence du rire," 10, 277
Beckett, Samuel, 64, 246
Berdoe, Edward, 261
Bieman, Elizabeth, 275
Biographie Universelle, 51
Blake, William, 222
Bloom, Harold, 15, 259
Boas, Louise S., 275–76
Booth, Wayne C., 253
Bourgeois, René, 266
Bright, Michael H., 274
Brooke, Stopford A., 267
Brown, Bernadine, 274
Browning, Robert: "Abt Vogler," 255; "Andrea del Sarto," 212;

Aristophanes' Apology, 268; "Artemis Prologuizes," 154, 162; *Balaustion's Adventure*, 268; *Bells and Pomegranates*, 119, 137, 145, 146, 170, 181, 189, 201, 231, 240, 254; "The Bishop Orders His Tomb at St. Praxed's Church," 203, **214–16**, 228, 250, 274; *A Blot in the 'Scutcheon*, **181–88**, 189, 197, 240, 271–72; "The Boy and the Angel," 203, **222**, 273; "Camp" (*see* "Incident of the French Camp"); "Camp and Cloister," 154, **159–60;** "Cavalier Tunes," 153, 154, 168; *Christmas-Eve and Easter-Day*, 254; "Claret and Tokay" (*see* "Nationality in Drinks"); "Cleon," 255; "Cloister" (*see* "Soliloquy of the Spanish Cloister"); *Colombe's Birthday*, **189–200**, 201, 202, 219, 220, 236, 240, 245, 273; "The Confessional," 203, **217–18;** "Count Gismond," 154, **155–59,** 162, 165, 270; "Cristina," 154, **164–65,** 271; "A Death in the Desert," 263; *Dramatic Lyrics*, 145, **146–69**, 201, 203, 228, 249; *Dramatic Romances and Lyrics*, **201–29**, 230; "Earth's Immortalities," 203, **222**, 275; "England in Italy" (*see* "The Englishman in Italy"); "The Englishman in Italy," 203, **210–11**, 273; "Epilogue" to *Asolando*, 3; "An Epistle [from] . . . Karshish" 255; *Essay on Shelley*, 6–7, 8, 12, 13, 247, 249, 265, 279; "The Flight of the Duchess," 203, **218–22**, 273, 274; "The Flower's Name," 203, **216;** "France" (*see* "Count Gismond"); "France and Spain," 203, 217; "Garden Fancies," 203, **216–17;** "The

Browning, Robert: *(Continued)*
Glove," 204, **224–28,** 273, 275–76; "Here's to Nelson's Memory," 214, 274; "Home Thoughts, from Abroad," 203, **212–14;** "How they Brought the Good News from Ghent to Aix," 203, **204–5;** "In a Gondola," 154, **160–62,** 270; "Incident of the French Camp," 154, **159,** 160; "The Italian in England," 203, **208–10,** 211, 273, 274, 276; "Italy" (*see* "My Last Duchess"); "Italy in England" (*see* "The Italian in England"); "Johannes Agricola in Meditation," 153, **166,** 262; *King Victor and King Charles,* **137–45,** 170, 187, 188, 240; "The Laboratory," 203, **217;** "The Lost Leader," 203, **211–12;** "The Lost Mistress," 203, **212,** 213; *Luria,* **230–40,** 241, 251, 276; "Madhouse Cells," 154, 166; "Morning" (*see* "Parting at Morning"); "My Last Duchess," 147, **149–53, 154–55,** 158, 166, 177, 182, 207, 215, 220, 250, 269; "Nationality in Drinks," 204, **223,** 228; "Night" (*see* "Meeting at Night"); "One Word More," 278; *Paracelsus,* **31–52,** 54, 55, 59, 63, 66, 68, 70, 73, 80, 84, 85, 90, 97, 104, 109, 112, 121, 131, 135, 136, 147, 148, 166, 171, 173, 213, 239, 247, 249, 251, 253, 261–62, 263, 265); *Parleyings with Certain People of Importance,* 27; "Parting at Morning," 203, **222,** 275; *Pauline* 3, **9–30,** 31, 34, 35, 36, 51, 63, 66, 79–80, 85, 97, 112, 116, 148, 166, 247, 249, 251, 254, 258–60, 278; "Pictor Ignotus," 203, **205–8,** 273–74; "The Pied Piper of Hamelin," 154, 168, 221, 270; *Pipa Passes,* **119–37,** 139, 145, 147, 149, 159, 228, 246, 252, 267–68, 277, 278; "Porphyria's Lover," 153, **166–68,** 271; "Queen-Worship," 154, **164;** *The Return of the Druses,* **170–80,** 232, 271, 276; *The Ring and the Book,* 254, 255, 266, 268, 272, 280; "Rudel and the Lady of Tripoli," 154, **164;** "Saul," 204, **223–24,** 275; "Sibrandus Schafnaburgensis," 203, **216–17,** 221; "Soliloquy of the Spanish Cloister," 154,**159–60,** 166, 214; "Song" ("Nay, but you, who do not love her"), 203, 222; *Sordello,* 35, **66–118,** 119, 120, 122, 127, 131, 135, 136, 137, 147, 148, 149, 151, 170, 173, 189, 191, 208, 228, 234, 240, 245, 247, 249, 250, 251, 253, 255, 263–67, 276, 277, 279, 280; *A Soul's Tragedy,* 230, 231, **240–45,** 246, 276–77; "Spain" (*see* "The Confessional"); *Strafford,* **53–65,** 66, 68, 69, 80, 85, 97, 118, 121, 135, 136, 137, 138, 139, 148, 193, 231, 262, 272; "Through the Metidja to Abd-El-Kadr," 154, 168, 270; "Time's Revenges," 204, **224,** 273; "The Tomb at St. Praxed's," (*see* "The Bishop Orders His Tomb at St. Praxed's Church"); "Waring" 154, **162–64,** 218, 270, 271
Bruns, Gerald L., 261
Bullen, J. B., 274
Bulwer-Lytton, Sir Edward, 139
Burns, Robert, 211
Burr, Michael, 258
Busk, Mrs. W.: *Sordello* 68
Butler, Samuel 86, 225

Cadbury, William, 270, 275
Canova, Antonio, 125, 267
Carlisle, Lucy, Countess of (historical figure; for RB's character based on her, *see Strafford*), 55, 59
Carlyle, Thomas, 14, 67, 232, 233, 276; *On Heroes and Hero-Worship,* 232; *Sartor Resartus,* 13, 37, 258, 263
Carnall, Geoffrey, 259
Cervantes, Miguel Saavedra de: *Don Quixote,* 72, 128, 264
Chaffe, Alan J., 264

INDEX *289*

Chandler, Alice, 271
Charles I, King (historical figure; for RB's character based on him, *see Strafford*), 59
Charlton, H. B., 262, 271
Chaucer, Geoffrey, 229; "Wife of Bath's Tale" 101
Chesterton, G. K., 178
Chevalier, Haakon M., 279
Christianity. *See* Religion
Clark, Helen C., 98
Coleridge, Samuel Taylor, 3, 32, 260
Collins, Thomas J., 266, 267, 275, 280
Columbus, Robert R., 265
Conrad, Peter, 251
Cook, Eleanor G., 258, 261, 268
Corn Laws, 210, 211, 228
Corneille, Pierre, 180; *Polyeucte*, 142
Cornwall, Barry (W. B. Procter), 33
Crawford, A. W., 275

Dante, 86, 99, 265; *Paradiso*, 99; *Purgatorio*, 265–66
Darley, George, 33; "Letters to . . . Dramatists," 33
Descartes, René, 81, 84
DeVane, William Clyde, 68, 145, 257, 273, 276
Dickens, Charles, 134, 271–72
Domett, Alfred, 68, 146, 199, 201, 258, 265, 275, 276
Donahue, Joseph, 32
Donne, John, 86
Dramatic mode, 9, 11, 15, 31–32, 33, 34, 48–49, 53, 54, 71, 137, 147–48, 149, 150, 153, 202, 204, 213, 218, 219, 223, 224, 247, 248–49, 250–52, 258
Drew, Phillip, 247, 259, 271
DuBois, Arthur E., 246, 269
Duckworth, Francis R., 277
Duerkson, Roland A., 259

Ecclesiastes, 214
Eggenschwiler, David, 271
Eglamor (in *Sordello*), 81, 86, 87, 89, 91–92, 113, 115
Eliot, T. S.: "The Love Song of J. Alfred Prufrock," 207

Erasmus, Desiderius, 47
Expansion and contraction, 24, 27, 30, 50, 92, 96, 206, 208, 234, 251
Examiner, 201

Faucit, Helen, 262
Felgar, Robert, 274
Fichte, Johann Gottlieb, 68
Forster, John, 201, 249
Fotheringham, James, 279
Fox, William Johnson, 67, 260, 278
Francis I, King (historical figure; for RB's character based on him, *see* "The Glove"), 225

Garrick, David, 31
German language and culture, 4, 67–68, 72, 264
Gilbert, William H., 258
Goethe, J. W. von, 8
Gothic Revival, 221
Govil, O. P., 258
Grandsen, K. W., 260
Griffin, W. Hall, 94
Guralnick, Elissa S., 265

Hair, Donald S., 272, 276
Hallam, Arthur Henry, 278
Halliday, F. E., 272
Haney, Janice L., 263
Harper, J. H., 266
Hartman, Geoffrey, 250, 266
Haworth, Euphrasia Fanny, 73, 137, 170, 173
Hawthorne, Mark D., 261, 264
Hegel, Georg Friedrich, 5, 54, 68, 265
Hellstrom, Ward, 275
Herford, C. H., 270
Holmes, Stewart W., 265
Honan, Park, 259, 260, 262, 267, 271, 276, 277, 278
Hood, Thomas, 214, 225
Hopkins, Gerard Manley, 117
Horne, Richard Hengist, 202
Hovelaque, H.-L,. 258–59
Huxley, Aldous, 116; *Point Counter Point*, 116

Ibsen, Henrik, 179

Irony 11, 18, 25, 36, 48, 49–50, 54–55, 59, 60, 61, 133, 167, 169, 171, 176, 179, 191, 193, 199–200, 201, 202, 207–8, 211, 212, 214, 216, 222, 226, 228, 232, 239, 244, 246, 247, 253, 254–55, 257, 260, 270, 279–80. *See also* Philosophical irony; Romantic irony
Irvine, William, 259, 262, 267, 276, 277, 278
Iser, Wolfgang, 269–70
Italy: RB's visits to 69, 92, 95, 101, 119, 120, 201, 254

Jack, Ian, 258, 269, 270, 276
James, Henry, 35, 256
Jamieson, Paul F., 274
Jankélévitch, Vladimir, 106, 149
Jerman, B. R., 269
Johnson, E. D. H., 268

Kean, Charles, 188–89, 230
Kean, Edmund, 9, 31, 32, 188
Keating, P. J., 258
Keats, John, 11, 32, 39, 121, 122, 267, 181, 259, 271; *Endymion*, 30; *The Eve of St. Agnes*, 167, 182, 271
Keenan, Richard C., 259
Kemble, John Philip, 31
Kemper, Claudette, 265
Kilby, Clyde S., 271
King, Roma A., Jr., 268
Kintner, Elvan, 7, 190, 210, 219, 230, 231, 232, 238, 239, 240, 241, 243, 244, 245
Knight, G. Wilson, 279
Knowles, Sheridan, 139

Landor, Walter Savage, 33, 73, 148, 228–29, 231, 262; "To Robert Browning," 229
Langbaum, Robert, 149, 152, 270, 271
Language and linguistic theory, 10–11, 26, 36, 37, 38, 41–42, 43, 46–47, g 62–64, 80, 81, 82, 83, 84–86, 123, 130, 150, 151, 161–62, 177, 184, 185, 196, 216–17, 250, 251, 252, 276–77
Loucks, James F., 274
Lounsbury, Thomas R., 272
Love, 11, 18–19, 20–21, 25, 38–39, 40, 42, 45, 50, 56, 97–101, 104, 124–25, 126, 127, 135, 139, 141, 160–62, 164–65, 166–67, 169, 170, 173–75, 176, 186, 190, 191, 199, 202, 217, 220, 222, 223, 224, 232, 234, 235, 239, 245, 262, 265, 266, 267, 270, 271
Lubbock, Percy, 272
Luther, Martin, 41, 47, 261
Lyric mode, 9, 14, 15, 32–33, 34, 44, 54, 81, 120, 121, 136, 137, 147, 148, 149, 151, 153, 168, 202, 213, 215, 248, 250, 258, 277, 279

Maclise, Daniel: "The Serenade," 160
Macready, William Charles, 52, 137, 138, 170, 179, 180, 181, 188, 230, 262, 271, 272
Man, Paul de, 253
Mandeville, Bernard, 259
Mann, Thomas: *Dr. Faustus*, 106; *Joseph the Provider*, 277
Marot, Clémet (historical figure; for RB's character based on him, see "The Glove"), 10, 26, 275
Martineau, Harriet, 68
Marx, Karl, 131
Mason, Michael, 263, 264, 280
Maynard, John, 259, 264, 269
Mazzini, Giuseppe, 276
McClatchey, J. S., 275
Medici family, 205
Mellor, Anne K., 257, 263
Mermin, Dorothy M., 270
Mill, John Stuart, 14, 33, 34, 85, 120, 137, 258, 260, 261, 264; "The Two Kinds of Poetry," 33, 261; "What Is Poetry?" 33, 85
Miller, Betty, 80, 277–78
Miller, J. Hillis, 28, 264, 269, 278
Milman, Henry Hart, 33
Milton, John, 181, 211; *Paradise Lost* 182
Minchin, Harry C., 94

Miyoshi, Masao, 258, 260
Monthly Repository, 85, 153, 260, 262
More, Paul Elmer, 264
Morning Chronicle, 228
Moxon, Edward, 119, 146, 153
Muecke, D. C., 263, 280
Muehlenfels, Ludwig von, 67

Narrative mode 34, 71, 72–73, 74–79, 136, 159, 162, 168, 204, 218, 222, 224, 248
Nelson, Horatio, Lord 274
Newman, John Henry, 32, 33, 274

Objective and subjective modes, 6, 8, 54, 92, 105–6, 149, 153, 248, 252, 258, 265, 280
Ong, Walter, 86
Orel, Harold, 279
Orr, Mrs. Sutherland, 28, 68, 120, 253–54, 258, 260, 274, 275, 276
Otten, Terry, 54
Ovid, 225

Palma (in *Sordello*), 69, 83, 97, 98–101, 102, 116, 191, 265
Paracelsus (historical figure), 35–36, 51, 73, 93
Parins, Marylyn J., 271
Paul, St., 259
Pearsall, Robert B., 276
Peckham, Morse, 259
Philosophical Irony, 4–5, 8, 24, 45–46, 51–52, 54
Pinter, Harold, 64, 246
Plato, 3
Porter, Charlotte, 98
Poston, Lawrence III, 271
Pottle, Frederick A., 259, 260
Pound, Ezra, 116
Power, 21–23, 24, 38, 39–40, 45, 50, 101, 103, 104, 105, 131, 136, 139–40, 155, 169, 171–72, 173, 177, 190, 191, 199, 202, 220, 232, 234, 235, 239, 244–45, 247, 265, 266
Preyer, Robert, 260, 278
Psalms, 223
Puseyism. *See* Anglo-Catholicism

Pym, John (historical figure; for RB's character based on him, see *Strafford*), 55, 59, 262

Racine, Jean Baptiste, 125
Rader, Ralph, 149–50, 152
Rajan, Tilottama, 257
Raphael, 205, 274
Raymond, W. O., 265, 271
Religion, 3, 11, 22–23, 25, 28, 36, 37, 39, 40–41, 45, 47, 67, 98, 103–7, 124, 131–32, 135, 159–60, 166, 172, 173, 176, 187, 188, 214, 215, 216, 217, 223, 232–34, 252, 258, 262, 275, 276
Reul, Paul de, 277
Rimbaud, Arthur, 83
Rivers, Charles L., 263
Robinson, Henry Crabb, 248
Role-playing, 36, 37, 39, 40–41, 43–43, 45, 48, 60–62, 64, 81, 122–24, 125–27, 128, 130, 142–45, 154–55, 156, 161, 168–69, 176–77, 182–84, 187, 193–97, 215, 217, 220–21, 236–38, 241, 250
Romantic Irony, 8, 28, 51–52, 54, 66–68, 72, 79, 104, 106–7, 109–10, 111, 132, 135–36, 139, 149, 152–53, 175, 185, 209, 216, 251, 262–63, 266, 280
Romanticism and the Romantic tradition, 3–4, 12–13, 13–14, 15, 18, 19, 28, 32–33, 38, 45, 85, 104, 110, 118, 121, 147, 208, 214, 247, 250, 251, 252, 257, 259, 261, 266, 271, 279
Ronsard, Pierre (historical figure; for RB's character based on him, see "The Glove"), 86, 224, 275
Rossetti, Dante Gabriel, 28
Ruskin, John, 228, 274

Saintsbury, George, 275
Salinguerra, Taurello (in *Sordello*), 69, 83, 89, 94, 99, 101–2, 114, 265
Santayana, George, 270
Schelling, Friedrich Wilhelm von, 68
Schiller, Johann Christoph Friedrich von, 91, 92

Schlegel, August Whilhem von, 31, 277
Schlegel, Friedrich, 4–5, 7, 54, 66, 70, 72, 79, 96, 104, 111, 114, 248, 257, 278; *Athenaeum* Fragments 7, 67, 71, 79, 97, 114, 248, 257; *Lyceum* Fragments 111, 278
Scott, Sir Walter, 71
Scott, William Bell, 53, 85, 262
Sedgewick, G. G., 270
Shaffer, E. S., 263
Shakespeare, William, 32, 181, 192, 211, 229, 259; *As You Like It*, 198; *Hamlet*, 32, 179; *Henry VIII*, 199; *Macbeth*, 32; *Much Ado About Nothing*, 182; *Othello*, 182, 270, 276; *Richard III*, 9, 32, 259; *Romeo and Juliet* 181, 182
Shaw, George Bernard, 246, 251
Shaw, W. David, 275
Shelley, Percy Bysshe, 3, 4, 12–25, 28, 32, 36, 80, 112, 115, 208, 211, 251, 255, 257, 259; *Alastor*, 9, 14, 18, 148, 258; *Defence of Poetry*, 251–52; *Epipsychidion*, 258; "Ode to the West Wind," 208, 211
Siddons, Sarah, 31, 32
Siddons, Henry: *Practical Illustrations of Rhetorical Gesture and Action,* 32
Simpson, David, 257
Slinn, E. Warwick, 268, 278
Smart, Christopher, 223; "Song to David," 223
Smith, Alexander, 31; "The Philosophy of Poetry," 33
Smith, Barbara Herrnstein, 264
Smith, C. Willard, 259
Sonstroem, David, 275
Sophocles, 54; *Antigone*, 54
Sordello (historical figure), 68, 73–74, 86, 93, 109
Spectator, 35
Stevens, Wallace, 252; "Another Woman Weeping," 252; "The Man with the Blue Guitar," 252; "An Ordinary Evening in New Haven," 252
Stevenson, Lionel, 264
Strafford, Sir Thomas Wentworth, 1st Earl of (historical figure), 53, 55, 59, 93
Strohschneider-Kohrs, Ingrid, 266
Subjective poet. See Objective and Subjective Poet
Sullivan, Mary Rose, 269, 276–77
Sutton, Max K., 271

Taylor, Henry: *Philip van Artevelde*, 52
Thompson, Alan R., 263
Tennyson, Alfred, 7, 34, 105, 167, 255, 261, 275; *In Memoriam*, 105; "Locksley Hall," 167; "Maud," 167; *Poems, Chiefly Lyrical*, 277
Tieck, Ludwig, 67, 263
Thirlwall, Connop, 54–55, 56, 59, 262
Tillotson, Geoffrey, 269
Times (London), 188
Tracy, C. R., 263, 271
Tucker, Herbert F., Jr., 112, 208, 259, 268

Vestures, 37, 38–39, 42, 44, 51, 171, 176–77

Wagner, Richard, 86; *Die Meistersinger*, 86; *Tannhaüser*, 86
Wagner, Robert, 264
Wenger, C. N., 262–63, 280
Wessell, Leonard P., Jr., 263
Woolford, John, 264
Wordsworth, William, 14, 19, 20, 32, 34, 36, 212; "Intimations Ode," 148; Preface to *Lyrical Ballads*, 34; *The Prelude*, 13

Yetman, Michael G., 265